Dear God

The price of religion in Ireland

Dear God

The price of religion in Ireland

Eamonn McCann

BOOKMARKS

London, Chicago and Sydney

Dear God: The Price of Religion in Ireland – Eamonn McCann
First published 1999
Bookmarks Publications Ltd, 1 Bloomsbury Street, London WC1B 3QE, England
Bookmarks, PO Box 16085, Chicago, Illinois 60616, USA
Bookmarks, PO Box A338, Sydney South, NSW 2000, Australia
Copyright © Bookmarks Publications Ltd

ISBN 1 898876 58 4 (Paperback)

Printed by Larkham Printing and Publishing
Cover by Sherborne Design

Bookmarks Publications Ltd is linked to an international grouping of socialist organisations:
- **Australia:** International Socialist Organisation, PO Box A338, Sydney South
- **Britain:** Socialist Workers Party, PO Box 82, London E3 3LH
- **Canada:** International Socialists, PO Box 339, Station E, Toronto, Ontario M6H 4E3
- **Cyprus:** Ergatiki Demokratia, PO Box 7280, Nicosia
- **Denmark:** Internationale Socialister, PO Box 5113, 8100 Aarhus C
- **Germany:** Linksruck, Postfach 304 183, 20359 Hamburg
- **Greece:** Socialistiko Ergatiko Komma, c/o Workers Solidarity, PO Box 8161, Athens 100 10
- **Holland:** Internationale Socialisten, PO Box 92025, 1090AA Amsterdam
- **Ireland:** Socialist Workers Party, PO Box 1648, Dublin 8
- **New Zealand:** Socialist Workers Organisation, PO Box 8851, Auckland
- **Norway:** Internasjonale Socialisterr, Postboks 9226 Grønland, 0134 Oslo
- **Poland:** Solidarność Socjalistyczna, PO Box 12, 01-900 Warszawa 118
- **Spain:** Socialismo Internacional, Apartado 563, 08080 Barcelona
- **United States:** International Socialist Organization, PO Box 16085, Chicago, Illinois 60616
- **Zimbabwe:** International Socialist Organisation, PO Box 6758, Harare

Contents

Foreword by Arthur Matthews
1

Introduction
3

Chapter 1
I can see Cleary now
5

Chapter 2
Ratzinger in the skull
29

Chapter 3
Faith of our fetters
45

Chapter 4
Daily, Daly sings to Mary
72

Chapter 5
It's alright ma (I'm only bleeding)
105

Chapter 6
London calling
122

Chapter 7
Rock of ages ago
137

Chapter 8
Child cares
147

Chapter 9
Black magic woman
166

Chapter 10
Home tales
185

Eamonn McCann is Ireland's leading radical journalist. His book *War and an Irish Town* has become the classic account of the origins and impact of the 'Troubles' on ordinary people in Northern Ireland. His most recent book, *McCann: War and Peace in Northern Ireland*, received very wide acclaim. Eamonn is a member of the Socialist Workers Party in Ireland.

Foreword

Arthur Matthews
(co-writer, *Father Ted* and *Hippies*)

Religion is a deep and mysterious subject. Eamonn McCann has given it some serious thoughts over the years, and this book is a compilation of many of his theories and conclusions on a subject which is the very definition of vast. It perplexes us all, and to those of us of a nervous disposition, ie me, it can be a very terrifying thing indeed. As a Catholic child, it never occurred to me that God and Jesus and the angels and saints and the Devil and all his evil works didn't exist. I was told by parents and teachers and everybody that they were very real in much the same way that maths and Irish and Australia and President De Valera were very real, so that was that.

But hang on. What is often overlooked about religion is something that Eamonn points his finger at immediately: it is mad. There is nothing rational about religion. There are great similarities between the language of religion and the language of the mentally disturbed. The problem is, if you can believe in God, Heaven and Hell, divine intervention, miracles, everlasting life etc, etc, etc, you really can believe in anything. That's when the madness begins. John Lennon once predicted that religion will die out and he may eventually be proved right.

Religion has always held out the promise of a reward for the faithful in the 'next world'. That surely is its great attraction. Everlasting life full of bowls of cherries and comfy pillows must have appealed greatly to a medieval peasant working naked in a gale force wind up to his knees in mud (remember too, this was an era before chips, tea and sweets), but to a large amount of people lucky enough to be living in the 'developed' world on the cusp of the 21st century, a warm house, a few cans of Budweiser, and football on the telly are really enough. Death being nothing more than a long sleep seems acceptable. Everlasting life as a reward for earthly misery is an outdated notion.

But, of course, people do still believe in it, and this book analyses this belief; it looks at the implications of religious devotion and points out the sheer ludicrousness of much of it. I can't be quite as clinical and rational as Eamonn is about religion and the supernatural. At the back of my mind is the thought that there might be something out there. I really hope there isn't, because the implications are just far too disturbing; so I shall enjoy this book partly because, as well as being amused and enlightened, I want to be reassured.

Of course, if Eamonn is wrong about all this, he's in for a severe kicking in the next world. If God does exist, there's no evidence at all that he's some benign Tony Blair type, and my bet is that he's more likely to be a Ming the Merciless-like flamboyant deity who will extract full revenge on Mr McCann for his reckless heresies. Everyone who reads this book should imagine all kinds of sharp objects being inserted into Eamonn's orifices just in case he's completely wrong about the whole religion thing. It makes you think. But in the end, surely, the rational must conquer the irrational. The sharp mind of Eamonn McCann sorts through the mighty maze of religious beliefs, practices and paranoias for you in these pages. Hold on tight through the theological minefield. You'll be greatly entertained along the way.

Introduction

'Magical' and 'mysterious' have been two of the words most commonly used to describe this year's eclipse of the sun. But, of course, impressive as the spectacle is said to have been in places less covered than Ireland by cloud, there was no magic or mystery about it. A total eclipse is a natural, precisely predictable phenomenon.

There was a time when such things did seem awesome, even terrifying, and only fantastical explanations appeared adequate. Hindus believed that the eclipse was caused by a demonic figure, Rahu, devouring the sun. In some pagan societies, it was thought that it marked the moment when an old sun died, its energy spent, and a new sun was born in the heavens to shine life down upon earth. In many Christian societies, an eclipse was taken as a portent of disaster to come, even of the end of the world.

We know better now. We know that it is science, not religion, which explains the world. The eclipse does remind us, though, how and why religion arose.

Religion emerged as an expression of human helplessness in the face of vast and seemingly inexplicable power. The wind, the waves, earthquakes and volcanic eruptions, thunder, storm, drought and deluge, plague and pestilence—primitive human beings were utterly at the mercy of them all, unable to understand, much less control, the forces unleashed. So they attributed all these terrifying auguries to 'gods', whom they sought to placate by ritual and sacrifice.

Eventually, in accordance with the law of supply and demand, specialists emerged in placating and interpreting the whims and wishes of imagined deities. Thus, priests.

Since the beginning of the division of the world into classes and the expropriation by a minority of the surplus produced by the majority, people have felt helpless, too, in the face of power in society beyond their control. The slave owner's rod on the back of the slave, the power of the monarch over the mass of the people, the capitalist's theft from the worker of the product of her labour, always, everywhere, churches have arisen to proclaim that this is the natural order

3

of things, god-given if you will, that to rebel against it is contrary to god's will.

Religion has meanwhile provided solace to the poor and the suffering, and held out a prospect of joy in a better world when life's done.

Surveying the wreckage of the ideals of the French Revolution, Napoleon put it plain: 'What is it which makes the poor man take it for granted that on my table at each meal there is enough to sustain a family for a week? It is religion, which says to him that in another life I shall be his equal, indeed that he has a better chance of being happy there than I.'

Religion can also be a vehicle for protest. The idea of a being, infinitely superior in power and glory to mere mortals as we scurry through our allotted years, can lead to acceptance that this is how god ordered our estates. But, depending on prevailing circumstance, it might lead just as well to a perception of all people as precious in god's sight, and thus point towards a conclusion that god smiles on revolt.

Socialists have to see religion in context. Marx didn't dismiss religion as 'the opium of the people'. What he wrote was that 'religion is an expression of real suffering and a protest against real suffering. Religion is the sigh of the oppressed creature, the heart of the heartless world and the soul of soulless circumstance. It is the opium of the people.'

Socialists in the classical Marxist tradition fight for a society from which religion will have disappeared because the ignorance, fear and oppression in which it is rooted will have disappeared. Introducing the Bolshevik decree which guaranteed freedom of religion, Trotsky declared in 1918: 'The complete abolition of religion will be achieved only when there is a fully developed socialist system... It can be attained only under social relations which are free from mystery, that are thoroughly lucid and do not oppress. Religion translates the chaos of nature and the chaos of social relations into the language of fantastical images. Only through the abolition of this earthly chaos can we end forever its religious reflection. The conscious, reasonable, planned guidance of social life in all its aspects will abolish for all time mysticism and devilry.'

August 1999

Chapter 1

I can see Cleary now

The absurdity of religion first occurred to me as a child, when, under pressure, I paid from my pocket money to go on a 'spiritual pilgrimage' to Lourdes. We spiritual travellers didn't actually go on the Derry Diocesean Pilgrimage. But our fares (half a crown, as I recall, return) helped subsidise those who did. The highpoint of our journey came on the evening when we assembled in St Eugene's Cathedral at the exact hour when the physical pilgrims, led by Bishop Neil Farren, were wending their way in solemn procession towards the Shrine of the Virgin in fabled, faraway France. We sang 'I'll Sing a Hymn to Mary', and were assured that we would share fully in the spiritual blessings allocated to the event. Thus, considered from the purely spiritual point of view, than which there is none more important, we gained as much as them we'd subsidised to travel—and at a fraction of the cost. So we were the winners.

There's a number of lessons in this story. One has to do with the differences between the Christian denominations. There never was a Protestant born who could have thought up a scam like the spiritual pilgrimage.

The entertainment dimension has figured prominently in much that I have written on religion over the years. Celebrity priest Michael Cleary, revealed after his death to have lived with his partner and to have fathered a child, and the flamboyant Bishop Eamon Casey, who was to flee the diocese of Galway with a wad of parish funds in his hip pocket after he, too, had been rumbled as a father, were among those who provided regular material for mirth. I am grateful to them for reminding us that, when all's said and done, the key thing to remember about religion is that it's ridiculous.

. . . .

Many of the pieces included in this collection have to do with the inadequacy of liberals when it comes to confronting religion. This has been the most consistent theme in my commentary on religion. I am aware of having perplexed and irritated comrades and friends by frequently taking aim, not at religion, but at mainstream critics of religion. But my point is made by a controversy under way as I write.

On 29 August 1999 a 72-year-old priest in County Leitrim called the gorgeous athlete Sonia O'Sullivan a 'slut' because, although unmarried, she'd had a child. Immediately, the old man was denounced by every paid-up liberal in the land, and officially disowned by the Church. But all he'd done was put forward the teaching of his Church on a matter of faith and morals.

There is a perverse conspiracy lurking here, involving cute bishops and lapsed-Catholic intellectuals. The bishops, if they were true to the beliefs they were proclaiming as eternal only a few years ago, would have endorsed the priest's sentiments, even if regretting his belligerent language.

Meanwhile, the halfway-house heretics wrote letters to the *Irish Times* welcoming the bishops' statement, issued through the official Catholic Press and Information Office in Dublin in the form of a statement of regret by the priest. None of them said that a Catholic priest calling Sonia O'Sullivan a slut illustrates how full of bile and hatred of women's sexuality the Catholic Church generally is, and how monstrous it remains that such a malodorous institution should have control of the education of the children of the nation.

None added that the Catholic bishops, by disowning the priest, showed themselves again as liars and hypocrites.

The liberals and the bishops regularly share living-space in an intellectual swamp and are unnerved by anyone, on any side, who takes a stand on firm ground. This is one of the factors in religion's survival as a major force in Irish society.

. . . .

Hot Press—20 October 1987

I'm beginning to warm to the Ayatollah Khomeini. He's a spaced-out old reactionary with views on sex, women, popular culture and social morality which, if it wasn't for his cranky approach to the Jesus-is-god question, would qualify him for membership of the Knights of Columbanus (aka the Knights of the Long Connives).

This is not a thought I'd entertain for longer than say, a Jesus and Mary Chain set, but I'm beginning to believe that, maybe, in relation to certain specific issues, it would not be entirely inappropriate to be, just, on his side.

I first experienced this odd and unsettling feeling a couple of months back while watching television coverage of the killing by

Saudi Arabian police of around 400 Iranians who had been on a pilgrimage to Mecca. You might recall the pictures—lots of Iranians running at lines of policemen, then lots of Iranian bodies swaddled in white cloth and lying like trussed pillows in serried rows in a public square under blinding sun.

You might recall the commentaries too, which explained what a fanatical lot these Iranians are, particularly when they've OD-ed on religion, and how dangerous this fanaticism potentially is to the political tranquillity of Saudi Arabia. There was a lurking hint that the Saudis had grounds to feel aggrieved at having been drawn into this messy event by the mad Iranians.

A couple of days later there were pictures of millions of Iranians in a turmoil of emotion as container-loads of bodies were brought home to Tehran for burial. Experts aplenty popped up to warn that the ordinarily-fanatical Iranians were now completely deranged altogether and that there was no telling what wild lunacy they might get up to.

By astounding coincidence these events took place at the same time as the now-annual Mayo pilgrimage to Medjugorje, Yugoslavia, where the Virgin Mary's one-woman show has been playing to packed houses for a record-breaking seven years. I took to thinking that if the Yugoslav cops were to fill the Mayo Mariolators full-of lead and send them back to be off-loaded in body-bags outside Tuam Cathedral there'd be a distinct air of perturbation in this country about the whole affair. It would rather colour the attitude of the generality of Irish people towards Yugoslavia. And we'd expect the rest of the 'international community' to signal disapproval too.

But since the Mecca massacre was of mad Iranians, no one—apart from Iranians themselves—seemed to mind. It occurred to me then that maybe the Ayatollah's side of this argument wasn't being given a fair show.

This thought elbowed its way back into the crowded forefront of my mind last week as I read those *Observer* extracts from the new book on the CIA by celebrity-hack Bob Woodward (the one who was played by Robert Redford or Dustin Hoffman in *All The President's Men*).

It seems that a couple of years ago the boss of the CIA, William Casey, was musing that the Ayatollah's main man in Beirut, a Sheikh Mohammed Hussein Fadallah, leader of the local branch of the Party of God (they've got one there too), would have to go. So he readied up an operation which resulted in the arrival of a car-bomb outside the Sheikh's lodgings in March 1985. On account of the US Congress not being minded to bankroll this imaginative initiative, Mr Casey had arranged for the Saudis to cough up the necessary cash.

The Sheikh was out shopping or whatever at the time, but the bomb went off efficiently enough, splattering 80 citizens around the resultant ruination of the local architecture. Reports had it that the Ayatollah was decidedly unchuffed about his main man in Beirut being the focus of such unfriendliness and even less chuffed at the dispersal of the four score passers-by, most of whom happened, it being that sort of neighbourhood, to be adherents of his variety of religious superstition.

I was reading Woodward's account of all this with my left eye, my right eye targetted the meantime on the television screen whereon flickered pictures from the Gulf of the US fleet, bristling with more fire-power than was available to all the combatants of the Second World War combined as it accompanied tankers which had been festooned with US flags so as to make them eligible for US protection against any Iranian barge, canoe or amphibious dinghy which might try to hinder their oil-laden progress, all this taking place some 5,000 miles from the nearest sandspeck of United States soil but about as far from the Iranian shoreline as from Howth to Bray on the DART.

Meanwhile, simultaneously, with my other eye, I'm scanning a (British) *Independent* story which reveals that the US is buying one third (633,000 barrels a day) of the Iranian oil which makes it out of the Gulf, the reasoning seeming to be that, other considerations notwithstanding, it would be sheer silliness of US companies not to grab a share of whatever free-enterprise action was going.

I myself personally am not at all mad. But if I were the Ayatollah I'd get mad.

. . . .

In Dublin—13 March 1991

Tomorrow, Good Friday, we celebrate a number of anniversaries.

In Dublin was first published on a Good Friday, 11 years ago.

Samuel Beckett was born on a Good Friday. Samuel Beckett went to Portora Royal in Enniskillen. As did Oscar Wilde.

Following his conviction for being gay, Oscar Wilde's name was removed from the Golden Roll of Old Portorans, only to be replaced many years later where, in its new gilt, it now outshines those of his faded contemporaries.

Oscar Wilde's father was born in Castlerea, County Roscommon. Castlerea is the birthplace also of J Waters, editor of this magazine. Small world.

The law under which Wilde was persecuted reflected the fundamentalist Christian belief that sex can properly be used only for purposes of procreation. This belief interlocks with another Christian notion— that the only person in history who was not procreated as a result of sex was Jesus Christ.

Jesus was all man, and all god. He was entirely human in that he began in the womb of a woman and developed there in the usual fashion until born. But I've been wondering: how did he begin?

All the billions of the rest of us began when a male sperm joined and interacted with a female ovum to form a zygote which in turn became an embryo which grew into a foetus which eventually developed into a baby. But there was no male sperm involved in the creation of the zygote which became the embryo and then the foetus which developed into the baby Jesus. What happened instead was that the zygote which was genetically coded to become Jesus appeared in an instant, attached to the wall of Mary's womb, all complete and ready to begin the process of cellular division and accumulation.

It follows from this that Jesus did not begin as a fertilised ovum of Mary's. The zygote which results from the fertilisation of an ovum does not consist of an ovum with a sperm added or attached to it. The zygote is not a sperm-and-ovum combination but an entity new, distinct and unique. Since there was no physical process of fertilisation involved in the 'conception' of Jesus it follows that the Jesus zygote was not an ovum of Mary's fertilised.

The Jesus zygote, then, arrived in Mary's womb in circumstances which are almost exactly repeated in our own time in cases of in vitro fertilisation. Mary was a surrogate mum, Jesus a 'test-tube' baby.

That is to say, Mary was a surrogate mum and Jesus a 'test-tube' baby if there is any truth in truth in the story of the Virgin Birth, which there isn't. We have previously discussed here the numerous Middle Eastern religions which taught of the Virgin Birth of a god in midwinter long before Jesus was a twinkle in the eye of the Holy Ghost. Christians simply stole the tale.

The implications for the Catholic Church's teaching today on surrogacy and in-vitro fertilisation are obvious. Not that the obvious nature of the implications will make a blind bit of difference to the teaching.

The idea of a Virgin Birth stems from the way people two millennia ago understood conception to come about. Then, and for centuries thereafter, it was assumed that a minuscule person-to-be was injected whole and complete into the woman's body by the man during intercourse, an assumption which accurately reflected a particular view of women's role in society generally, passively to carry and painfully bring to life the products of men-only.

In the light of that understanding, it made a sort of daft sense to believe that a person-to-be might be magicked into the woman by, for example, the spirit-dove which flapped into Mary's bedroom on the Day of Annunciation. But now it doesn't make even daft sense.

This should be kept in mind as controversy continues about whether facilities for in vitro fertilisation should be provided in hospitals in the 26 counties.

Ominous signs already abound that many who regard themselves as radicals are preparing to do battle with the hierarchy by arguing that the Church's policy on this matter lacks 'compassion'. Of course it does. But to demonstrate this is to say nothing of fundamental relevance.

It's not the policy which is wrong. What we need to concentrate our fire on and blast to bits is the bedrock on which the policy is based, of anti-woman bigotry, ignorance and primitive superstition.

. . . .

Hot Press—15 May 1996

The most miraculous thing about god is that although there is only one of him there's one for everybody in the audience.

I am prompted towards this paradox by the recent contretemps between Tony Blair and the pious tendency of the British Tories over Blair's suggestion that if Jesus were alive and well and living in Britain he'd be a member of New Labour.

Blair didn't say it was actually impossible to be true-Blue and truly Christian at the same time. Blair doesn't say anything about anything as clear-cut as that. What he said was this: 'My view of Christian values led me to oppose what I perceived to be a narrow view of self-interest that conservatism—particularly its modern, more right-wing form—represents. Every human being is self-interested. But Tories, I think, have too selfish a definition of self-interest.'

Some of the Tories, in the course of denouncing Blair for seeming to associate Christianity with his own party, came close to suggesting that as a matter of fact it's their party which uniquely embodies Christian ethics in British politics.

There's no need for this fractiousness. They are all right. God supports New Labour and the Conservative Party. Not to mention the Lib Dems, the Scot Nats, Plaid Cymru, Nicky Kelly, Fianna Fail, Fine Gael, Lord David Sutch, Irish Labour, the Stickies, the other Stickies, the Provos and Dangerous Dan McGrew (Independent). In fact, he backs everybody except the Progressive Democrats. Even god draws the line.

That apart, there is no political or ideological construct of any kind which god cannot be persuaded to endorse.

This doesn't apply only to the transient affairs of parliamentary politics. God has an infinite elasticity of purpose in the real world as well.

The Proclamation declaimed by Patriot Pearse outside the GPO at Easter 1916 'place[d] the cause of the Irish Republic under the protection of the Most High God, whose blessing we invoke upon our arms'. Three months later there were Orangemen with dog collars in the trenches astride the Ancre explaining to men of the Ulster Division that 'God is on our side' as they went over to total slaughter in the Battle of the Somme.

Given that concatenation of circumstances from just a few months of our small island history, we should know better than to join in the dispute between Blair and the Brit Tories.

We might stand on one side of the Ormeau Road and sing 'Oh, God Our Help In Ages Past', or on the other side singing 'Faith Of Our Fathers', and imagine that ours is the song that most pleases god's ears. But god is singing back a hymn of a different colour: 'Any way you want me, that's how I will be.'

. . . .

Hot Press—12 June 1996

'Give the devil his due', we say. But we don't. A county Carlow priest has spoken of his 'fears' that local teenagers are 'practising devil worship'. Fr Edward Dowling (PP, retired) last month told churchgoers in Bagenalstown to be 'permanently vigilant' for signs of involvement in 'the occult' by local youngsters.

Fr Dowling revealed that 100 candles had been stolen from St Andrew's church in the village: some of these had later been discovered 'scattered around' at Church Road. Others were found 'in the grass in the park at Fair Green'.

Fr Dowling also informed a 'hushed' congregation that he had been made aware of reports of unidentified teenage boys 'walking in the area with a ouija board'.

Fr Dowling has won the public support of the chairman of the Bagenalstown Town Commissioners, Mr Paddy Kiely (FF) who, according to *The Irish Times*, 'said he had seen for himself five blue signs of a sinister nature on a wall at a local railway bridge.'

An unnerving experience, no doubt. We must hope that by now Mr Kiely is sitting up in bed, and perhaps taking light nourishment.

But what we really should be asking is, where's the equity? Is this report not thoroughly biased against the devil? Does it not simply take for granted that worship of the devil is something to be 'feared'. Imagine the outcry if that were said about the devil's rival, god!

Whatever happened to balance, objectivity, the right of reply?

It sometimes seems to me that the devil—or Lucifer, Prince of Darkness, foul fiend, call him what you will—is used as a scapegoat, never given a fair crack of the whip.

You don't find followers of the devil descending on neighbouring villages with bayonets in their teeth, shouting, 'The Devil is great!' as they cut children's throats.

You never hear of warmongers geeing people up for slaughter by assuring them that 'We have the devil on our side'. No.

Remember that schlock-jock Jones, who bewildered hundreds of all ages in 'Jonesville' in Guyana to swallow poison and die in mass suicide? Did he tell them to do it so as to join the devil in hell? No, he did not. He told them to do it to join god in heaven.

So who's the good guy and who the bad man, eh?

When's the last time you heard a news item from the North telling that members of the devil-worshipping community had gathered outside a competitor's gig belching hatred and threat?

Is it followers of god or followers of the devil who are creating most of the bother and misery in this world? Go on. Tell the truth, and don't shame the devil.

I know of many bad things done in Carlow, and the devil had nothing to do with it. God's crowd, though, were well involved.

In Dublin—5 February 1987

It is not nearly well enough known that bestiality is only a venial sin.

The theological basis for this classification of the offence—if 'offence' it be at all—has to do, I understand, with the fact that dumb animals don't have souls to be sullied; neither, then, are they capable of giving, and are equally incapable of withholding, informed consent to the commission of the act.

So feel free with a frolicky ferret.

It is relevant also to point out that there is no recorded case of anyone catching AIDS from sex with an animal, a fact to which suspiciously little attention has been paid in the avalanche of earnest exhortation to 'Safe Sex' with which we are presently engulfed. (By 'Safe Sex' I refer only to the question of transmittable ailments. I do not imply that having a poke at a polecat is a no-risk activity.)

My own interest in bestiality had, I confess, waned in recent years (time takes its toll on us all) not least on account of a futile fortnight spent criss-crossing the back roads and greens of Connemara by bicycle in an effort to locate the sex shop which, according to jackeen legend, does a roaring trade in inflatable sheep.

I had been disappointed, too, by my failure (so far) to establish a factual basis for the valuable story of the Cullybackey man marooned for years on a desert island with a comely pig and a jealous Alsatian who, when a beautiful woman arrived deshabillée on the beach on a piece of driftwood and offered in her gratitude for landfall to do anything he desired, asked would she ever mind taking the dog for a walk.

My interest was rearoused, as indeed I was myself, by the discovery that there is a considerable body of English case law setting precedents relevant to Southern Ireland—dealing with the question of whether a duck is an animal in the context of the laws forbidding bestiality. The question ruffled so many feathers in the 1870s that it eventually reached the British cabinet.

What had happened was that a judge, a Lord Huddleson, having sentenced an unfortunate Warwickshire youth called Hone to 15 years in the slammer for committing an 'unnatural act' with a hen, subsequently discovered that the Court of Appeal had previously quashed the conviction of a chap called Dodd who had allegedly done a duck on the ground that a duck was not an animal 'within the meaning of the act'. ('Act', presumably, in 'Act of Parliament'.)

Huddleson wrote to Home Secretary John Cross asking whether the decision in the case of Dodd and the duck set a precedent for Hone and the hen and whether, in light of this, the conviction of Hone might be accounted unsafe.

Cross called for advice from Attorney General Sir John Holker who subsequently submitted a report to the cabinet suggesting that the appellate court's decision re Dodd and the duck had itself been based on Collins and the turkey, but that the Collins decision had since been overruled anyway in the case of Brown. (With what fowl deed Browne had been charged, I have been unable to discover.)

Moreover, Sir John informed the cabinet, the decision in Dodd and the duck had been grounded not only in precedent but also in the court's opinion that the act with which Dodd had been charged was physically impossible, a consideration which apparently did not arise in the matter of Hone and the hen. There are things which you can do with a hen which you can't do with a duck. Obviously.

Eschewing the temptation to hold forth at length on the relevance of all this to stories from our own religious tradition featuring fruitful relations between revered personalities and feathered callers, let me say merely that there's reasons aplenty, to do with both public health and eternal salvation, for us to shrug off the last traces of species-ist bigotry and adopt instead the attitude epitomised in the exchange between prosecuting counsel and Albert Harris in the case of one George Gilbert.

Prosecutor: 'Mr Harris, on the day in question were you proceeding along a lane adjacent to the farm of Mr Clarke?'

Harris: 'I was.'

Prosecutor: 'Would you describe for his Lordship what you saw?'

Harris: 'Well, George Gilbert was standing in the doorway of the barn with a sheep.'

Prosecutor: 'Yes, and what was he doing?'

Harris: 'Well, he was messing about with the sheep.'

Prosecutor: 'By that statement, are we to understand that the accused was having sexual intercourse with the sheep?'

Harris: 'Er, yes.'

Prosecutor: 'Mr Harris, what did you do when you observed this shocking spectacle?'

Harris: 'I said, "Mornin', George".'

Isn't there a lesson in that for us all?

Hot Press—12 December 1991

I imagine that Terry Waite rang a few faint, distant bells last week when he arrived back in Britain and spoke of the pestilential fellow who invented Vanity Fair.

The long Waite recalled that he had had no communication from the outside world for the first four years of his Lebanese captivity: then a guard handed him a postcard depicting John Bunyan in prison.

'You were a lucky fellow, Bunyan,' Waite remembered transmitting a thought across the centuries, 'with a window to look out from, a chair and a table, writing materials…'

Many of those who listened to Waite will have remembered Bunyan vaguely, as a religious writer from way back, author of *The Pilgrim's Progress*, one of those books which almost everybody has heard of but hardly anyone has read. Which is a bit of a pity. *The Pilgrim's Progress* is well worth reading today and can be especially recommended to sky-pilots and opponents of constructive begrudgery…

Bunyan lived at a time and in a place when there was more to religion than bullshit and spoof. His version of Christianity was sufficiently spot-on to be denounced by the government of the day as 'licentious and destructive' and likely to lead on to 'the subversion of all government'. When he went on a preaching tour to London he was accused of 'going thither to plot and make insurrection…this pestilential fellow'. From all of which it can immediately be deduced that this was a decent guy.

Bunyan's ideas were shaped in the Cromwellian Revolution of the mid-17th century when the Catholic notion of the 'divine right of Kings' was swept away by the Protestant Parliamentary Army. In the turmoil of the time, all manner of liberating, radical ideas flourished, and new groups fevered by the thought of freedom sprang up—Diggers, Levellers, Ranters and the like, many of whose manifestos still rattle with relevance today.

Bunyan was only 16 when he joined the Parliamentary Army and threw himself into a hubbub of argument, speculation and planning for a new future. He aligned himself with those who held that the Church should consist of individuals coming together in self-governing congregations and argued that the plain people had no need of bishops or professors or of guidance from the State to interpret the Word of God. He continued to preach these sensible things even after the Restoration of the Monarchy in 1660 and the reimposition of religious uniformity.

What alarmed the establishment about Bunyan was not so much what he said as the way that he said it. He spoke and wrote in blunt, accessible terms, not in the discreet language of the educated elite. His appeal was always to the poor and powerless to rise up against the oppressive rich. And even when he was arrested, charged with illegally 'calling together the people' and sentenced to 12 years, he continued to proclaim the Good News of liberation.

In prison he wrote *The Pilgrim's Progress*, which was eventually to become the world's best-selling book after the bible. It is an allegorical tale of a journey from the City of Destruction to the Celestial City, full of fighting, heroism and feats of derring-do. The pilgrims are poor and humble folk, the unsavoury characters who strive to thwart them— Mr Two-Tongues, Lord Time-Server and so forth—rotten-rich.

The best passage describes how two pilgrims happen on a town, Vanity Fair, where belief in privatisation and the market economy is of Progressive Democratic proportions. Everything is for sale: 'houses, lands, trades, places, honours, preferments, titles, countries, kingdoms, lusts, pleasures and delights of all sorts...whores, bawds, wives, husbands, children, masters, servants, lives, blood, bodies, souls, silver, gold, pearls, precious stones and whatnot'.

And no doubt problems to do with planning permissions can be solved at a price.

One of the pilgrims, Faithful, suggests that this is not the most moral way to live, and is arrested, tried and executed, one of the burghers of the town observing that 'if all men were of his mind...not one nobleman would any longer have his place in this town.'

Bunyan was given the Connolly treatment after his death. Chunks of his writing which could be presented harmlessly out of context were popularised, while his political message was smoothed over and suppressed.

The suppression didn't always work. In the last century, Protestant missionaries who offered *The Pilgrim's Progress* to converts as a purely spiritual tract could find that its meaning shone through clearly enough. The single most massive rebellion against imperialism in the 19th century, the Taiping revolt in China, was led by people who took their inspiration directly from Bunyan's book.

There is very little in the works of today's leading 'liberation theologists'—Boff, Camara, Kung, Schillebeeckx—which Bunyan wasn't on to more than three centuries ago.

Those who contemplate the weary, stale, ugly and repressive role that the Christian sects play in our own time and place and who wonder how religion might be made to seem meaningful again, could do worse than thank Terry Waite for reminding them of John Bunyan, and of the message from his pilgrim soul, that religious ideas acquire life and become real only when and insofar as they reflect, albeit, inevitably, in distorted form, the material struggles of the mass of poor people.

. . . .

Hot Press—2 July 1992
The Archbishop of Canterbury, George Carey, said an interesting thing a couple of weeks back—something of an event.

George wings in from the 'evangelical' faction of the Anglican crowd, which puts more stress on whooping it up for Jesus than engaging in rational discourse.

But on 5 June he was quoted in the London *Independent* saying that without religion there can be no morality: that 'no god means no goodness'. It's not often these days that the old lie at the heart of all organised religion is set down in such plain and pithy terms.

The question at issue here has been rowed about and ruminated over since way back when. Socrates himself was breaking no new ground when he invited young ravers gathered around him on the slopes of the Acropolis to ponder the question: 'Is an action good simply because the gods enjoin it?'

It leapt starkly from the dialogue which followed that—aside and apart from the sheer impossibility of ever getting everyone to agree on what it was that the gods were enjoining—to answer 'Yes' to the question was to accept that we humans have no way of working out for ourselves what's good and what's not.

Once god or 'the gods' are allowed in as arbiters, blind obedience becomes the only basis of morality. Which is as good a reason as any for giving up on gods.

Religion, far from providing a basis for morality, has ever been a force for immorality. The Christian religion in particular has opposed and obstructed every advance in moral evolution for almost 2,000 years, sanctioning and sanctifying every imaginable cruelty and form of oppression, regarding those who sought the liberation of humanity as dangerous enemies to be destroyed, endlessly and obsessively endeavouring to keep people corralled in ignorant superstition, in thrall to foolish priestcraft.

All this is well-known and undeniable, which is not to say that it deters the representatives of Christianity from droning dishonestly on about the relevance of their religion to human morality.

So the Church went in for mass murder, slave-holding, intolerance, perversity, bestiality and diverse other dark practices all down through the ages? Ah yes, say the purple propagandists, but that was on account of the human element, which the spiritual essence of religion inevitably transcends.

In fact, the exact opposite is the case. The human element has always cried out against the cruelties of religion. And religion has always defended its cruelties precisely on the ground that mortal life is of no account.

The humanist argument against religion has always been that it is not how we die but how we live which matters—the only sound basis for any moral code.

All this is of some obvious relevance to much current argumentation in the South. There is a line of argument that 'the bishops'—almost invariably a reference to the Roman Catholic bishops—have a legitimate function in commenting on and even laying down the law with regard to 'moral issues', but ought to steer clear of 'politics'. (Since the 'moral issues' in question require political action, the line of argument is wobbly. But no matter.)

This is the standard approach of those who regard themselves as 'progressive', 'liberal', even 'radical'. But, in fact, it represents an enormous and unnecessary concession to the bishops. It is precisely their claim to authority on moral issues which needs to be challenged head-on.

More than half a century ago, during the dark days of fundamentalist terror in the United States, the prolific, freethinking publisher and essayist Emanuel Haldeman-Julius wrote: 'A great deal of water has passed under the bridge since the days when no sinner was safe and only marauding, murdering saints could lay down the moral law to mankind…'

'Religion,' he went on, 'for all its babble of morality, has appeared in history as an immoral force that has been compelled, from age to age, to accommodate itself to the progressive morality of the race: a morality growing up outside of the Church and perforce asserting itself generally in opposition to the Church and to religion.'

Instead of making the timid argument that the bishops have it wrong on this or that issue, or complaining that they have intruded into 'political' territory, those who want freedom in this society should be asserting themselves generally in opposition to the Church and to religion.

. . . .

Hot Press—26 January 1994
Michael Cleary bit the dust. I remember him mainly for two things. First, his manic antics at the Ballybrit racecourse at Galway in 1979, prior to the arrival of the sicko from Cracow, John Paul II, for a 'Youth Mass'.

The demented Cleary, drafted in as master of ceremonies by a hierarchy which reckoned that some OTT flamboyance might be helpful for the day, whirled and windmilled like a crow-clad dervish on acid as he strove to whip the crowd up into a frenzy of anticipation of the Great Whited Sepulchre's arrival, orchestrating Nuremberg rally-style chants of 'We Love the Pope' and relentless choruses of the worst spiritual ever written, 'He's Got The Whole World In His Hands', and occasionally yelling out about what a happy wee woman the 'Virgin Mary' must be this minute looking down from high heaven upon this wonderful sight.

Local bishop Eamon Casey bullshitted afterwards about Cleary's supposed credibility with young people lending weight to the papal sermonising—which had to do with the necessity for the most strict adherence to the Church's teaching on sexual morality, else you'd roast in hell forever. Now that I come to think of it, I'm surprised Casey managed to stay so calm throughout the proceedings.

Then there was Cleary's performance at the time of the X case, when he first seemed to suggest that the 14-year-old girl who was pregnant as a result of rape and who wanted an abortion either wasn't pregnant at all or, alternatively, had become pregnant deliberately as part of a convoluted plot designed to discredit the constitutional prohibition on abortion. He then changed tack and said that had he been the girl's father he'd have procured an abortion in England and lied to the gardai about it afterwards, thus preventing public scandal and controversy.

He did have a certain significance in that Casey and himself accurately represent two important strains within the RC church in Ireland as we come to the close of the 20th century, the one an oul bull, the other an oul bollix.

. . . .

Hot Press—22 February 1996
I see that the Catholic bishops are worried about falling attendance

at mass along the West coast and have suggested that this can be taken as evidence of continuing depopulation of the region. They could be right. Then again, maybe it's just that fewer people are going to mass.

There's little evidence of a declining population in Liverpool, Portsmouth or Newcastle, where the numbers of Catholics attending church on Sundays is also in steep and accelerating decline. Last month the Latin Mass Society called on Catholics in both Britain and Ireland 'to face up to the reality of a Church in deep crisis'.

The latest figures published in the 1996 *Catholic Directory* show that between 1988 and 1995 the numbers of Sunday mass goers in Britain fell by 200,000 to an average of 1,190,037. A separate study on behalf of the Catholic overseas relief agency Cafod predicts a halving of mass attendance to 600,000 in the next nine years.

I read in the *Catholic Times* (28 January) that officials of the Latin Mass Society have blamed the gathering crisis on the trend towards 'liberalism' and 'modernism' since Vatican Two. They might be on to something. Religion is like a single malt scotch. It should be taken neat or not at all. To dilute it is to deprive it of its very essence.

Says Latin Mass man Leo Darragh: 'Most of those traditions and practices which clothed the Church so gracefully and effectively for generations have been contemptuously cast aside by a very tiny but powerful and influential pressure group, and now it is in a state of serious embarrassment.'

'We have the strength of centuries behind us,' he continued. 'So let us wipe away the rhetoric and jargon. Let us say things the way they really are.'

True enough, Gregorian chant, ornate processions to High Mass and contemplation of the complexities of Thomistic Philosophy could turn the tide. Fewer nuns saying 'fuck' would help, too. Most of all, the Church should adopt a stern approach to the class of Catholic who holds forth in saloon bars and television studios about the 'institutional Church' being one thing but that 'in the end' a person has to be guided by 'his or her own conscience'. This is not Catholicism. This is Protestantism. Some will recall from Church History lessons that there was quite a to-do about the distinction once upon a time.

The bishops in the West would be better advised to take this line rather than hinting that the emptying churches of Achill betoken something the rest of us should be worried about too.

Meanwhile a piece in the *Guardian* (30 January) expresses puzzlement that so many British Catholics are drifting away from the Church 'despite the glamour of a string of celebrity converts' such as airhead idler the Duchess of Kent, three-in-a-bed arms-to-Iraq salesman Alan Clark and Tory Minister Ann 'Immigrants Out!' Widdecombe. I'd have thought that an organisation which allows people like that in shouldn't be surprised by a rush of others getting out.

Even more meanwhile, an *Irish Times* article (20 January) by the distinguished scientist Richard Dawkins debunking astrology has drawn a predictable succession of spluttering rejoinders. Many people have written, freely giving their names and addresses for publication, unconcerned about embarrassment to themselves or their children, proclaiming their belief that the position of stars and planets at the time of birth can dictate, day to day, the entire course of one's life. I suppose this is no more ridiculous than the notion that the moon's a balloon. No, I tell a lie, it is a lot more ridiculous. Still, it's in line with the common experience of meeting sane-looking people who ask you smilingly, 'What sign are you?' and nod meaningfully that they'd thought so when you lie.

Astrology arose at a time when it was commonly assumed that the earth was at the centre of the universe and that all other bodies moved in intricate harmonious patterns around it. It mustn't have seemed then such a daft thing to believe—although it should be noted that astronomers like Eudoxus were lampooning believers as long ago as 300 BC.

That was then. Now the standard astrological chart still in use refers only to those planets which were visible to the naked eyes of the ancients. The 'telescope' planets—Uranus (discovered 1781), Neptune (1846) and Pluto (1930)—don't figure at all.

There has been no excuse for this nonsense since Copernicus: since 1543 to be exact, when the great man published *De Revolutionibus Orbium Caelestium*. And I have even more compelling evidence.

Some years ago, I worked as news editor of the *Sunday World* when the late Kevin Marron was brilliantly the editor. The 'stars' column, contributed by a famous syndicated 'expert' whose name now mercifully escapes me (Pertrungo?), was one of the paper's most popular features. The pair of us decided to have fun with it. So for months we distributed the paragraphs of prediction at random among the signs, putting Virgo under Cancer, slotting Pisces into Gemini and so forth.

The letters of congratulation on the accuracy of our man's predictions continued to arrive in, if anything, even greater and more enthusiastic profusion.

. . . .

Hot Press—16 May 1996

My attention has been caught by a modest flurry of liveliness among the Catholic rank and file across the water. Some Catholics there are concerned about the possibility of a right-wing traditionalist being appointed Bishop of Liverpool.

This is particularly upsetting to progressives, since the last Liverpool Bishop, the late Derek Worlock, had been one of their leading icons for close on 20 years. This may say more about English Catholicism than about Dr Worlock, but no matter. The point is, Worlock was there, frequently arm-in-arm with his Anglican counterpart, the former Test batsman David Sheppard, expressing concern about social problems, communing with the street people and so forth. This gave people who crave that their religion seem relevant to the secular world a satisfying sense of purpose.

Now, more than a year after his retirement and three months after his death, the word is out that John Paul wants an incense-impregnated traditionalist in Worlock's place. The chagrin of the progressives has been heightened by squeaks of anticipation from the likes of novelist Alice Thomas Ellis. She used her column in the *Catholic Herald* to dismiss the Merseyside trailblazer as a light-minded follower of fashion whose activities and doctrinal perspectives served only to 'dilute' the Catholic faith.

Ms Ellis's column is regularly worth reading for the sheer implacability of her hostility to change. In the current controversy, she has been blunt in claiming that she 'speak[s] for the thousands of Liverpudlians who are totally against the progressive ideas of Worlock'.

What is certain is that she speaks for those Liverpool Catholics who back the pope in wanting more emphasis on liturgical and sacramental matters and less time spent on social and political affairs. And she's entitled to feel vindicated by the recent switch to Catholicism of prominent High Anglicans like Tory Minister Ann Widdecombe, the Duchess of Kent and *Daily Telegraph* editor Charles Moore. It is precisely the adherence to traditional structures, beliefs and practices which had attracted this element away from the à la carte ambience of the Anglicans.

Ms Ellis and her co-thinkers haven't had it all their own way. Influential Catholic liberals like John Wilkins, editor of the not-bad weekly magazine the *Tablet* have rushed to defend Worlock's legacy. The *Guardian* reported (although we should always be suspicious of this stock claim) that lines to phone-in programmes on Radio Merseyside were 'jammed' with outraged members of the faithful anxious to speak up for their late Bishop. The editor of the *Herald*, the scatty American Cristina Odone, has now genuflected to Worlock's memory and apologised for having printed Ellis's column.

This hasn't been a full-tilt controversy such as has convulsed Catholicism in continental Europe, the Americas and India. We haven't seen Catholics lying in the cathedral aisle to block the passage of the Pope's appointee towards his enthronement, in line with events at Chur in Switzerland a little time ago. Nor have any clergy summoned a press conference to denounce Vatican disregard for local wishes, as has happened more than once recently in the US. By general contemporary standards, the Liverpool contretemps has been discreet, reticent, low-key.

Not by Irish standards, though. It will be recalled that about a year and a half ago, the popular Bishop of Derry, Edward Daly, was replaced by a far-right supporter of the Opus Dei organisation, Seamus Hegarty. In private, many priests of the diocese didn't hide their disgruntlement. The required welcoming editorial in the *Derry Journal* was decidedly stiff and formal. But there was no public expressions of protest, nothing that would qualify as 'controversy'.

This docility of Irish Catholicism was just as evident in the excitement last month about a statement by Bishop Willie Walsh that he found it hard to understand the ground for confining the priesthood to unmarried men. This struck news editors at RTE as such a dramatic outburst as to require national news coverage. Declan Kiberd in the *Sunday Tribune* near swooned at the drama of it all, hailing the pronouncement as marking a 're-emergence of Irish Catholic pluralism'.

In fact, Walsh had been at pains to make it clear he wasn't challenging Church teaching but merely confessing to a personal difficulty. 'If our faith and our church is to be a living one then we have to face questioning and doubts and difficulties... I don't like people talking about "loyal opposition". We are not in the business of democracy', he'd gone on to say.

The Catholic propagandist Joe Foyle put Kiberd right when he explained that Walsh 'knows well that 1,000 difficulties don't make a single doubt, and that...[we] would be wise to bow to the collective wisdom of our worldwide church as enunciated by our Pope'. Nothing Willie Walsh has said before or since challenges this view.

That as keen a mind as Kiberd's can seize up dealing with a middle-rank bishop's slight personal doubts says a lot about how unused Irish Catholic intellectuals are to serious doctrinal dispute. There's more vibrant life in English Catholicism these days. Now isn't that a thing?

Mention of Seamus Hegarty reminds me... Jean Doherty (not her real name) tells me that she is 'demented' at the seeming impossibility of processing complaints that children attending St Mary's National School in Ardara, County Donegal, had been violently abused over a period of more than a dozen years by the head teacher, James Boyle. Mr Boyle was suspended from his position 20 months ago by the Department of Education. Parents had taken their complaints to the department, having failed to get satisfaction from the local Church and State authorities.

The department's investigation under a leading lawyer collapsed when it emerged that it had no powers to compel witnesses, or to order discovery of documents, or indeed any relevant powers at all. The only inquiry now under way is being conducted by a Monsignor James MacDwyer—the manager of the school. His mandate is to report to Dr Phillip Boyce, Seamus Hegarty's recent successor as Bishop of Raphoe.

Boyce is under no legal obligation to give the Department of Education sight of the report.

Parents at another national school in the Raphoe diocese met a few weeks ago to discuss how to proceed with allegations that their own children had been violently abused by a senior teacher. Some of them are minded, in raging frustration, to allow the matter to drop. Their own experience, combined with the Ardara incident, gives them no hope of satisfaction.

It was merely a coincidence that Hegarty was transported from Raphoe to Derry just as these stories broke. He wouldn't have had time or space to look back over the border once he had settled into Derry, given that the sex abuse scandal involving the Derry priest Gerald McCallion burst into the open almost before he had his feet under the mahogany dining table in the Bishop's Residence.

What conclusions are to be drawn from this sad tangle of circumstance? Well, Labour minister Niamh Breatnach has concluded that this is the time for a new law giving the bishops a veto over the appointment of teachers to schools funded by the State.

Meanwhile, no address by a bishop is complete without a coded message to the faithful that they needn't take at face value further stories of savagery tumbling out of Church institutions, reminders that these things just weren't understood in those days, suggestions that the media, in fairness, ought also to highlight the great work done by the decent majority of religious, and references to interesting new research on false memory syndrome.

. . . .

Hot Press—27 May 1998
What's the next world coming to?

Cardinal Basil Hume told BBC Radio 4's *Today* programme that comments by two Sunday School teachers from the West Midlands to the effect that the late Diana Spencer was probably roasting in Hell were 'upsetting for us all'.

'Nobody can judge another person except God', said the Cardinal. 'He knows all the circumstances'.

Well, quite so, God being, after all, omniscient. So he must have known Diana Spencer's circumstances. That she was in the company of a man with whom she'd committed adultery when she died. And on her own admission, he wasn't the first she'd commited adultery with.

What's the attitude of the Catholic Church to adultery these days? Is it still a mortal sin, or not?

Hume admitted that Diana hadn't been without sin, but went on to claim that she had done 'a great deal of good. She was by no means a saint...clearly a flawed person... I think whenever a person does things which are wrong, and we don't have to pretend that wrong is right, that one does have to put it in the context of their whole lives.'

By which he presumably meant that her (as he seemed to believe) generally virtuous life softened the offensiveness of her adultery in the eyes of God.

This is unscriptural and contrary to the teaching of the Church which Hume purports to speak for.

The injunction against adultery does not appear in scripture in any elusive or elliptical form. It is in the Commandments: 'Thou shalt not commit adultery.' This isn't a poetical or allegorical remark. It's an Instruction.

What's more: to suggest that adultery is a mere misdemeanour which might be offset by acts of kindness or charitable works is to deny the sacramental nature of the solemn marriage vow. Hume's remark was little short of heresy.

As for Hell: some say, or hint, that there is no Hell in the 'old-fashioned' sense of a vast pit of fire where souls suffer unimaginably for all eternity.

But in Matthew 25:41 the words which God will utter to the damned on Judgment Day are set out clearly: 'Depart from me ye accursed, into everlasting fire…' Not much room for ambiguity there.

Hart's *Catholic Doctrines* puts it plain: 'It is of Faith that there is a Hell; that its duration is eternal; and that the wicked will there be tormented for ever in company with the devil and the lost angels.'

No Catholic is permitted to believe other than that a man or woman who has died in adultery is currently, and for all time, writhing in indescribable agony in the punishment furnace of Hell.

If a person can commit adultery and yet escape hellfire on account of a generally good life, this should surely be proclaimed from the pulpits and spelt out in religious knowledge classes in our schools.

But, of course, this is a nonsense. Hume's remarks had no basis in scripture or tradition or in the general body of Church teaching. And he wasn't making a general point, applicable to all.

What we have here is another example of one divine law for the rich another for the poor, of Faith as a matter of fudge and nudge, immutableTruth in constant flux as the interests of the institutional Church are maintained in constant adaptation to passing circumstance and fashion.

Once there were cardinals who would at least make a show of sticking to their doctrinal guns.

. . . .

Hot Press—30 September 1998
'Black and blue from the punching and pinching of children, Mickey Mouse and Donald Duck have asked a French Government agency for protection.'

I am reminded of Croke Park and Fr Michael Cleary.

The quote comes from the *Daily Telegraph* of 16 September and refers to a dispute at the EuroDisney theme park east of Paris where workers who daily don daft costumes and prance around the park as cartoon characters have found themselves hit, kicked and spat on by small children. The entire *Alice in Wonderland* team has quit. Now the others, mad as hatters, say they aren't going to stand for it any more.

On the final August weekend security guards had to link arms to escort Mickey and Minnie Mouse through a leering throng of six to ten-year-olds. The workers' representatives have written to the Inspection du Travail, the agency charged with enforcing safety-at-work provisions, demanding a stronger security presence and court action against the culprits.

The workers say that while they are allowed to retreat to 'rest areas' if they feel in peril the children seem to sense weakness and panic when they notice Donald Duck, Kanga, Roo, Kevin Myers, Tigger or whomever edging in that direction and take it as a signal to launch concerted mass attacks.

After a threat of industrial action, the company has dropped a threat of disciplinary action against Winnie the Pooh for allegedly pulling off his head and kicking a pram.

Just like Fr Michael Cleary on National Children's Day

National Children's Day was dreamed up by one of the useless Southern governments of the '80s as a wheeze to deflect attention from their betrayal of all promises relating to children's issues. Free toothbrushes were distributed in the schools as part of the same scam. I am not at all sure Charlie Haughey wasn't involved.

The centrepiece of the affair was an event at Croke Park, with all manner of star-studded surprises and fantastical delights promised.

A brass band marched around the field playing Christian Brothers tunes and then marched around it again, after which it marched around the field playing Christian Brothers tunes. Fr Michael Cleary was emcee, perched on a podium in the middle of the pitch, waving his mad arms in a desperate effort to orchestrate clapping along to the beat of the band. 'C'mon now, boys and girls, sure yeez all know this one!'

Many of these youngsters would never see six again, and were seriously cheesed off by the insanitary old fraud's patronising patter. 'Heh, heh, an' howse all da mammies and daddies, heh, heh heh?' he'd gibber, puffs of dandruff billowing from his beard and floating in thick flurries over the clean heads of the children on the terraces.

Then Mickey Mouse arrived in a helicopter. He climbed down onto the pitch and made towards Cleary's podium with that scampering, arms-akimbo saunter which the Disney corporation thinks looks cute. Cleary was lathering himself into an even higher state of frenzy. 'Ya-ya-ya-ya-ya, Mickey Mouse! It's Mickey Mouse, boys and girls!' as if this were truly the most amazing spectacle any of us had ever set eyes on. Mickey Mouse hopped and skipped in even jauntier style, and diverted from his path towards the podium to head over to the sideline to greet the excited children.

But both Mickeys had misinterpreted the elemental howl arising from the throng. The instant they had the Mouse within range, avenging hordes of Dublin toddlers swarmed over the barriers like Visigoths storming the gates of Atrium. The last I saw of Mickey Mouse was a gloved paw waving feebly as he was engulfed in a huge suffusion of callow rage.

Then the gardai baton-charged, grabbed Mickey Mouse under the oxters and, slashing on all sides like Braveheart surrounded by Englishmen, fought off the more persistent of the pugnacious tots and ran, half pulling, half carrying the limp Mickey Mouse back towards the centre of the field where, rubicund faces sweat-streaked from their exertions, they formed a protective circle around the quivering rodent. All the while, Fr Micheal Cleary, distraught, was tearing at his tufty hair and issuing shrieked imprecations, along such lines as, 'Stop kicking Mickey Mouse, yeez wee bastards.'

My children and I agreed afterwards that it had been a smashing day. Disney's characters are terrific for kids. You just have to know how to handle them.

And then there's the Rev Dr Balducci of the Vatican's Congregation for Evangelisation of Peoples, who says in a new book that stories of alien encounters and abductions are perfectly plausible and are not to be dismissed.

'The existence of extra-terrestrials cannot be denied. There is too much evidence of flying saucers', states the authoritative Church spokesman.

He says that the first question he would ask an alien is, 'What is your concept of god?'

The Catholic Media Office in London takes a different view, suggesting the first query should be 'whether Christian atonement was applicable to them'.

Possible major doctrinal split in the making here. Clarification urgently needed. ET, phone Rome.

Chapter 2

Ratzinger in the skull

Generally speaking, the Catholic Church in Ireland has been intellectually inert throughout the 20th century. It didn't have to fight to carve out or protect its area of influence. The national movement which succeed in ending British rule in the South was steeped in Catholicism. The State which resulted was born Catholic. Questions of how the Church should relate to the State were largely unasked, much less answered. Political radicalism didn't tend to be associated with anti-clericalism. The contrast with Italy, France and Spain is as striking as is the resemblance to Poland. No wonder John Paul loves Irish Catholicism so well.

Ireland has produced no major theologian in this century. 'Liberation theology' has never caught on, despite the number of fervent Catholics in arms against the Northern (and occasionally the Southern) State. The handful of 'radical priests' who have emerged in the North have been extreme Nationalists, not socialists. Genuinely radical Irish priests have been more likely located in Africa, Asia or Latin America.

This is not to deny that the ideological battles within Catholicism worldwide have had direct relevance to Ireland. I have occasionally surveyed this broad battlefield.

. . . .

In Dublin—23 February 1989

The last act of the sinister Sicilian, Gaetano Alibrandi, before retiring as Ireland's Papal Nuncio, was to transubstantiate Senator Des Hanafin into a Knight of St Gregory. Senator Hanafin is now doubly benighted, having already been a member of Columbanus's crowd.

The eminent knight was accorded this latest elevation on account of his tremendous work in raising money for the referenda campaigns which ensured that people whose marriages are over will find no solace in civil law and that women in Ireland who become pregnant will be constitutionally required to bring the pregnancy to full term whether or not this is their wish or in their interest or in accordance with their own conscience.

Many people contemplating the pictures of Sir Hanafin shrouded in incense and surrounded by ancient men garbed like warlocks will have assumed that he has now acquired even more immense influence that hitherto. This is not true, as he'll discover if he ever tries to wither a heretic's willie or turn a Presbyterian into a toad.

The significance of his becoming a member of the Gregory coven is altogether different. This Gregory was an interesting chap. Not nearly enough is taught about him in our schools.

The order into which Hanafin was inducted was founded by Gregory XVI, although this is NOT the Gregory the order is named after. Popes? You couldn't be up to them.

Gregory XVI (1831-46) named the order after Gregory I (590-604), possibly just because he wanted 'Gregory' in lights, more likely because he genuinely admired the guy. They had a fair bit in common.

Here's a couple of things which Gregory XVI believed, and required all Catholics to believe.

He believed that democracy was a mortally sinful idea.

In *Mirari Vos*, published in 1832, he declared the belief that people had the right to make up their own minds on any matter of morality 'insane'.

Freedom of the press? 'Heretical vomit.'

He was stern on the Jewish question, too. He decreed that any Jew who insulted the Catholic Church or a Catholic priest should be killed. That's killed dead.

And there's more, but we'll leave that for another day because it's the real Gregory, Gregory I, 'Gregory the Great', who's our main man here.

Gregory the Great you might remember from your school days as the guy who was so struck by the beauty of fair-haired Anglo-Saxon youths on sale in the Roman slave market that he (a) bought a couple and (b) sent St Augustine and a team of monks over to England to convert the rest of them.

Gregory I was no dunce. He is accounted among the four great 'Latin Doctors' of the early Church…although it must also be admitted that much of what he wrote was a mite zany. His *Dialogues*, for example, tell of miraculous happenings all over Italy, considerable numbers of folk turning themselves or others into all manner of creatures, holy people levitating and flying around the countryside in veritable flocks, and so forth.

But the main reason Gregory I is called 'Great' is that he, arguably more than any other single pope, established that the Catholic Church has a temporal as well as a spiritual role in this world. He taught, and practised, that the Church can and should make civil as well as moral law and indeed, having made civil law, can and should intervene to enforce it.

Gregory was the chief civil magistrate in Rome before he became Pope. He then merged the two offices. He personified the unity of Church and State. In this role he raised armies, waged war, made treaties, on all occasions seeking to impose the authority of the Church by secular, civil means.

He hated women, and sex. He taught that every sexual act, even in marriage, must be atoned for. Women were the source of the sin inherent in sex. After intercourse, a man had to perform a ritual act of washing and then do penance before entering a Church.

Taking pleasure in sex was always sinful. The notion that procreation is the only acceptable purpose of sexual activity was not invented by Gregory I. But it was he who was most influential in feeding it into the body of Christian belief.

I don't suggest that Des Hanafin believes in all the things Gregories I and XVI espoused. But given some of the things they believed in, there's an aptness about John Paul II conferring on him the order instituted by the last of the Pope Gregories in honour of the first.

I saw a picture in the *Irish Catholic* of himself and Alibrandi staring at the sky, as if in search of inspiration. But they were probably just looking out for low-flying nuns.

. . . .

In Dublin—9 November 1989
The intellectual emptiness which characterises the internal life of the Irish Catholic Church was evident last month in the silence which greeted two significant developments in the long-running battle between the repressive centralists around John Paul II and the advocates of a looser doctrinal regime.

First, the Brazilian Franciscan, Leonardo Boff, reacted angrily to the latest restrictions placed on him by Cardinal Joseph Ratzinger, head of the Inquisition (or the Vatican Congregation for the Doctrine of the Faith, as it now styles itself). Second, it was announced that all 22 German diocesan bishops will meet with Vatican officials in mid-November to convey the German Church's objections to 'the new Roman centralism'.

Boff, the single most influential of the 'liberation theologists', announced that he had accepted an order from Fr Estavao Ottenbreit, provincial leader of the Franciscans in San Paulo, that he should not travel or give interviews outside Brazil until next January at the earliest. Boff made it clear he believed the order had come from the Franciscan superior general in Rome, Fr John Vaughan, and that Vaughan was acting on the express instructions of Ratzinger.

Commenting on the fact that Ottenbreit, Vaughan and Ratzinger had all denied point-blank that the order had been passed along this chain of command, Boff said: 'They are all liars. They arrange from behind, so when someone asks, they say, "I don't know." In the end, I'm the one who has to put up with it.'

Describing the restrictions put on him as 'persecution', Boff left little room for doubt that if the measures are extended beyond next January he will consider an open breach with the Vatican. 'While this Pope is alive, with this Curia with Ratzinger, we are going to see only control, and very little freedom… There's a vigilance all over the Church, a repression that you accept, that you suffer, and if you want to continue on, you do it. I hope this is the last time, because I'm getting tired of it.'

Boff is hardly a household name in Ireland, but he's well enough known among the clergy and to a layer of Church activists, particularly those who consider themselves radical. And it is well recognised in such circles that at the heart of his disagreement with the Vatican is an issue of sharp and dangerous relevance to the Catholic Church in Ireland.

Boff has argued that in a capitalist society where, by definition, the mass of the people are excluded from the exercise of real power, the Church, in fulfilling its role as the 'Church of the people', ought to be in an antagonistic relationship with the machinery of the State. The arguments arising from this are complex. But in, say Darndale in Dublin, not to mention West Belfast, the practical implications are straightforward. Perhaps it is this which dissuades our home-grown Catholic radicals from expressing an opinion on Boff's case?

The impending visit of the German bishops to the Vatican follows a formal declaration of dissent last year by 163—*one hundred and sixty three*—German-speaking theologians. The declaration came in the wake of a bitter dispute over the appointment of a bishop to Cologne: after a year long wrangle the Vatican appointed its own man over the heads and the loud objections of local laity and the German Church as a whole.

The objection by the theologians to Vatican high-handedness was then extended to the underlying issues. The 'Cologne declaration' attacked John Paul II's 'fixation' on contraception and bluntly rejected his attempt to make hard-line opposition to contraception an article of fundamental faith.

Whether the German bishops will mend fences or formalise differences with Rome remains to be seen. In the meantime, let us wonder why one can't imagine the Irish bishops heading for Rome as a group to present a distinctive, mildly dissident point of view on anything at all.

. . . .

In Dublin—20 September 1990

I think we can all agree that there's no way the world community could sit back and allow the puffed up dictator of a tin-pot state to impose his will on other people. All who are acquainted with history will know where that leads.

So why haven't the Americans bombed the Vatican?

Last month the Vatican launched a no-warning attack on hundreds of innocent theologians throughout the world. Nothing has been heard from some of them since, despite the anxious enquiries of distraught relatives and friends.

The guided missive was entitled 'Instruction On The Ecclesial Vocation Of The Theologian' and was signed by Vatican strongman Cardinal Joseph Ratzinger, prefect of the Inquisition, aka the Congregation for the Doctrine of the Faith).

The Instruction is aimed at 'the bishops of the Catholic Church and through them her theologians'. Essentially, it says that theologians who disagree with Vatican directive should keep their disagreements to themselves.

Which might sound no more unreasonable than many another religious edict until we focus on the fact that this instruction applies to the Instruction itself.

That is to say, no theologian is allowed to publicly challenge the Instruction not to publicly challenge Instructions.

This is wonderfully reminiscent of my own favourite Stalinist decree which laid down that when Uncle Joe declared you a non-person not only was it an offence to mention you, it was an offence to mention that it was an offence to mention you.

When Uncle Joe zapped you, you were zapped good.

And thus with John Paul. And there's more, and better.

The document bans Catholic theologians from saying that the Vatican might be wrong even when the Vatican admits that it might be wrong. It happens like this. There are, as we all know, different levels of certainty in Catholic teaching. There's your infallible pronouncements, which were instituted by Pius IX, the self-styled 'Prisoner of the Vatican', at the First Vatican Council just over 100 years ago.

When the Pope makes an infallible pronouncement—*ex cathedra*, as we experts say—it's game over, end of story, argument finito. The teaching that the 'Blessed Virgin Mary' was conceived without Original Sin is an example of an infallible doctrine.

Then, at a somewhat lower level of certainty, there are policies, rules, requirements, beliefs backed up by the Magisterium: that is, by the teaching authority of the Church. The Instruction breaks new ground by defining more narrowly than ever before what constitutes the magisterium.

It has generally been taken to refer to the authority of all the bishops of the Church, meeting together or at least acting in concert. However the new document declares that 'the Roman Pontiff fulfils his universal mission with the help of the various bodies of the Roman Curia and in particular with that of the Congregation for the Doctrine of the Faith… Consequently, the documents issued by this congregation expressly approved by the Pope participate in the ordinary Magisterium of the successor of St Peter.'

In other words, the Congregation, currently controlled by John Paul's two closest doctrinal advisors, Cardinal Ratzinger and Archbishop Alberto Bovone, has now declared itself capable of entering new items into the Magisterium, with the agreement of the Pope but without reference to any other institution or area of authority within the Church.

This despite the fact that, within the text of the Instruction itself, the Congregation accepts that the teaching of the Magisterium is 'reformable', that is, it might be wrong and might have to be changed.

The Congregation is saying, 'Even though we might be wrong,

theologians have no right to say so.'

One, understandably anonymous, Catholic theologian told the semi-official Church newspaper the *Universe*: 'Any criticism of a document from the Congregation is [now] forbidden so I cannot comment officially. In practice, the effect of this document means the level of theological disagreement and debate in the Church is to be taken out of the public arena... There will be fear that even showing moderate disagreement will be seen as disloyalty.'

More daringly, the leading Catholic theologian, Dr Geoffrey Turner, Head of Theology at Trinity and All Saint's College, allows himself to be quoted by name, saying: 'The Congregation is certainly flexing its muscles. Its model of theology is that the Magisterium makes definitive statements on faith and practice, and theologians must agree—even on reformable matters!... This is a political, ideological document about the power struggle in the Church... It's certainly not a piece of theology.'

Another leading theologian, writing in the *Catholic Herald*, warns that: 'We now have theological justification for what used to be called "creeping infallibility"... Dissent is out. The Congregation accepts that not all the teaching of the Magisterium is irreformable. Yet even if the validity of the Magisterium's view is not evident, even if the opposite opinion is more probable, disagreement cannot be justified. The freedom of research so proudly proclaimed early on (in the Instruction) becomes a freedom to conform to the "truth"—an unexceptionable proposition in itself, were the "truth" not identified with the teachings of the Magisterium as interpreted to the faithful by the Congregation for the Doctrine of the Faith. The meaning of the word "freedom" has been stood on its head.'

If the Ayatollah Khomeini had issued a decree that no Islamic scholar could question his rulings, even rulings which he himself admitted might be wrong, I fancy the item might have figured on the RTE *Six O'Clock News* as an example of the sort of daft totalitarianism Muslims put up with.

But about this, in a country still nominally overwhelmingly Catholic, not a dicky bird.

I don't suggest seriously that the Vatican should be bombed.

But if somewhere had to be bombed, and I was the unfortunate someone forced to select the target, I'd have to include the Vatican somewhere in the prime list of possibles.

In Dublin—13 March 1991

That old joke about the Church's side winning referenda in Ireland 'with a ballot paper in one hand and a Carmelite in the other' may soon have to be changed. It's now possible to have a Carmelite in both hands. The old Order is rapidly changing.

John Paul has just approved new constitutions for 92 discalced Carmelite convents, mostly in Spain, removing them from the authority of the Carmelite Order worldwide and making the prioress of each house directly responsible to the Vatican rather than to the Superior General of the Order.

This is the first serious split in the Carmelites since its foundation by St Teresa of Avila in 1562. The superior general, Fr Felipe Sainz de Baranda, is said to be 'enraged'.

In 1984, John Paul tried to reverse a gradual process of change within the Carmelites by directing Vatican officials to draw up a 'new' constitution—based on the original 'Rule of 1581'. The document which emerged—essentially proposing a return to pre-Vatican II disciplines—was rejected by a 70-30 vote of Carmelites worldwide. The Carmelites then produced an alternative document themselves which was submitted to the Vatican last summer. They were still awaiting the go-ahead to vote when—without prior warning or any consultation with the Order—John Paul announced as a fait accompli that 92 convents with 1,500 nuns were to be separated from the Order and would henceforth operate under a constitution in all essentials identical to the one which the Order as a whole had overwhelmingly rejected.

The Vatican statement also made it explicit that each of the 700 other Carmelite convents around the world would have Vatican support if they decided to opt out of the 'official' order and join the 92.

Carmelites in the US have publicly pointed to the similarity between this manoeuvre and the process whereby John Paul removed the far-right Opus Dei organisation from the jurisdiction of the bishops and made it a 'personal prelature' with 'chains of command' from all around the world bypassing local bishops and connecting directly with Rome. Are there the makings of a full-scale, Pope-induced split here?

. . . .

Hot Press—6 October 1993

My columnist colleague Sam Snort confessed in the last issue that he dreams of being promoted to Pope and issuing Papal Encyclicals advocating sensible sex.

He's just the man. He'd be elected by excited acclamation once the College of Cardinals were able to feast their glassy eyes on the gargantuan Snortian pecker. This is confirmed in recent correspondence to the prestigious *New Internationalist* magazine.

Not many people know that erections are necessary for papal elections. During the ceremony, says a Mr Guy Lambert of Oxford, who sounds like the sort of fellow who would know, the cardinals are required to take a gander at, which is not to say give a goose to, the prospective Pontiff's genitals.

This is in order to avoid a repetition of the disastrous case of Pope Joan, who dressed as a man in order to get a classical education in Rome and who proved so incredibly brilliant that she was elected Pope. For seven centuries since—and here I quote directly from the *Catholic Encyclopaedia*—'all candidates for the papacy had to undergo a physical examination to prove their sex.'

Confirmation that the prelate is indeed possessed of the appropriate equipment is ceremonially announced in the form: *Testiculos habet en bene pendentes*. Or in English, 'Testicles he has, and well-hung ones too.'

Those of us who know what we speak of don't doubt that a glance at Snort's beautifully-proportioned, tasty and well-used appendage would be enough to sew up the election.

. . . .

Hot Press—24 August 1994

I see that the Pope is blaming 'the permissive society' for sex crimes by priests.

Revealing the latest twist in what must already be a spectacularly deformed psyche, John Paul has written to the Catholic hierarchy in the US complaining about the media using incidents in which children have been abused by clergy 'as an occasion for sensationalism'. If he meant that there's so much of it going on it hardly amounts to big news any more he might have a point. But what he was hankering after was a cover-up.

In the same communication he announced the formation of a 'committee of experts' in the Vatican on child sex abuse. He'll have no problem finding Vatican experts in the area, I imagine.

Simultaneously one of his familiars, Joaquin Navarro-Valls, spoke about the pain the Church in the US is now suffering as a result of having had to pay out $400 million (so far) in damages to victims of clerical sex abuse. Navarro-Valls continued: 'One would have to ask if the real culprit is not a society which is irresponsibly permissive, hyperinflated with sexuality [and] capable of creating circumstances that induce even people who have received a solid moral formation to commit grave moral acts.' (Presumably, he meant immoral acts, although such is the inversion of morality in the Vatican these days it's impossible to be sure.)

So it's people who live sexually-liberated lives who are responsible for the sex-crimes of repressed celibates? And freedom causes oppression and democracy is to blame for dictatorship and it's the honesty of the poor which corrupts the rich.

. . . .

In Dublin—7 December 1990

How depressing that there hasn't been a single comment from within the Catholic Church in Ireland about the presence of the Papal Nuncio, Archbishop Emanuele Gerada, at the mass in the Pro-cathedral in Dublin to mark the deaths of six Jesuits and two lay workers killed in San Salvador by the death-squads of the Christiani government.

Gerada's last posting before coming to Ireland was as Nuncio to El Salvador. In that position he used his considerable influence to support the regime on whose behalf the Jesuits were killed and to oppose what the Jesuits represented.

In the *Guardian* last March, the Catholic writer Peter Hebblethwaite described how Gerada used the office of Papal Nuncio to marshal opposition within the Salvadoran church to Archbishop Oscar Romero, who was to be assassinated in his church in 1980 by the same elements who have now slaughtered the Jesuits. According to Hebblethwaite, Gerada personally organised four of the five other Salvadoran bishops into a faction which set out systematically to undermine Romero in the eyes of the laity.

Interestingly, Hebblethwaite claims that Gerada expressed alarm that Romero had 'fallen into the clutches of the Jesuits'.

In her book, *Oscar Romero—Martyr for the Poor*, Anne Daly says that shortly before his death Romero had written to the Vatican complaining that he was being undermined by Gerada and that the Nuncio seemed more influenced by government and business interests than by pastoral considerations.

The fact that Gerada was posted to Ireland—a prestigious position in the Vatican diplomatic hierarchy—indicates that the complaints of Romero, and Gerada's association with the regime on whose behalf he was assassinated, did not unduly trouble the John Paul administration.

Indeed, Gerada is credited—if that's the right word—with ensuring that John Paul did not once refer to Romero as a 'martyr' during the 1983 Papal Visit to El Salvador. Instead, John Paul repeated and emphatically referred to the 'sacrilege' involved in the killing, suggesting that the shocking thing was not that the Catholic Archbishop of the country had been shot to death by forces from within the machinery of State, but that this had happened during mass.

Now Gerada parades with clasped hands and head bowed at a mass in Ireland for the latest victims of the same death-squads.

And it seems there isn't a colleague of the murdered priests or of the murdered Bishop willing to say a word out loud about the mockery it makes of their martyrdom.

. . . .

Hot Press—4 March 1996

There has been a great deal of confusion about Catholic teaching on women priests not only in newspapers like the *Indo* and the *Times*, which we wouldn't expect to know much about anything complicated, but also in trade press publications like the *Universe* and the *Irish Catholic*. Let me clear the confusion up.

The question is: has John Paul II infallibly declared that women cannot be ordained priests? If he has, how come relatively conservative theologians like Enda McDonagh insist that the matter is still open for debate?

Here's the situation. In 1994 John Paul II issued an apostolic letter, 'Ordinatio Sacerdotalis', declaring in unambiguous terms that the ban on women becoming priests was not a matter of Vatican policy, but of Church doctrine: it wasn't that the church chose not to ordain women but rather that it was doctrinally impossible for women to be ordained.

Campaigners for women's ordination were naturally disappointed at this hard line. Some made it publicly clear that they wouldn't give up. Citing scripture, precedent and tradition, they argued that in his apostolic letter the Pope had not been speaking infallibly. There was still room for debate.

In November, however, the Vatican Congregation for the Doctrine of the Faith intervened. The teaching contained in the apostolic letter, it announced firmly, had been set forth 'infallibly'. Spokesmen for the Congregation, including its Prefect, Cardinal Joseph Ratzinger, repeated in statements and interviews that there was no room for debate now. To advocate the ordination of women was to place oneself outside the Church.

Understandable, then, that there should be puzzlement at churchmen like McDonagh continuing to argue for women priests and suggesting that John Paul's line might not survive his papacy.

Let's get this down.

While the Church says that it's an infallible teaching that women can't be ordained priests, it doesn't say this infallibly.

The Pope was not speaking infallibly when he confirmed the infallibility of the teaching.

Cardinal Ratzinger's declaration that there is no room for debate on the issue is open to debate.

And as the distinguished US Jesuit theologian Avery Dulles has put it, the Pope 'by his extraordinary and non-infallible teaching authority [has] vouched for the infallibility of the teaching'.

So that's that. There you go. Here you come back again.

. . . .

Hot Press—July 1999

So the Pope wants Vatican diplomats to intervene more decisively in world affairs to ensure that Catholic teaching is given greater weight in decisions to do with human rights, aid programmes and population control.

At the same time, UN officials are complaining that a Vatican campaign has stymied efforts to fulfil pledges made at Cairo five years ago to reduce the numbers of women dying in childbirth and to improve the reproductive health of young people.

The coincidence of the two reports prompted me to ponder how come the Catholic Church has diplomats accredited to various countries and is represented at the United Nations and in a wide range of international bodies. After all, it's a church, not a country. The Protestants, the Jews, the Muslims, the Hindus, the Buddhists, no other religion is involved in global politics in this way.

It's commonly assumed the dual remit arises from the status of Vatican City as a State. But it's not as simple as that. Religion rarely is.

In fact, it isn't Vatican City which is recognised at the UN and in the chancelleries of the world, but the Holy See, which at first sight is strange. Vatican City may be a State, albeit of the micro variety—less than half a square kilometre in area and with fewer than 500 citizens—but the Holy See is an altogether more nebulous affair.

Vatican City's statehood derives from the Lateran Treaty of 1929, negotiated between Pius XI and Mussolini. The purpose was to ring-fence Church property and central administration from the secular law of the surrounding society.

The Holy See, on the other hand, defines itself as 'the supreme organ of both the Catholic Church and the Vatican City State'. It might be imagined as the apex of a trinity, the micro-State and the institutional Church being the two other components. It has no temporal or territorial existence of any kind. Nevertheless, the Holy See is mandated to conduct international relations as the 'juridical personification of the Church'.

In itself, this isn't to be wondered at. Treating abstract constructs as material realities is the stock-in-trade of all religion. What's wonderful is that the arrangement has been accepted by governments and international agencies. As well as being represented at the UN, the Holy See maintains diplomatic relations with 157 countries.

The Holy See has a seat at the UN as a Non-Member State Permanent Observer (NMSPO). There is no provision in the UN Charter for the accreditation of any such entity.

The designation originated in an ad-hoc way in the infancy of the UN in 1946, to make provision for Switzerland—which was affiliated to a number of international bodies being brought within the UN's remit but was prevented by its constitution from taking up UN membership.

Five years later, in 1951, Pius XII, citing the Vatican City's affiliation to two international bodies, the Universal Postal Union and the International Telecommunication Union (the City State ran its own postal service and radio station) claimed a comparable right, and appointed an Auxiliary Bishop from New York to attend the UN on a part-time basis. The Bishop's status was uncertain. UN documents from the time refer to him as the representative of 'the State of the Vatican City'.

By 1964, the presence of the pope's man at UN Plaza had become accepted as custom and practice. Then, Pope Paul VI wrote to Secretary General U Thant, announcing that the Holy See wished formally to appoint a Permanent Observer on the Swiss model. There was no discussion of the proposal at the General Assembly or in any other UN forum. Within three weeks, U Thant had replied, welcoming the Holy See as the organisation's second NMSPO. Ever since, nominees of the pope have been able to attend and speak, but not to vote, in the General Assembly, and to participate fully in UN-sponsored international bodies.

Thus, the Holy See operates as a member of the World Health Organisation, the UN Educational, Scientific and Cultural Organisation, the International Atomic Energy Agency and so forth. It also attends and has played a prominent role in gatherings such as the Conference on the Environment and Development in Rio in 1992, the International Conference on Population and Development in Cairo in 1994, the World Conference on Women in Beijing in 1995 and so on.

Given the UN's propensity to seek consensus rather than majority decisions, the Holy See has been able at assemblies of this sort, frequently in alliance with conservative Latin American and Muslim delegations, to block initiatives which it considers out of line with Catholic teaching. When it has failed, it has then mounted worldwide campaigns against the programmes and initiatives it had failed to defeat.

The Cairo conference, for example, in the face of Holy See-led opposition, launched a Programme of Action to address 'the critical challenges of interrelationships between population and sustained economic growth in the context of sustainable development'. The five years since have been marked by a Vatican-inspired effort to prevent the programme being put into practice.

The Holy See was particularly upset by the programme's stress on the 'right of all couples and individuals to decide freely and responsibly the number, spacing and timing of their children, and to have the information and means to do so', and by the conference's more explicit call for measures to 'ensure that women and men have information and access to the widest possible range of safe and effective family planning methods'.

In a recent briefing document, the dissident group Catholics for a Free Choice detailed the Church's 'campaign of obstruction' against the recommendations of Cairo:

* The campaign was the context for the publication of John Paul's March 1995 encyclical 'Evangelium Vitae' (The Gospel of Life) which condemned not only contraception, but the treatment of infertility.

The encyclical claimed that unspecified international institutions were engaged on a 'conspiracy against life'.

* In June the same year, bishops from Asia and the Middle East forthrightly condemned 'safe sex' education, saying, 'We insist that the only reliable remedy to the spread of AIDS is fidelity within marriage and chastity outside marriage.' They added that 'periodic abstinence' was the only acceptable method of family planning.

* Three months later the Brazilian bishops attacked a government health programme involving the use of condoms. 'Sickness isn't fought by degrading morals and hurling people to hell.'

* In September 1995, the Vatican denounced any focus by UN agencies on the sexual and reproductive health of women and demanded that governments interpret all references in Cairo documents to sexuality to mean sex within marriage.

* In March 1996, the church in Brazil rejected a marriage application on the ground that the man was paraplegic and therefore impotent.

* In August 1996, Kenyan President Daniel Arap Moi responded to pleas from Church leaders and cancelled all sex education in primary schools. 'Our religions are against this immorality,' he explained.

* In the same month, the Nicaraguan bishops declared that the country was suffering from 'anti-reproductive colonialism' and that the terms 'reproductive rights', 'reproductive health' and 'safe sex' really meant 'abortion, promiscuity and the arbitrary use of sex'.

* In July 1977, the Vatican newspaper *L'Osservatore Romano* highlighted and welcomed a report by a consultant in bioethics saying that people with physical or mental disabilities shouldn't have sex. The disabled should 'collaborate with God to avoid creating further pain and sorrow'.

* In November 1977, the Holy See's UN deputation protested against the distribution of contraceptives in UN refugee camps.

* In April 1998 the New York and Connecticut State Catholic Conferences launched a lobby to dissuade insurance companies from covering health plans which included contraceptive drugs and devices.

* In June 1988, the Vatican condemned proposals to include 'enforced pregnancy' in the International Criminal Court's list of war crimes, lest this provide a basis for women raped in wartime to obtain legal abortions.

The examples, chosen from a catalogue which could have been 20 times as long, have this in common: that they weren't random outbursts by reactionary clerics responding to this or that development; each was an element in a coordinated effort to combat attempts to put the Cairo recommendations into practice.

The Holy See operates in world forums after the manner of a State. But when it doesn't get its way it self-transubstantiates into a religion and mobilises its agents and adherents across the globe to set the majority decisions which it disapproves of aside.

All of this activity affects the lives and legal rights, not only of Catholics, but of many millions of people of all religions and none.

What is at stake here is the health, contentment and life expectancy of an entire generation. Every day, 7,000 people under 24 become infected with AIDS; half of all rapes and sexual assaults in the world are inflicted on 15-year-olds and under; complications from pregnancy and childbirth are the most common cause of death among teenage girls.

These are world problems which the Catholic Church doesn't want confronted, other than with piety and prayer-beads.

The cynicism and dishonesty of the deception shouldn't shock us. But we should be shocked that they have been allowed to get away with it for so long. It's time these malevolent illusionists were kicked out of the world bodies they've conned their way into.

Chapter 3

Faith of our fetters

That Northern Ireland atheists are to be asked in the 2001 census whether they are Catholic atheists or Protestant atheists illustrates the extent to which the religious division has become accepted as the defining characteristic of Northern society. In fact, it's a mere by-product of our colonial history. The practical way in which a division based on politics and economics came to be expressed in religious terms emerges from the piece included here on the Catholic Church in Belfast.

The greatest recent achievement of the Christian denominations in the North has been to absolve themselves from all responsibility for hatred between 'the two communities'. The hand-washing of Catholic and Protestant bishops after the Orange-inspired massacre of three children in Ballymoney in 1998 is a case in point. The truth is that the Churches sustain the division in order to sustain themselves.

Everywhere, those who believe they are fighting in god's name must, perforce, believe that their opponents are god's enemies. Believers thus provide thugs without a religious thought in their heads with a ready-made rationale for murder.

In the North, as in the South, mainstream politics has not kept pace with the drift of the young away from religion. Parties based on appeals to communal soilidarity cannot break easily from the ideologies delimiting the communities. The need for class politics to underpin opposition to sectarian hatred is clearer in the North than anywhere else in Europe.

. . . .

Magill—11 August 1988

Catholic West Belfast has been the bane of British governments for longer than a century and never more so than now. About 90,000 overwhelmingly working class people live in the huge fan-shaped area which runs south west from Castle Street in the city centre along Divis Street and Falls Road and opens out along Andersonstown Road and the Glen Road to Poleglass and Twinbrook ten miles away on the outskirts of Lisburn. Over the past two decades its streets have seen more violence than any other urban area in Europe.

It is, in the fashionable phrase, the most 'alienated' area of the North, not only the biggest and most densely-populated Catholic district, but with the highest proportion of intransigent supporters of Republicanism. It returns seven Sinn Fein representatives to Belfast Council. Gerry Adams has been its MP since 1983.

In St Luke's Church in Twinbrook on April 24, the month after the Milltown Cemetry and Andersonstown Road killings had made the area the focus of intense media scrutiny, the Catholic Bishop of Down and Connor, Cathal Daly, delivered a sermon in which he analysed and prescribed a remedy for West Belfast's social ills. He cited unemployment and housing statistics, and attacked the Industrial Development Board for 'writing off' the area, while praising the efforts of the Housing Executive. He referred to discrimination against Catholics in employment and specifically criticised the records of Shorts Ltd and the Harland and Wolff shipyard. Dr Daly condemned the security forces for a 'lack of sensitivity' in their dealings with local people and forthrightly denounced the IRA for allegedly operating a 'revolutionary strategy' designed to deepen deprivation. He called on the Northern Ireland Office to formulate a 'comprehensive plan of overall development' for the area and suggested the recruitment into the civil service of talented people 'with sufficient understanding of and empathy with' the local community to supervise the implementation of the plan.

Thousands of copies of the sermon were later printed under the title 'The Way Forward' and distributed free in West Belfast parishes. It drew an enraged response from radical activists in the area, of whom Fr Desmond Wilson has been much the most trenchant. Wilson, the North's best-known 'dissident priest', has been engaged in a polemical battle with the Down and Connor diocese for the past 20 years. He argues that Daly is motivated not so much by genuine concern for the interests of his flock but by a desire to establish, or re-establish, control over them. Wilson has co-authored a rebuttal of the Twinbrook sermon, published last month as a pamphlet, 'The Way Forward?'; a wealth of derision is implied in the question-mark.

'Over the past 20 years', says Wilson, 'people around here have created alternative political parties, alternative forms of education and job creation, even alternative forms of worship. The Church authorities want to bring all that activity under control... The Church authorities are offering themselves to the political authorities as the main agency for social control in this area.'

The Catholic Church in Belfast has always found it difficult to balance between the need to speak for its own people and the need to maintain a business-like relationship with governments whom its own people regarded as hostile. And given the radical nature of political ideas sometimes generated by the Catholic's sense of exclusion from the established order of things, it has had to confront movements emerging from the Catholic community itself, both to maintain its authority and to ensure that its institutional interests are not put at risk in political turbulence. Cathal Daly is by no means the first diocesan chief who has had to gird himself for political battle.

Daly's first predecessor as Bishop of Down and Connor was Cornelius O'Devany, ordained in the late 16th century. Belfast was little more than a cluster of houses. The main area of Church activity was the Antrim countryside where O'Devany ministered to scattered enclaves of the faithful. He appears to have had an ambiguous attitude to Catholic rebelliousness but was nevertheless accused by the Lord Deputy, Sir Arthur Chichester, of involvement with Hugh O'Neill and Red Hugh O'Donnell, the Earls who took flight in 1607. Chichester, after whom Belfast's Chichester Street is now named, was the main architect of the Ulster Plantation, intended to scour popish disloyalty from the land. He had an unsqueamish approach. O'Devany was arrested, tried in Dublin and sentenced 'to be taken back to prison and then drawn on a cart to the place of execution, there hanged on the gallows and cut down while alive, stripped, disembowelled, his heart and bowels burnt, his head cut off and his body quartered'. An old man of 79, O'Devany died in this fashion in 1612.

There was no official Catholic presence in the environs of Belfast for some time thereafter. In 1677 came the appointment of the first priest specifically accredited to Belfast. This was Philomy O'Hamill, ordained in that year by Oliver Plunkett. It was a bad time to become a priest. O'Hamill led a miserable existence in and around Belfast, where there were few Catholics and few obvious candidates for conversion. He survived the period of the Williamite Wars, but continued to be hunted in a rather desultory way until he surrendered in 1708 and died in prison.

At the time of O'Hamill's ordination, Belfast consisted of a castle, the Protestant church of St George and about 20 streets along the riverside. If there were Catholics among the populace, they weren't advertising their presence. However, judging by O'Hamill's experience, Belfast's Protestants were not the intolerant bigots of caricature. They petitioned the authorities for his release and, after his death, petitioned that he should be allowed burial according to the rites of the Catholic Church. In a survey the year before his surrender, 1707, seven Belfast Catholics proclaimed their religion, the first recorded Catholics of the city.

By the middle of the 18th century, Belfast was a middling-sized port with a few industries servicing trade, and already a centre of small-scale linen production. It had a population of 8,549 of whom 556 were Catholics. The town's priest, John O'Mullan, said mass on Sundays at a sand-pit by Friar's Bush in Stranmillis just outside the town. He appears not to have been harrassed or his services attacked. By the 1770s it was being publicly advertised that mass was said on Sunday mornings at the home of a Catholic businessman, John Kennedy.

Catholics drifted slowly into Belfast through the 18th century to find work in emerging industries, such as linen, salt, beer, rope and pottery. Already, they were beginning to congregate in the Falls area to the west of the town centre. There is scant evidence of inter-communal bitterness. This is partly explained by the fact that the Catholics were such a small minority that they presented no real threat and by the generally quieter conditions following the upheavals of the previous century. But just as important was the fact that the Belfast Presbyterians, who increasingly provided the town's intellectual leadership, although they did not labour under the harsh, penal disadvantages suffered by the Catholics, were themselves disadvantaged in relation to the Anglican establishment and had come to make common cause with the Catholics.

The first Catholic Church in Belfast, St Mary's in Chapel Lane, was opened in 1784 to cater for a flock which now numbered perhaps 3,000. Much of the money to build it was subscribed by Presbyterians. At the opening ceremony, the Belfast Volunteers lined up splendidly arrayed in scarlet and black uniforms under the command of Captain Waddle Cunningham to provide a guard of honour for parish priest Hugh O'Donnell—himself in full-dress regalia—as he and the Catholic populace arrived in procession for their great day. The Anglican sovereign of the town paid for the pulpit.

The Belfast Presbyterians were the most radical political element in Ireland. They had enthusiastically welcomed the American Revolution against George III: 'The Presbyterians of Belfast are all Americans in their hearts', opined one official report. In 1794 the Belfast Volunteers were the first in Ireland to allow Catholics to join. These were the people of Hope, McCracken and Russell, people of small property and great spirit. But while the ideas they espoused led them to embrace the cause of the Catholics, the same ideas were anathema to the Catholic Hierarchy in Ireland, as everywhere. This was eventually to be significant for the shaping of Belfast's Catholic community.

At the beginning of the last century, Belfast had a population of around 20,000, of whom between 3,000 and 4,000 were Catholics. By the end of the century it was a city of 340,000, between a quarter and a third Catholic.

Belfast's rising commerce was remarkably undisturbed by the '98 Rebellion. The collapse into chaos and defeat of the Rebellion had a sobering effect on Presbyterian politics in the city, but Presbyterian liberalism in the form of Whiggery was to survive as a distinct political tendency through the century. Meanwhile the entrepreneurial genius of the Protestant merchant class was put to good effect.

As industry expanded, large numbers of Catholics and Protestants poured in from the rural hinterland. They tended to cluster together with their own kind in areas which rapidly developed into appalling slums. Although the conditions of Protestant slum-dwellers were scarcely, if at all, better than those of their Catholic counterparts, the position and self-image of the communities differed in that the Protestants had co-religionists of wealth and substance in the town and a resultant sense of identification with the civic establishment. To an extent, Catholics settled in already alienated. Competition for jobs and territory was inevitable, and always with a potential for sectarian strife. Belfast experienced its first inter-communal disturbances in 1813. By later standards it didn't amount to much but, as in all such circumstances, the divisions it reflected were reinforced by the fact of its happening.

The tremor of nervousness which the first sectarian battles caused in the Catholic community strengthened the tendency of newcomers to huddle into their own area. Catholic Belfast bulged out on both sides of the Falls, clumps of mean streets encircling the mills they depended on: the low wages, long hours and early-morning start made it necessary to live alongside the workplace. The Catholics were desperately poor, uncertain of themselves and mostly illiterate, ravaged by fever, tuberculosis and malnutrition. An open sewer ran the length of the Falls. As the linen trade expanded and spawned subsidiary activities such as brickworks and haulage and sucked in more immigrants, one commentator observed: 'The one great question which builders in the neighbourhood have to meet is how to get at that channel of abomination in order to contribute to its nastiness.' In the 1830s, 45 percent of all deaths in the city were from contagious disease. The death-rate for under-30s was more than double that for Ireland as a whole. In this situation, the Church was the one institution capable of providing Catholics with a sense of identity and belonging and of their own human worth.

For most of the century, however, the Church was ill-equipped for the task. The second Catholic church, St Patrick's in Donegall Street, opened in 1815, the third, St Malachy's, in 1844. The first school, St Patrick's, was opened in 1828. But there was a shortage of priests and Church organisation consistently lagged behind the growth in the Catholic population.

William Crolly, appointed to Down and Connor in 1825, was the first Catholic bishop to become an important figure in Belfast life. Crolly well understood the delicacy of the Catholics' position and constantly counselled good citizenship and respect for the law. His influence was appreciated by the civil authorities. His successor, Cornelius Denvir, a scholarly professor of philosophy, seemed unnerved by the ferocity of anti-Catholic feeling whipped up from the early '30s by Protestant demagogues such as the prototype Paisley Henry Cooke, who at a mass rally in Hillsborough in 1834 proclaimed the 'political marriage of Presbyterianism, the Church of Ireland and the Tories'. Denvir rarely ventured out.

Cooke's Hillsborough marriage was by no means fully consummated. The voice of the liberal Presbyterians, the *Northern Whig*, regularly poured scorn on his rantings. It had welcomed Catholic Emancipation in 1829, which had boosted the morale of Belfast Catholics while having negligible impact on their conditions of life. And Presbyterian liberals remained well-disposed generally towards the Catholic community. At the laying of the foundation stone for St Malachy's Church in 1841 the toast was: 'To the Liberal Protestants of Belfast', some of whom had dug deep to fund the building.

Still, the trajectory of events was ominous. The first deaths from sectarian violence happened in 1832, the first mass Orange attack on the Falls in 1835. And other developments were putting a strain on relations between liberal Protestants and the Church.

The *Northern Whig*, although recognising the legitimacy of Catholic grievance in relation to education and much else, nevertheless strongly supported the ideal of non-sectarian schooling. This brought it into repeated conflict with Catholic clerics. An important example was the introduction by Peel's Liberal government in 1845 of a Bill to establish 'Queen's Colleges' in Belfast, Galway and Cork to give both Catholics and Presbyterians free access to third-level education. Irish Presbyterians overwhelmingly welcomed the measure as, briefly, did a few Catholics.

The Bill offered both churches the right to provide on-campus religious instruction and chaplaincy services and to nominate representatives to governing bodies. It was denounced by the Catholic Archbishop of Armagh as 'pregnant with danger to the faith and morals of the youth of this country'. The Church issued a series of demands, including that the professors of a number of departments, including zoology, history, logic and anatomy, should be Catholics if any Catholics were to take these courses: in effect, separate Catholic departments. When Peel's administration rejected the demands, Catholics were forbidden to attend the new colleges. Thus Queen's College, Belfast, opened in 1849 as an all-Protestant institution. The distinguished Celtic scholar, John O'Donovan, no Protestants having opted to take his course, attracted no students to the lectures he patiently prepared every year until his death in 1861. The *Whig* and those it spoke for were appalled.

The *Whig* also welcomed an 1854 Bill providing for the inspection of convents to ensure that young women hadn't been pressurised into entering religious orders. Bishop Denvir and his clergy reacted with fury.

These and other controversies, frequently concerning education, happened at a crucial time in the development of Belfast and in the determination of what the Catholic community's position in Belfast would be.

The city's expansion accelerated from the 1840s onward. The first railway, to Lisburn, was laid down in 1839 and extended to Portadown four years later. A new dock was built in 1841, then the Donegall Quay extended and modernised and the Victoria Channel gouged out to allow heavier ships to use the port. Thousands continued to pour in from the countryside. Insanitary working-class areas seeped outwards. By 1860 there were 41,000 Catholics among the city's 140,000 people. From 1857 onwards there were regular minor outbreaks of sectarian violence and occasionally major strife.

Meanwhile, shipbuilding and heavy industry became fully established. The linen trade received a major boost when the American Civil War devastated the Lancashire cotton trade and opened up vast new markets for an alternative textile. Within a decade, just short of a million new spindles were installed in Belfast. This provided the basis for Belfast to become the world's largest producer of linen manufacturing machinery. A new layer of skilled workers emerged, no longer ragamuffins who coughed their lungs out in the mills, but men who went to work in sturdy boots and bowler hats and whose skills gave them status and bargaining power. Inevitably, Catholics lost out in the competition for these jobs. And as the jobs were defended, to be 'passed down', the systematic exclusion of Catholics from the major areas of industry became a settled fact of Belfast life. By no means all Protestant workers benefitted from these developments, but those workers who did benefit were all Protestants. It was during this period that, in asserting its institutional rights, and its authority over its 'own' people, the Catholic Church cut its community off from that section of Belfast Protestantism which was ideologically in support of full citizenship for the Catholic people.

At the same time, the Church was in organisational chaos. Through the '50s Dr Denvir, a naturally timid man, increasingly averted his eyes from the violence and squalor of Belfast to concentrate on tending his flock in the more serene areas of Antrim. Drunkenness, licentiousness and inattention to religious duty were rife along the Falls and in other Catholic areas. One estimate suggested that as many as a thousand Catholics a year were 'lapsing'. Great numbers were still illiterate: while disapproving of 'Protestant' state schools, the Church had not managed to provide an adequate alternative. There was change of a sort when Patrick Dorrian was appointed Coadjutor Bishop in 1860, and more so when he assumed full episcopal authority in 1865. Dorrian was a remarkable man. More than any single individual he created the Catholic Church as it is today in Belfast. He was intellectually formidable, politically astute, an organiser of genius and possessed endless energy.

Dorrian moved swiftly to revitalise the Church in the city and to stamp his authority upon it. His first target was instructive. The Catholic Institute had been set up in 1859 by businessmen of impeccably orthodox opinions who had purchased a house near the city centre, intending it as a centre where respectable Catholics, excluded from much of civic life, could meet to discuss business or socialise, and to hold meetings and other functions. It had a small library and newspaper reading room. In 1865 Dorrian stunned the members of the Institute by informing them that they had challenged the authority of the Church. When some Institute members resisted this view Dorrian threatened 'to debar them from the Sacraments, all and every one'. The Institute was wound up to the gleeful distaste of Belfast Protestants of all persuasions who saw it as proof positive of the Catholic Church's totalitarian nature and the timidity of even its most substantial members in the face of clerical censure.

But Dorrian would have been unconcerned about Protestant reaction. He was asserting Church authority over Catholics. It was in the matter of obedience to authority that Catholics differed most fundamentally from Protestants, and in particular from Presbyterians. Throughout his priestly life he welcomed Protestant support for causes endorsed by the Church. But in matters internal to the Catholic community—and he adjudged the Institute, being a specifically Catholic group, to come within that category— only the Church had authority to initiate or regulate. 'Some of my own people wish to have themselves entirely free of Ecclesiastical control in what they have called the "Catholic Institute",' he wrote later. 'I have to make a stand to purge if from the Presbyterian leaven.' Dorrian's next defence of Church authority over its 'own' was against an external opponent. In 1866 the town council bought land off the Falls for a cemetery. It offered ten acres to the Catholics and 17 to the Protestants, the rest of the land to be open to all comers. Dorrian demanded total control over the Catholic patch, in effect legal ownership by the diocese. He argued that while Catholics must be buried in consecrated ground, he was debarred by canon law from consecrating ground over which a non-Catholic body retained rights. (This was highly questionable.) To placate him, the council had a six-foot deep trench dug around the intended Catholic section and an underground brick wall built. Dorrian was unimpressed. He cited possibly canonical difficulties, such as that a Catholic might buy a plot in the Catholic section, then become a Protestant but have had it stipulated in a will made while a Catholic that he or she was to be buried in the Catholic plot: Would the Church have a legal right to turn the ex-Catholic corpse away? Dorrian rallied the Catholic community in a fund-raising drive for land for a Catholics-only cemetery and eventually bought a site at Milltown. Twenty thousand Catholics turned out to join in lusty hymn singing to celebrate the opening in 1870. An address presented to Dorrian at a banquet to mark that year's Vatican Council expressed relief that 'we are no longer exposed to the danger of being interred in desecrated ground and having our bones disturbed by unhallowed hands.'

Dorrian poured much of his great energies into expanding the Catholic school network. In the course of his 20 year reign he opened new schools in the diocese at an average rate of one every six months. He brought the Christian Brothers to Belfast to cater for boys and the Dominican nuns to found a school on the Falls where efforts to inculcate 'industrious, orderly and lady-like habits' into young Belfast women continue to this day. He preached constantly against the dangers presented by mixed, national schools and stamped hard on the few daring Catholics who argued for a non-denominational system: 'I am absolutely appalled by their disregard for authority. [The bishops] must lay down the law for them, for teachers, and for all.' He appointed Ireland's first full-time diocesan religious knowledge inspector, a priest who visited each Catholic school at least once a year to examine pupils and report back on standards of instruction.

He set about attracting Catholics back to the sacraments with some style—1865 saw Belfast's first city-wide 'general mission', which opened with a public procession to a sung High Mass in St Mary's. Twenty-four extra priests were drafted in to hear confessions ten hours a day, six days a week, for a month and to say masses each morning and conduct devotions in the evenings. The Holy See contributed a plenary indulgence to all who participated faithfully. An air of pietistic excitement enveloped Catholic Belfast. By the end of the mission 30,000 had been to confession and communion, many for the first time, and two Protestants had been converted.

Dorrian reorganised the city's parishes, altering boundaries to take account of the changing population, codifying the exact duties of parish priests and curates and making each parish responsible for its own fundraising. Door-to-door collections were introduced. Weekly door-to-door collections gave rise to a regiment of Church activists in every parish, and provided every Catholic family with a regular reminder of the parish to which they 'belonged'. Even today, Belfast Catholics, asked, 'What area are you from?' are as likely to reply 'St Matthew's' or 'St Peter's' as 'the Short Strand' or 'the Lower Falls'.

The institutions of the Church came to dominate day-to-day life in Catholic Belfast. In 1867 Dorrian had opened St Peter's Church off the Falls. It was an ornate, solid-stone, gothic-style, twin-spired building, as impressive as any church in the city, as it still is. The dedication was accounted the most impressive religious spectacle ever witnessed in Belfast. Cardinal Cullen, 12 bishops and scores of priests took part in the solemn ceremony. A choir and full orchestra performed Haydn's No 3 Grand Imperial. Four years later St Paul's further up the Falls Road was added. Further along still, St Joseph's opened in 1880. St Matthew's, Ballymacarret, followed in 1883. If the material conditions of Catholics in Belfast remained dreadful, if the community was still excluded from power and decent employment, they at least had imposing churches, schools and halls to take pride in and derive an identity from.

Dorrian set a style and modus operandi which the Church has followed, or tried to, in Belfast ever since. It developed as an efficient, disciplined organisation which has sought the widest support for its own institutional interests while defining these as being co-extensive with the interests of the Catholic people. Logically, given this perception, it has sought to stifle any dissident or alternative voice claiming to speak for any section of the Catholic people. It has been logical, too, that it should tend to support conservatives of any religion who backed, say, denominational education against advocates of mixed schools who pursued social reform. Dorrian pushed this to the limit in 1877 when the Church in Belfast publicly backed Charles Stewart Vane-Tempest-Stewart, Sixth Marquess of Londonderry, aka Lord Castlereagh, a Conservative who was sound on the schools question, in a by-election against a Liberal who was out for social reform but wobbly on the education issue.

Then, as ever, in Belfast as everywhere, the litmus test was: what's in it for the Church? And the outcome has generally been that the Church contained its 'own' people, shielding them from Protestant contamination as they headed towards collision with political authority, thereby ensuring a resolution which left social and economic grievances unremedied, but Church interests and institutions intact.

Hot Press—16 November 1994

Times change, and not always for the worse. A new Catholic bishop has been appointed to the diocese of Derry but this time we won't have petal-strewers.

Seamus Hegarty, currently Bishop of Raphoe (Donegal), is set to take over from Eddie Daly whose consecration in the early '70s was an affair of great ceremony and mighty pageant. The new Bishop was carried in procession—and with, I should say, a certain saving appearance of embarrassment—through the Bogside under a fringed canopy, glittering with gold and held aloft by a solemn squad of prominent Catholic laymen clad in the gowns of some esoteric order. Behind the mitred Bishop bestowing blessings on the awed crowds lining the pavements came contingents of white-surpliced priests, hymn-singing members of various confraternities, flocks of nuns and babbles of children.

And, before the Bishop, came a dozen or so shiny-faced school-children each carrying an urn from which they scattered fistfuls of rose petals at his feet. Those chosen for this prized role were identified by name in the local press as 'the petal-strewers'.

It's as good a mark of the changing times as any that if they tried that stunt today, the petals would be blown away in gales of laughter.

But there are other aspects of Hegarty's appointment which aren't funny at all.

It is now widely acknowledged that John Paul II has systematically been slotting into dioceses, in Ireland and elsewhere, men of his own mind, that he is particularly intent on key posts going to the most reliably retrogressive. In this connection, Derry is a significant appointment, the fourth biggest diocese in Ireland with 200,000 nominal Catholics, and with a particular political importance.

It is with this in mind that we should look at the selection of Hegarty, brought in from a rural area to take 'control' of the biggest single concentration of urban, working-class Catholics in the still-turbulent North.

It is not accidental that Donegal was one of only two counties which voted No, No, No in last year's referenda on abortion, abortion information and travel for the purpose of having an abortion. No other bishop gave such open and unequivocal support to the fundamentalist crazies. Hegarty emerged deservedly as one of the super-heroes of the Youth Defence crowd (the fanatical right-wing Catholic anti-abortion group).

He cannot, of course, be held responsible for all that happens in Donegal with regard to women's rights, sexuality and fertility. But he has been important in the formation of the ideological climate in the county whereby, for example, a woman who enquired in Letterkenny Regional Hospital about sterilisation following a desperately difficult sixth pregnancy was visited in the maternity ward by a consultant who gave her a lecture and a prayer book.

A few years back I got to know a Donegal girl who had been repeatedly raped by a group of local men and who, when 13, had become pregnant and, at 14, had given birth. I am honoured that she has become my good friend. We talk now and then. On the surface at least she has survived the horror to which she was subjected with a most remarkable resilience. This was no thanks to the Catholic Church in Donegal.

The case was the talk of her home area long before it came to court. The courts treated her disgracefully. No representative of the Catholic Church ever darkened her door to offer sympathy or comfort, or prayer. This was at a time when public discussion of abortion and related issues was, in Donegal anyway, at a pitch of frenzy, with daily statements from councillors, priests and campaigning groups dominating the news, and no 'pro-life' pronouncement complete without a ritual protestation of compassion for rape victims and other women with unwanted pregnancies.

But there wasn't an ounce of compassion available for my young friend who during that period was trembling with pain and on the edge of suicide.

No reference to these appalling events, which surely had implications for the moral life of the Catholic community in the diocese, was ever made from a pulpit. The animals who savaged the youngster were able to attend mass without fear of embarrassment, while she for a time hid herself away, out of a misplaced sense of shame.

Again, we cannot blame Hegarty for this. But he certainly knew of the case. And while he was never short of subject matter for public statements on sexual morality, he sang dumb about her suffering and, by implication at least, sanctioned the furtive silence of his priests.

Hegarty's willingness to associate himself with fundamentalist groups on the far-right fringe of Catholicism was made publicly plain two years ago when he led a 'pilgrimage' from the Raphoe diocese to

Medjugorje in Bosnia-Hercegovina where six fraudsters have claimed to meet and talk with the 'Virgin Mary' at twenty to seven, local time, every evening.

The 'visionaries' have been denounced as phony by the local Bishop of Mostar, Pavao Zanic, who has repeatedly pleaded with his fellow bishops to try to dissuade Catholics from travelling to Medjugorje or giving the 'apparitions' credence.

Dr Zanic's pleas fell on deaf ears in Donegal. Hegarty placed himself at the head of a procession through Medjugorje which included as grisly a selection of Irish 'pro-lifers' as has ever assembled anywhere with nefarious intent. The chief warlock of the Medjugorje conspiracy, the aptly-named Fr Slavko Barbaric, thinks him a great man.

No doubt, they'd carpet the processional route through Medjugorje for him with flowers. But not along Rossville Street.

Dark and all as the scene sometimes looks, there's been progress up here.

. . . .

Hot Press—19 April 1995

The opening of Derry's Gay Pride festival was a most splendid affair. About 150 of us gathered at the Tower Museum just inside the walls to hear Mayor John Kerr of the SDLP speak about the need for an open, pluralist society where differences were a matter for celebration rather than condemnation. Then we sipped white wine in the evening sunshine and gently mocked the small contingent of Free Presbyterians who had assembled at Magazine Gate to sing mournful hymns and bark biblical quotations—the word 'abomination' seemed to crop up a lot—through a squawky loud-hailer.

SDLP and Sinn Fein councillors mingled easily with gay activists. But not a single Unionist representative showed up. Which, many agreed through the munching of canapes and small triangular sandwiches, suggested that Nationalists have grown more tolerant and progressive in their attitudes, while Unionists remain mired in the narrow ground of the old bigotries.

How, then, to explain the news from the United States that Irish Nationalists have been celebrating a new legal right to express hatred of gays?

In a landmark decision, the US Supreme Court has ruled that the organisers of the Patrick's Day parade in Boston can stop gay organisations joining their march. This overturned a decision by Massachusetts courts which had last year upheld an appeal from the Irish American Gay, Lesbian and Bisexual Group against their exclusion.

The Supreme Court based its ruling on the proposition that the parade was an expression of Irish identity, and that the organisers had a right to define this identity as excluding gay sexuality. It would be a violation of their constitutional right to free speech to force them to 'say' something about Irish identity which they disapproved of, the court held.

The wide significance of the judgement has not been lost on Irish-American homophobes. 'Every racial, ethnic and religious group that wants to maintain the integrity of its heritage has a right to insulate its parades from those who would insult and degrade its culture,' said the Catholic League for Religious and Civil Rights.

The League's Boston-based operations director added: 'Irish Catholics may now publicly honour their patron saint without having that celebration exploited by those who scorn the religion and morality of St Patrick… The aggression of an extremist group against the Catholics of South Boston has ended in failure.'

Thus, to demand equal rights for gays is to 'insult and degrade [Irish] culture'. The conflation of Irishness, Catholicism and homophobia is laid out openly for all to inspect.

The Supreme Court ruling will apply to all St Patrick's Day parades throughout the US. The campaign of the Irish Lesbian and Gay Organisation (ILGO) in New York, which has attracted considerable publicity over the past three years, has no legal avenue left open.

However, there is a way forward—if those in the North with relevant influence do what's necessary. Northern Nationalist leaders have more clout than ever in Irish America. If John Hume or Gerry Adams or both were to say loud and clear that this anti-gay bigotry is unacceptable to them, the balance of debate in Irish-American circles would be significantly affected.

If they were to call on their US supporters not to take part in events from which gays were excluded, outfits like the Catholic League would be seriously undermined, and the confidence of Irish gays would be significantly boosted.

But Hume has never ventured a comment on the issue. Adams, when asked for support by the IGLO in New York last March, responded with a statement which might kindly be described as equivocal.

This shouldn't be good enough for Sinn Fein and SDLP supporters of gay rights. They cannot be content to be associated in the US
with people who, had they been in Derry a few weeks ago, would
have taken their stand with the loudspeaker Paisleyites rather than
with the glad gays.

Bit of pressure on the Nationalist leaderships wouldn't go amiss here.

. . . .

Hot Press—February 1998

'Those who perpetrated this murder are anti-Christian', declared the
priest at the funeral of Loyalist murder victim Liam Conway last
month. Mr Conway, the breadwinner for two disabled brothers, was
shot dead as he sat at the wheel of a mechanical digger off the Crum-
lin Road in Belfast on 23 January, another Catholic killed in supposed retaliation for the INLA slaying of Billy Wright before Xmas.

Most of those listening will have understood well what was meant.
The word 'Christian' is commonly used to convey decency, tolerance,
mercy, love. It is taken to indicate the very antithesis of vengeance,
bigotry, violence, hate. To characterise the killers as 'anti-Christian'
will have seemed obvious common sense.

But the sectarian murder-gangs make just as much sense when
they claim to act out of Christian conviction.

The life and death of Billy Wright shows how naturally Christian
fervour shades into evil. Wright was a religious man. He had been a
lay preacher. He banned swearwords and other 'unChristian practices' on his wing in the Maze. He left instructions that the emphasis in his funeral oration should not be on political salvation in this
world, but on eternal salvation in the next.

Many took a cynical view of Wright's protestations of religious
motive, dismissing it as no more than a handy excuse for hate...
Bernadette Martin, innocently asleep in her Protestant boyfriend's
home when Wright's killers erupted into the room and riddled her
head and body with bullets... Eileen Duffy, 19, and Katrina Rennie,
only 16, shot to bits in a mobile sweet-shop by cowards... Charles and
Teresa Fox, old age pensioners, pitilessly dispatched in their isolated
home in Tyrone.

To concede religious motivation to such a man strikes many as
throwing a cloak of respectability over sectarian thuggery.

But look at it in the light of the slogan in pride of place in the cell
of Wright's friend, Johnny 'Mad Dog' Adair: 'Kill Them All—Let

God Sort 'em Out.' From where did he come up with that?

From 1205 and the Crusade against the Cathars.

The Abbot of Citeaux, head of the Cistercians, at the time one of the most powerful men in Christendom, was asked as the Crusaders set out from Montpellier how they might distinguish between heretics deserving of death and innocent folk who chanced to be in the same place at the same time. The Abbot decreed 'Kill Them All—Let God Sort Them Out.'

It might seem ironic that Adair, a UDA thug from the Shankill, should adopt the slogan of a Catholic monk. But the sense of the slogan—that followers of false versions of Christianity deserve death, and that only god can separate the just from the unjust—is not specific to any particular Christian denomination.

The Crusade against the Cathars was itself undertaken by one Christian denomination against another. (The real purpose was to consolidate the power of the Duke of Burgundy in what is now southern France.) The Crusade was prosecuted with focussed ferocity: in the town of Beziers 30,000 people, every man, woman and child the Crusaders could root out, were cut to death. Seven thousand were slaughtered where they had gathered for refuge, in the Church of the Magdalen in the centre of town. The killers were granted a plenary indulgence.

Over and over again, Christian convictions have been expressed in the slaughter of people identified as heathens or apostate. This has happened so frequently and through so many centuries that it makes no sense to present it as out of character for Christianity.

In Ireland, Protestantism has been associated since the 16th century with an antiCatholicism so virulent as implicitly to deny the humanity of Catholic people. Again, there have been material reasons for this.

In 1615, half a century after its foundation, the Church of Ireland rejected the 39 Articles of the Church of England, preferring a stricter version of predestination, one which held that those not 'elect' were utterly irredeemable, their very existence offensive to the eyes of god. This provided a religious justification for cleansing whole areas of the native population, suppressing their culture, exterminating them where 'necessary'.

The greater 'need' for such measures in Ireland than in England dictated the difference in doctrine.

In seeing Catholics today as disposable people, Billy Wright was in harmony with this Christian tradition. Respectable Protestant leaders have portrayed Wright as beyond the pale of 'proper' Protestantism. But the murderous attacks on Catholics which he inspired and organised were well in line with Protestant, and, more generally, Christian tradition.

One of the ways Christianity has affected the conflict here has been to render it more implacable, to lend it greater ferocity, to make it more scornful of the sanctity of life.

The people who killed Liam Conway were Christians, not anti-Christians.

. . . .

Hot Press—13 May 1999

Wendy Austin ruminated last week on that silly old nonsense about it being possible to tell Catholics from Protestants by the distance between their eyes.

Sh didn't say it it was so. She couldn't. There's never been a scientific study of the matter. But who's to say that a properly-conducted survey involving statistically-reliable samples wouldn't show that the median distance between Catholic eyes is two and half or even five millimetres greater than the median distance between Protestant eyes?

Members of the SDLP have often struck me as unusually wide-eyed. You'd wonder if they are capable of focussing on a fine point at all. Whereas, DUP people appear naturally equipped for the narrow perspective. These are mere impressions, of course, of no objective value.

What's needed is a wide-ranging study conducted by qualified researchers spread out across the country, equipped with calipers, meticulously measuring the exact distance between the left and right eyes of matched samples of Prods and Taigs. There's little doubt, given the other projects they have poured resources into, that the University of Ulster would readily supply the necessary personnel and the Community Relations Council full funding.

It was Aloysha Enumo who, on *Talkback* on Radio Ulster, provoked Wendy into raising the possibility that the eyes have it. Ms Enumo, from Rwanda, had just explained that the differences between Hutus and Tutsis in her country had to do with the size of their noses.

The detail is to be found in a book, *We Wish To Inform You That*

Tomorrow We Will Be Killed With Our Families, by *New Yorker* writer Philip Gourevitch, an investigation into the genocide in Rwanda in 1994 which followed a Hutu government call for the extermination of the Tutsis.

The killing was on a scale so vast as to require an act of imagination rather than of intellect to comprehend it. I'd assumed at the time that, whatever the immediate triggering circumstance, this was a bubbling to the surface of age-old, tribal hostility...ethnic animosity, its origins lost in the jungle mists of time.

But not at all.

The first account of Rwandan life to appear in a European language was published in 1863 by John Hanning Speke, famous for 'discovering' a great lake which it pleased him to call 'Victoria'. He announced that he'd also discovered proof of the biblical story (Genesis, 9) of the casting-out of the children of Ham, son of Noah, who'd been cursed for the sin of giggling at his father naked. Ham's family, the story went, were, or became, the first black people on earth.

A chapter in Speke's *Journal* headed 'Fauna', began: 'In treating of this branch of natural history, we will first take man—the true, curly-headed, flab-nosed, pouch-mouthed negro... As his father did, so does he. He works his wife, sells his children, enslaves all he can lay hands on, and unless when fighting for the property of others, contents himself with drinking, singing and dancing like a baboon, to drive dull care away.'

Speke recognised these immediately as sons of Ham. Living alongside them, he recorded, was an altogether different race: 'Men who were as unlike as they could be from the common order of the natives...fine oval faces, large eyes, high noses, denoting the best blood of Abyssinia.'

A lost race of Christians, then, who with preferment and education might prove themselves 'as superior in all things' as Englishmen.

Speke never spoke to a Rwandan of any face-shape or eye-size, nor set foot in Rwanda, but researched his theories by gazing upon the region from a handy vantage point in what is now Tanzania.

Nor is there any record of a German entering the area prior to 1885 when a gathering of European leaders in Berlin gave the country to the Kaiser. After World War One, ownership of Rwanda passed to Belgium. It was the Belgian administration which, in the '20s, set out scientifically to test Speke's theory.

Teams of qualified researchers spread out across the country, equipped with calipers, meticulously measuring noses. They found that the median Tutsi nose was five millimetres narrower and two and a half millimetres longer than the median Hutu nose. Proof positive of two nations.

Ethnicity was made into the defining feature of Rwandan existence. After a census in 1931, every citizen was given an identity card, allocating him or her to one or other group. The Belgian administration stabilised its rule by giving those deemed to be Tutsis preference over Hutus in politics, business and education.

This affected only an emerging Tutsi elite. The vast majority of Tutsis continued to live and work alongside and to marry Hutus. In the countryside, most Hutus were arable farmers, most Tutsis were pastoralists. But there wasn't a single all-Hutu or all-Tutsi area or village in the land. 'Transfers' from one group to the other, frequently as a result of marriage, were so common as to be unremarkable and to go unrecorded.

By law, however, all political organisations were based on ethnicity. The first academically-respectable history of Rwanda, by a Belgian missionary, Monsignor Louis de Lacger, observed: 'One of the most surprising phenomena of Rwanda's human geography is surely the contrast between the plurality of races and the sentiment of nationality unity. The natives of this country genuinely have the feeling of forming but one people.' This was published in 1958.

Lacger noted that beneath the veneer of colonial administration, real life in Rwanda differed from Belgium, as from most European countries, in that all the people spoke the same language, Kinyarwanda, worshipped the same god, Imana, and accepted the same king, the Mwami. 'There are few peoples in Europe among whom one finds these three features of national cohesion.'

Another Belgian missionary, a Fr Pages, recorded that, far from any section of the Rwandan people living the brutish life of Speke's wild fantasy, '[They] were persuaded, before the European penetration, that their country was the centre of the world, that this was the largest and most powerful and most civilised kingdom on earth.' They believed that while god might visit other countries by day, he returned at night to rest in Rwanda.

Gourevitch—his interest in Rwanda germinated under the teaching of the naturalist Dian Fossey at Cornell University during one of her sojourns from studying the habits of mountain gorillas in north west Rwanda—speculates that it might have been this very sense of national unity and high level of cultural self-confidence which led the Belgians to impose such an all-embracing, rigid and irrational system of ethnic organisation. Unusual means were necessary to divide such people against themselves.

Formal politics having been constructed solely around the idea of ethnic identity, the various Hutu and Tutsi parties vied with one another as to which could best secure the interests of its own side vis-à-vis the other. As independence approached and power beckoned, rivalry intensified within and between the two groups—1957 saw the publication by a number of Hutu intellectuals of *The Hutu Manifesto*, endorsing an inverted, modernised version of Speke's two-nations theory and demanding a Hutu State for a Hutu people.

When a leading Hutu politician was beaten near to death by Tutsi political activists in the district of Gitarama in December 1959, Hutu leaders, many of them young and European educated, called for a general Hutu mobilisation 'to defend ourselves and our nation'. There followed the first-ever ethnic massacre in Rwandan history. In 1960, the Belgian military commander in the country appointed a Provisional Government under Gregoire Kayibanda, one of the authors of *The Hutu Manifesto*.

Thereafter, in short, violence begat violence. Tutsis forced into exile, mainly to Uganda, formed the Rwanda Patriotic Front and waited for the moment to fight their way home.

In the early 1990s, Rwanda, like almost all of sub-Saharan Africa, was plunged into economic crisis as the government slashed wages and public spending in order to meet the repayment demands of the International Monetary Fund. The supposed remaining privileges of the Tutsis made them prime candidates for scapegoating. When the Hutu president, Habyarimana, was killed in a plane crash, State radio, wrongly, blamed the Tutsis and urged Hutus to take up arms to 'cleanse the country of the cockroaches'.

Tens of thousands, including doctors, priests, women and children, answered the call. At least 7,000 Tutsis were butchered every day, for a hundred days, a faster rate of killing than the Nazis ever managed with the Jews.

The point is this. That the extent of real difference is not a factor in determining the intensity of hatred or fear people can feel against one another. In the right contrived circumstances, the length of a nose can be enough to spark genocide.

And so, too, the width between eyes.

. . . .

Belfast Telegraph—14 July 1999

The Orange Order regularly and reverently commemorates soldiers who died in the Great War and in the War against Hitler. But one of the Protestant boys who followed the drum to Ormeau Park on Monday seems to have missed the message.

He was pictured on the front page of the *Independent* yesterday, beefy back ornamented with a huge tattoo depicting armed men in orange colours and swastikas beneath the Hitlerite slogan 'Blood and Honour'.

He wasn't typical, of course. But he appears to have been tolerated. And his presence highlights the extraordinary disparity between the way many members of the Orange Order see themselves and the message their marching sends out to the wider world.

The confusion runs deep with the institution itself. The estimated 10,000 brethern who gathered at Larne didn't vote on the resolution calling for the disbandment of the Parades Commission. Maurice Wilson, District Master of Sixmilewater, explained from the platform that a political call of that sort would be wholly inapprropriate on such a 'purely religious' occasion.

But simultaneously at Ormeau Park, Grand Master Robert Saulters was arguing for the removal of the commission on grounds which, it appears from reports, were purely political and not at all religious.

At Portadown, Armagh Grand Master Denis Watson was the voice of sweet and reasonable moderation as he regretted the 'unashamedly sectarian' behaviour of the parades body and insisted that, far from wanting confrontation with people living along the contentious Portadown route, 'accomodation is all we seek'.

It seems, however, that there was brisk trade at a number of venues in babies' bibs with the slogan, 'Born to shit on the Garvaghy Road'. If Masters, Grand Masters, Chaplains or anybody else voiced objection to infants being paraded in public with such a declaration of contempt for people of a different religion tied around their necks, it must have been out of earshot of the scores of journalists alert everywhere for an incident to report.

The source of all this confusion was indicated in those speeches which conveyed the ideological essence of Orangeism: that is to say, which made no distinction between religion and politics.

At the Ormeau Bridge, Ballynafeigh Chaplain William Hoey, having revealed his belief that the SDLP is Sinn Fein 'under another name', went on to warn against the 'continuing danger' of the Catholic Church.

At Ormeau Park, the Rev Ronald Johnston denounced the Parades Commission and then cautioned the brethern to be mindful that 'our faith is under attack from Romanism'.

In the most interesting speech of the day (judging from the various media reports), the City of Derry Grand Lodge Chaplain, the Rev Stephen Dickinson, numbered himself among many Protestants who, he claimed, were 'baffled' by Protestant clergy who supported the Multi-Party Agreement.

A 'Yes' vote in the referendum, he argued, meant, 'Yes for the destruction of the Protestant and Unionist cause'. Where, he demanded to know, 'do they get their text from scripture for any of that?'

Mr Dickinson's language and references will have been considered old hat by the more self-consciously modern, media-friendly elements of Orangeism. But his was the true voice of the authentic tradition.

Maurice Wilson at Larne may have been expressing a certain unease at the implications of intermeshing religion and politics. But the idea at the heart of Orangeism is precisely that the cause of 'Ulster' and the cause of Protestantism are one and the same thing, that the fight to keep Ulster British in 1999 is the fight for biblical truth in the modern world. It follows from this that compromise with Nationalism is near-enough blasphemy. Even to concede that Nationalists might have a legitimately-held grievance—with regard to Drumcree, for example—is to give ground to sinful error.

Herein lies the ideological nexus which at various times and places has provided a link between fundamentalist religion and the politics of race-hatred. This is the area where the ideas of the yob with the Nazi tattoos overlap with the thoughts of the pastor on the platform.

Orangeism is irrational, out of place in the western world, out of time in the late 20th century and offers Protestant people no way forward.

. . . .

Socialist Worker—July 1999

There's been no end of giggling and guffaws at the news that Northerners who identify themselves as athiests in the next census will be asked whether they are Catholic atheists or Protestant atheists. But it's no joke.

The draft census form, published earlier this month, reveals that atheists—or agnostics or humanists—taking part in the 2001 census will be directed to a supplementary question: 'What religion, religious denomination or body were you brought up in?'

No such question will be on the census form in England, Scotland or Wales.

The Northern Ireland Office tells me that the point of the question is so government can monitor the working of equality legislation. In order to maintain a balance between Catholics and Protestants in the distribution of jobs, houses or whatever, it's necessary to know what the existing balance is in any workplace or area, and which side new applicants come from.

This is ridiculous. To give a job or a house to an atheist is not to give it to a Catholic or a Protestant. But the fact that the idea is barmy won't worry the New Labour regime at the NIO. It's well in line with official practice across a wide range of political activity.

Ever since the publication of the Belfast Agreement, the SWP has highlighted the fact that the structures it envisages are not designed to end sectarianism, but to manage it. The intention isn't to bring people together, but to police people part.

Thus, members of the Assembly are required to register on their first day as Nationalist, Unionist or 'other'—with the significant addendum that when it comes to electing an Executive or taking any other 'key decision', the 'others' don't count. The Agreement is explicit that what's needed is 'parallel consensus' between Nationalists and Unionists only.

There is no provision in the Agreement or in the Standing Orders of the Assembly for the existence or emergence of any bloc of 'others', not even in the far distant future. Ending sectarianism isn't acknowledged even as an aspiration now.

This notion of the entire Northern population being naturally and forever divided into a Green tribe and an Orange tribe is the underlying assumption of British and Irish government policy and is implicitly accepted by all the major Northern parties. It is a highly convenient assumption, particularly for British governments, which can present themselves as benign and neutral outsiders heroically striving to broker a peace between two tribes which have been at irrational war for hundreds of years.

But this is the greatest nonsense of all. It's impossible to understand the development of sectarian politics in the North, or in Ireland generally, other than by reference to the involvement of Britain in Irish affairs. And this includes very recent history. The new Bloody Sunday Inquiry has reminded us that by no means all the atrocities of the last 30 years can be fitted into the 'two tribes' model.

Revelations about the murder ten years years ago of solicitor Pat Finucane, and the killing of Rosemary Nelson this year, point to the direct involvement of the RUC and, in the Finucane case, of the British security services. That apart, on the formal political level, successive British governments have wielded executive power in the North since the collapse of the old Stormont parliament in March 1972. Tony Blair's 'Nothing to do with me, guv, I'm only trying to help' stance is both contemptible in itself and contemptuous of the Northern Irish people.

Imposing a sectarian identity on the entire population—including people who have no sense of identity with any sectarian group—lets Britain off the hook, while intellectually imprisoning the population within the narrow rigidities of Green-Orange politics. It boosts the likelihood of argument within the new structures being dominated by disputation about how each tribe is faring vis-à-vis the other.

The mechanisms established under the Agreement will operate to direct anger and discontent arising from below along sectarian channels. Competition for votes between the various Nationalist and Unionist parties will, more or less automatically, be on the basis of who can secure the greatest advancement for 'our' side against 'the other side'.

'Justice' will refer solely to keeping a balance between Catholics and Protestants. Which, like the proposed census questions, is no joke.

. . . .

Socialist Worker—August 1999

Ruth Dudley Edwards has made what she believes is a major discovery about the Orange Order—that when you meet some Orangemen close-up and in friendly circumstances, they aren't such a bad bunch.

In *The Faithful Tribe*, Ms Dudley Edwards examines the history of the Order since its foundation in 1795 and unearths evidence that, along the way, there have always been decent sorts involved. From this she concludes that the Order has been demonised by Nationalist commentators who have managed in turn to demonise Orangeism to the world. She writes with the zeal of the convert (she's a Dublin-born cradle-Catholic) and with a view to influencing thinking on current Northern crises, particularly the rows over disputed Orange marches.

Her discovery that all Orangemen aren't devils all the time isn't the blinding revelation she seems to imagine. She writes in tones of wonderment of the days when Orange and Hibernian bands loaned one another drums, or when Catholic farmers and neighbours in the Orange Order helped one another out at harvest, and suggests that knowledge of this dimension of members of the Order has, in effect, been suppressed by Nationalist propagandists.

If truths like this were known, she argues, nobody could present an Orange march along Garvaghy Road as inherently hostile to the Catholic people of the area.

But folksie tales of this sort have been part of the currency of political and literary discourse for many years. Although often exaggerated in the more syrupy writings of Northern nostalgics, they are not entirely inaccurate. But neither are they the point.

The fact that there are members of the Orange Order who'd have the kettle on before you'd finished knocking the door tells us nothing about the role of the Orange Order in history or of the significance of its implacable refusal even now to break breath with Catholics through whose districts they propose to parade.

In much the same way, the fact that there are decent men in the Catholic priesthood doesn't make us shift our opinion of the Catholic Church as a thoroughly reactionary institution which continues to play an evil role in Irish society.

Orangeism presents itself—and is accepted in this light throughout Ms Dudley Edwards' book—as the authentic and defining expression of the 'culture' of the Protestant people. The implication is that it's natural and inevitable for Protestants of all classes to bind themselves together, and to define their interests in religious terms and as separate from and contradictory to the interests of Catholics.

There is no space in this perspective for the many thousands of Protestant socialists and trade unionists who have struggled over the years to make common cause with Catholic workers against the common class enemy. Nor, indeed, for poets like Louis McNeice, playwrights like Sam Thompson, or musicians like Van Morrison, all of whom are identifiable from their work as products of the Northern

Protestant backgrounds they came from, but who express a culture which, far from being containable within the narrow ground of Orangeism, opens out to and draws sustenance from the wider world. Her cultural commentary is thoroughly philistine.

The notion that it's natural for a community to express itself in politics solely by reference to its religion is the very essence of sectarianism. It has provided the ideological fountainhead of Unionism through the years, structured into the ruling party through the affiliation at the highest level of the Orange Order. The Order has thus supplied the organising principle behind Unionism's construction of a political slum in which working class people were kept powerless and pitched against one another while land-owners, employers and elements of the professional classes held a monopoly of political power, enforced by repressive law and their own private police force.

Cherry-picking history in order to rehabilitate the Orange Order, Ms Dudley Edwards invites us to believe that this past wasn't such a bad place after all. There's no future in that sort of thinking.

Chapter 4

Daily, Daly sings to Mary

The 20th anniversary of the September 1979 visit of Pope John Paul II prompted a spate of newspaper articles chronicling the decline in Catholic influence in Southern Ireland over the intervening years. Most underestimated opposition to the Papal visit at the time, and overestimated the rate of progress since.

Southern liberals, who dominate the media, have always been nervy about facing the truth about the Catholic Church's role in a society with which they are generally well-pleased. Writing on religion in the South, I have tended to polemicise as much against what I believe to be the inadequacies of the Church's liberal critics as against the Church itself.

There is little acknowledgement in the South of the extent to which the 'fight for Irish freedom' was a fight to be free to make Ireland Catholic. Nationalism wasn't as closely intermeshed with Catholicism as Unionism was with Protestantism, but the entanglement was intimate nonetheless. As a result, the quasi-official ideologists are reluctant to oppose the Church head-on, for fear of damaging irreparably the only source of moral authority they can think of to keep unruly elements in check. This has been a major factor in the feeble referenda campaigns on abortion and divorce in the '80s and '90s.

The liberals' dearest wish is that the Church itself become more liberal, thus to avoid any need for unpleasantness. Some of these pieces try to make the point that this aspiration is unlikely to be realised.

The forecast in the *Hot Press* piece of March 1996 that two US clerics operating a ministry to gays would soon be silenced by the Vatican has since been proven accurate.

. . . .

In Dublin—27 October 1988
'Ireland and the Irish Church experienced the great honour of finding themselves centre stage in Vatican affairs yesterday when the Pope beatified Fr Charles of St Andrew, the Passionist priest who, from 1857 to his death in 1893, was based in Mount Argus, Dublin.'

So ran the first paragraph of the *Irish Times* report of a Vatican ceremony on 16 October.

Now it may well be that the two journalists whose names were appended to this story, Joe Carroll and Paddy Agnew, felt greatly honoured that a person who had lived in Ireland was being declared 'blessed' by the Pope. Quite likely, the editor of the *Irish Times* shared this pleasurable experience. And good luck to them, say I.

It may even be true that a majority of the people of Ireland likewise felt greatly honoured, although it's my own impression that a clear majority didn't feel greatly involved in the business one way or the other.

Whatever about that, the statement that 'Ireland' felt greatly honoured carried with it an assumption that 'Ireland' and 'Catholic Ireland' are synonymous terms.

But Northern Protestants will hardly have felt 'greatly honoured' at 'finding themselves centre stage in Vatican affairs yesterday'. Indeed, it will have come as news to them that they were to be found yesterday in any such place.

And there is a not insignificant number of other people, North and South, who feel that they have a right both to be included in 'Ireland' and not to be included among those who felt 'greatly honoured' by the beatification.

Moreover, the use of the phrase 'the Irish Church', when what is clearly meant is the Irish Catholic Church, is an unthinking insult to non-Catholic Churches.

When Ian Paisley declares or implies that Northern Ireland is a Protestant state, the *Irish Times* is rightly, if rather too righteously, outraged. Yet so pervasive is Catholic ideology in Southern Ireland that all non-Catholics can be casually discarded from 'Ireland' in what purports to be a straight news story.

. . . .

In Dublin—16 March 1989

We ought, I suppose, to feel some vague sense of satisfaction that so many Irish writers have publicly declared their solidarity with the beleaguered Salman Rushdie. But where, I wonder, were these doughty defenders of freedom of expression two years ago when Zionist pressure kept Jim Allen's play *Perdition* off the Dublin stage?

Perdition was originally written for the Royal Court Theatre in London and was in the final stages of rehearsal—with, if it matters, Gabriel Byrne in the lead—when an outcry well-orchestrated by leading British

Zionists unnerved the Royal Court's management. The play was cancelled a few days before its scheduled first night.

Perdition's theme was the collusion between Zionist leaders and Nazis in Eastern Europe during World War Two, a collusion which might at first sight seem grotesquely unlikely but which was based on the fact that Zionism and Nazism share one key idea—that Jews are different, to the extent that they cannot be, and should not seek to be, assimilated into non-Jewish society.

After the Royal Court management shamefully backed down and cancelled the play, Jim Allen and his director Ken Loach tried assiduously, but in vain, to find a London theatre willing to defy Zionist wrath. At last they came to Dublin and believed that they had reached agreement with the Olympia. But howls of protest from local censors persuaded the relevant authorities that staging the play would prove an unprofitable venture, and *Perdition* was dropped.

If mention of these events doesn't clang any loud bell it's because only a small fuss was raised at the time. Indeed I have recently read a number of articles and editorials in Irish publications about the Rushdie affair which, reasonably enough, have ranged over examples of censorship and abuse of writers in Ireland through the decades. *The Playboy*, the *Plough*, the *Rose Tattoo* etc: in none of them that I have seen has the suppression of *Perdition* been mentioned.

It's as if Irish literary society has blotted the fact out of its collective memory.

. . . .

In Dublin—16 March 1989

I greatly regret that the Pope could not see his way to granting Archbishop Paul C Marcinkus's reported wish to become Papal Nuncio to Ireland.

Marcinkus has been cloistered in Vatican City for the past seven years, resisting demands by the Italian authorities that he come down to the station and answer a few questions about his dealings, as head of the Vatican Bank, with Roberto Calvi of Banco Ambrosiano, who was found hanging under Blackfriars Bridge in London, and about the collapse of the Ambrosiano, from the coffers of which, it was discovered, £800 million sterling had gone missing. Marcinkus has beaten the rap by citing a treaty signed between the Vatican and Mussolini which, inter alia, prevents extradition for religiously-motivated crimes.

John Paul II finally sacked Marcinkus a fortnight ago, just ahead of the trial in Milan of Licio Gelli, boss of the P2 Masonic Lodge, which is widely believed to have used much of the missing £800 million to fund extortion, right-wing terrorist atrocity and political corruption.

Italian papers now suggest that Marcinkus will be 'kicked upstairs' —made a cardinal and appointed pro-President of the Vatican State, a purely formal position.

The *Observer* (5 March) suggested that Marcinkus's offer to accept exile in Ireland was refused because 'Curial hearts grew faint at the vision of a cigar-smoking, golfing American plenipotentiary dropping into Dublin's hotels on his pastoral round.'

Rather too tender for my taste, these Curial hearts. I'd have thought that Marcinkus would have fitted in well in today's Dublin, and that if the nuncio's job wasn't considered suitable he'd have made a perfect spiritual adviser to the Oireachtas Joint Committee on Commercial State-Sponsored Bodies.

. . . .

In Dublin—31 August 1989

I earnestly hope that Cardinal O Fiaich is right when he predicts that boatloads of black African priests will soon be arriving in this country to take up positions in parishes left undermanned by the fall-off in Irish vocations.

The matter is, of course, no direct concern of mine. But I suspect that black Africans would be more fun than the pasty-faced priests which Maynooth has been turning out in recent times.

Speaking on RTE's lunchtime news programme on 21 August the Cardinal claimed an aptness about Africans coming to priest in Ireland since, after all, hadn't the Irish gone out to Africa from the last century until fairly recently, to make up for a shortage of priests in that continent?

I fear that the Cardinal has fallen into a subtle but by no means insignificant error here.

The Irish priests in Africa were missionaries. Their purpose was not to strengthen the predominant religion of the areas they went into, but, on the contrary, to convince local people that their religion was mere superstition which should forthwith be abandoned in favour of the white priests' beliefs.

The main reason Christian missionaries in sub-Saharan Africa had some success in this enterprise was that the social and economic basis of African tribalism, and therefore of tribal religions, was in the process of being destroyed by the enormously more powerful force of European imperialism—of which Christianity was an ideological reflection. As Dr Livingstone put it: 'If we establish our commerce, our religion will follow naturally.'

There is a parallel between this process and the process whereby Catholicism in Ireland now finds itself short of vocations, but it is not the parallel which Cardinal O Fiaich appears to imagine.

A major reason for the current 11 percent per annum fall-off in Irish vocations, and for the decline in religious practice generally, has to do with the steady and unstoppable incorporation of Ireland into the global, US-dominated economy and the consequent undermining of ideas which flourished at an earlier stage of Ireland's development. Catholicism in Ireland is in the position of a tribal religion whose hocus-pocus has begun to lose its allure and which, as a result, is experiencing difficulty finding new recruits to train up as witch-doctors.

Coca-Cola salesmen and franchise barons for Burger King are the high priests of the new ideological order. I do not suggest for a moment that their rule would be altogether a good thing, nor that resistance to their rule should be in any way discouraged. But importing priests from Africa in an effort to resuscitate the old order is hardly an answer.

. . . .

Hot Press—17 February 1990
Dublin Archbishop Desmond Connell must surely be a most perplexed prelate as, alone in his palace at Drumcondra, he ponders the wickedly illogical ways of the secular world.

The Archbishop is currently in serious soapy bubble with the progressives for having referred to persons of the gay predilection as suffering from a 'disorder'. Writers of letters to the editor of the *Irish Times* continue to nibble and ruminate on the issue.

They complain that the Archbishop is unChristian in failing to show charity to his fellows.

Now it may well be that the Archbishop ought not to have said what he did. But if so, it was a Christian thing which he ought not to have said. Because if there's one thing we can say with certainty about the god of Christianity it is that he was dead set against gays.

Is it not most plainly set down in Genesis 19 that the Lord God was wont to react to gay sexual practices by sentencing the practitioners to eternal hellfire and zapping their brothers, sisters, neighbours, casual visitors and all belonging to them?

Did not the Lord God dispatch his Angel of Death to Sodom on the night before the scheduled firestorm to give the tip-off to the one just man, Lot?

Did not a crowd of the local hooligans gather outside Lot's front door demanding to know what the dark, winged person was doing in the vicinity?

Yea.

Did not the Lord God on the following day blast and ruin the city until there was left not a stone upon a stone? Were not many hundreds of the citizenry consumed in the flames, far exceeding in their numbers those who perished in the recent unfortunate occurrence in San Francisco?

Is it not perfectly plain from this that the Lord God of Christianity regarded homosexuality not just as a 'disorder' but as a foul and pestilential condition so abhorrent as to warrant the utter destruction of all and any who tolerated it in their midst?

I am aware, naturally, of common practice among progressive elements of interpreting the entire bible as analogy and parable, thus to facilitate the dismissal of passages of awkward literal meaning. But with what hidden, poetical meaning can the story of Sodom be invested so as to deprive it of its obvious import?

Would it not be more convenient, and generally conducive to intellectual dignity, if campaigners for the rights of gay people were to say straight that Archbishop Connell is accurately articulating the Christian attitude to homosexuality? And, further, to say straight that the Christian attitude is wrong?

. . . .

Hot Press—29 March 1990

Amid the maelstrom of controversy over the draft pilot programme on AIDS education, which is to be introduced to schools in the South next September, not enough attention has been paid to the views of Senator Willie Farrell of Fianna Fail.

Herein lies one of the more puzzling of recent Church-State controversies. Even now that they've had sight of the document for a couple of months, there is still no explicit, authoritative statement of the bishops' attitude.

It's been left to Senator Willie to wade in where bishops balk.

At a meeting of the North Western Health Board, the Senator declared that not only was there no need for mention of condoms in the health education programme, there was no need for health education. What was needed was no more dirty movies on television.

In his day, Senator Willie told the enthralled gathering, 'these diseases' presented no problem to the Irish people because 'they had high moral standards'. Health education in this area should be 'forgotten about'.

'How did we make a success of our lives without any health education?' he demanded to know.

Now some regular readers will see Senator Willie's intervention as the outburst of an antediluvian gobdaw. But it could also be closer to official Catholic teaching than the indistinct line of the bishops.

The most recent Vatican pronouncement on AIDS came from Cardinal Joseph Ratzinger, head of the Congregation for the Doctrine of the Faith, John Paul's numero uno ideologist.

Cardinal Ratzinger travelled to Washington DC to convey the Vatican view to the John Paul II Institute for Studies on Marriage and Family.

The AIDS virus, he said, has become 'a portrait of the interior sickness' of the modern age. It could be combated only in the context of a crusade against 'rampant moral evil'. The central, strongly-argued theme was that Catholics must treat AIDS as a spiritual, not a medical, problem.

He spelled it out: 'Positive thinking'—by which, in the context, he meant the tendency to regard AIDS as an illness of the body—'offers the spiritual organism no ethical resources for maintaining immunity; it is rather the ruination of the spiritual defence system, leading to an important surrender to death's deceptive promises.'

In view of this, even if medical researchers succeeded in finding a vaccine for AIDS, their efforts would ultimately prove futile: 'It will only shift the field of devastation somewhere else.'

Could it be that the reason the Irish bishops have been coy on the issue is that they fear that this line would meet with considerable resistance, even from committed members of their own flock?

Whatever about that, it does appear that it's Senator Willie Farrell, and not the bishops, who speaks for the Pope on this important matter.

. . . .

Hot Press—19 April 1990
Who fears to speak of Easter Week? The Southern Irish establishment and its journalistic and academic hangers-on.

'Officially', the Easter Rising was the most glorious single episode in Irish history. But these days, it's hard to praise the memory of it without seeming to offer support to the Provos. Hence the shiftiness of the establishment.

This is commonly expressed in the assertion that the people who followed Pearse were different in character and motivation from present-day Republicans. One of the most important of the supposed differences has to do with sectarianism.

The leaders of '16 were high-minded men (and a few women), it's said, scholars, aesthetes and trade union militants. They would have regarded with revulsion any suggestion that their struggle was intended to advance the interests of Irish Catholics, as opposed to the nonsectarian interests of the 'nation as a whole'. Unlike the Provos, it is claimed.

But in fact, the Provos are nowhere near as Catholic as the people of '16 who seized the GPO.

In *The Soldier's Story of Easter Week*, Brian O'Higgins, a rank-and-file member of the Volunteers who was stationed on the roof of the GPO throughout the fighting, recalled how the men there took turns reciting the Rosary every half hour day and night for the duration.

This was no mere eccentricity on the part of one particular group.

Pearse himself believed that the Irish people—not people in general, not 'humanity'—had been created 'in the image and likeness of God'. He regarded Irish Nationalism as 'a divine religion'. And part of the purpose of this religion was to redeem the Irish nation from the sin of national apostasy just as Christ had redeemed mankind.

It was for this reason that the Rising was arranged for Easter. To Pearse, the Rising didn't just have religious connotations: it was, itself, a religious event, a sacrifice, not unlike the sacrifice of the Mass.

It won't do to argue, as some have, that while this was Pearse's personal approach it wasn't characteristic of the Rising generally.

The British Marxist historian John Newsinger has pointed out: 'Only by recognising the religious fervour that gripped these men and women does the Military Council's despatch early in April 1916 of George Plunkett, a papal count, to Rome to seek Pope Benedict XV's blessing for the imminent rising become in any way explicable.'

Newsinger also explodes the notion that the prominent participation in the Rising of James Connolly, a professed Marxist, brought a secular element into the heart of the affair.

There is no record of Connolly ever distancing himself from the Catholic element in the Rising's ideology. He was reconciled with the church before his death. (Ruth Dudley Edwards records that Pearse, when he heard that Connolly had confessed to a priest and agreed to receive the Last Rites, said: 'Thank God. It was the one thing I was anxious about.')

The second-in-command of the Citizens' Army, Michael Mallin, wrote to his wife while awaiting execution, asking that his daughter be persuaded to become a nun and his son a priest 'as a penance for our sins'. He went on: 'I do not believe our Blood has been shed in vain. I believe Ireland will come out greater and grander, but she must not forget she is Catholic; she must keep faith.' (What an interesting initial capital that 'B' is).

Countess Markievicz was converted to Catholicism as a result of observing how the intense devotion to their religion of the rank and file of the Citizens' Army brought solace to 'these simple unlettered men' as they faced death.

Any objective reading of history of the period leaves no room for doubt that both the Volunteers and the Citizen Army, at leadership as well as 'grass roots' levels, saw and felt the Rising not just as an assertion of Irish Nationalism but of Irish Catholic Nationalism.

And there is nothing surprising in this. It resulted from colonialism, from the fact that British imperial power expressed itself in Ireland through the oppression of the Catholics. The struggle against colonialism tended 'naturally' to become a specifically Catholic struggle.

Something similar is happening today across Eastern Europe. Religions long suppressed by Stalinist thuggery are suddenly flowering again and providing the dominant ideology of popular revolts.

Neither the Rising nor, for the most part, the War of Independence which it detonated, involved hostilities with the Protestant community. The most important reason for this is that the Rising and the War of Independence took place mainly in those parts of Ireland where the Protestant community was scarcely represented.

The Provos represent the ideology of the Rising and of the War of Independence much more accurately than any other political tendency today, and they do it in a context much less congenial than was available to Pearse, Connolly, Collins etc.

This is not to say that one is an exact replica of the other. For example, none of the signatories to the 1916 Proclamation acknowledged a right to divorce. (Connolly argued that 'the divorce evil' was a capitalist institution!) In contrast, when all the members of the Northern Ireland Assembly were polled in 1986 and asked how they urged people in the South to vote in the divorce referendum, Sinn Fein was the only party all of whose members called for a 'yes' vote.

On the particular issue, Grizzly Adams' crowd would appear to be a mite more secular than James Connolly, one of the reasons the Catholic Church gives Grizzly a hard time.

. . . .

Hot Press—20 May 1991

It would be in the Catholic Church's interest to give up its influence over civil affairs in Southern Ireland. So Prionsias de Rossa told the Worker's Party Ard-Fheis the weekend before last.

The Catholic Church is damaging itself when it weighs in against divorce? It would be doing itself a favour by staying silent about contraceptive slot machines in pubs?

Prionsias knows better than the bishops what's good for the Church?

Eh?

The double-jointed reasoning arises from the fact that Mr de Rossa, like many another vote-hunter, wants to be regarded as 'liberal', 'progressive' and so forth but not as 'anticlerical'.

Unwilling to confront the power of the Church, they plead with the Church to avoid confrontation.

The bishops will have been touched by Prionsias' plea. Touched as with a tickling-stick. If there's one thing Catholic bishops understand—and some say there's only one—it's power, and how to hold onto it.

That emerges starkly from Gerald McElroy's just-published *The Catholic Church and the Northern Ireland Crisis*. Mr de Rossa might usefully while away a few hours Euro-commuting in its company.

The book examines how the Church has reacted to the chaos of the North over the past 20 years, the way its 'line' has changed from time to time, with blithe disregard for the supposed immutability of its teaching.

But some things never changed. Always, the Church has been guided by a single, central consideration: how to hold onto its power.

The Church in Belfast was warmly disposed to the Provos when they emerged in 1969/'70/'71, seeing the new movement as a possible bulwark against the Leftism of some civil rights leaders.

The 1970 Lenten Pastoral read in all Belfast churches fulminated against socialism—which wasn't exactly sweeping the community at the time. The violence gathering ominously all around rated scarcely a mention.

But within a few years, the Provos had become 'devil-people'. They had managed to marginalise the civil rights Left—but in the process had themselves acquired enough strength in the community to challenge the authority of the Church.

Or consider the Church's attitude to Protestant rights in a united Ireland.

Replying to Brian Lenihan of Fianna Fail at the New Ireland Forum in 1984, Bishop (now Archbishop) Cathal Daly said that in a united Ireland the rights of Protestants (in relation to health, education, contraception, divorce etc) would be defended by the Catholic Church as 'a matter of plain justice and not just of political expediency'.

This was seized on by Senator (as she then was) Mary Robinson, who wondered whether, since it was 'a matter of plain justice', these rights ought not to be available to Protestants in Southern Ireland now. The bishops explained that, ah no, sure, that was a different question altogether...

The point is made even more sharply in Mr McElroy's examination of the Irish Church's line on 'mixed' marriages, an issue which has embittered Irish Protestants to an extent which is rarely acknowledged by Catholics.

The Church's attitude everywhere is that the Catholic partner in a mixed marriage must strive to have the children brought up 'in the faith'. But the way the obligation is to be fulfilled varies.

The Irish hierarchy, in Dr McElroy's phrase, is 'virtually unique' in giving the obligation the status of divine law. 'These obligations are not imposed by the Church's regulations, nor can the Church remove them; they come from God', the *Irish Directory on Mixed Marriages* announces.

But god sings from a different hymn-sheet elsewhere. The French, Belgian, Swiss and German hierarchies, for example, explicitly acknowledge that the religious upbringing of children must be acceptable to the consciences of both partners.

The tougher line of the Church in Southern Ireland reflects the extent to which it has had effective control of the civil law of marriage since the formation of the State. In this situation, it is fatuous to argue that separation from the State would be of benefit to the Church. It wouldn't. It would weaken the Church.

On this and adjacent issues, what's needed is an unambiguous campaign against the influence of the Church in civil affairs. But there is no party in Leinster House willing to come within a barge-pole's length of that line.

. . . .

Hot Press—August 1995

I was reading Dermot Keogh's horribly fascinating *Ireland and the Vatican* (Cork University Press) the other night when I chanced on a quote which I had to share with somebody, so it might as well be you. It's the text of a 1930 letter from the leadership of the IRA to Pope Pius XI about the proposed appointment of a Papal Nuncio to Ireland.

The Republicans were complaining that while the Catholic Church was organised on an all-Ireland basis, with the premier diocese (Armagh) in the North, the accreditation of a nuncio to the Dublin government amounted to a recognition of the 26 County State and therefore to an acceptance of the legitimacy of partition.

Here's how the Army Council of the IRA conveyed its complaint: 'Prostrate in spirit at the feet of your Holiness in Whom we revere the Vice-regent of Jesus Christ, we humbly declare ourselves faithful children of the One Holy Catholic Church of which your Holiness has been appointed by Divine Providence the Supreme Head and Guardian.

'In bringing before Your Holiness certain protests and complaints, we do so in entire submission to the laws and teachings of our Holy Church, and humbly submit that these protests and complaints impinge in no wise on those sacred laws and teachings. We wish to renew the congratulations we have already had the honour of having had conveyed to your Holiness on the recovery of the temporal independence so essential to the dignity of your Holy Office and your exercise of the governance of the Universal Church, and we pray God to confirm and continue the peace and dignity thus restored to the Holy See.

'We desire to keep the relation between our ancient nation and the Vatican on a more exalted plane than an alleged adjustment, by which the Nuncio is accredited to a native garrison in the arbitrarily-established Southern province, while the Cardinal Primate is under the civil jurisdiction of a bigoted alien garrison avowing its allegiance to England…'

(The mention of the Vatican's 'recovery of…temporal independence' is a reference to the 1929 Treaty between Pius XI and Mussolini which restored the political independence of Vatican City in return for Church acquiescence in fascist rule in Italy.)

. . . .

Hot Press—5 March 1996

A telling indication of the way the Catholic Church is reacting to the crises now surrounding it came with a gathering under the chairmanship of Cathal Daly at a country house in Dundrum, County Tipperary, during the week ending 17 February.

At a series of workshops and plenary sessions, 'facilitated' by the newly-appointed Bishop of Limerick, Donal Murray, and the leading Jesuit, Joe Dargan, the Irish bishops spent four days discussing a 'crisis of dissent' in the Church and planning the restoration of the Church's authority.

Despite much recent talk about openness, transparency, dialogue and so on, the Dundrum meeting took place in strict secrecy. The gathering had obviously been scheduled some time in advance. It will have required considerable, detailed preparation and exchange of information—finalising a date, setting an agenda, making catering arrangements for their lordships' needs. But there was no advance announcement. Only Andy Pollock of the *Irish Times* caught wind that something was up. Nor was there anything in the shape of a communiqué afterwards.

It wasn't until the following week that there was even a whisper of what had transpired. The *Irish Catholic* (22 February) told on its front page: 'Bishops prepare for year 2000 in secret session… Exclusive.' The story was scarcely enlightening. What was provided was a summary of the 'mood and tone of the gathering', in the form of a quote from the Auxiliary Bishop of Cork, John Buckley:

'It was a joyful period of relaxation and reflection. We emphasised the essence of our mission which is to present the person of Jesus Christ to the people of our time who are searching for a meaning and purpose in life. The search and the message of Jesus are made for each other. It is through Jesus that we realise the greatness of our humanity.'

There was also a reference to the desirability of peace in the North. And that, for what it's worth, is as much as the people in the pews have been permitted to know.

It may come as a surprise to some that this is still the approach in 1996. But it shouldn't really. In Ireland, as elsewhere, the main priority of Catholic Church bosses at the moment is to re-impose order on an unruly flock. In this context, the bishops will have seen the Cleary, Casey and Comiskey affairs, the various money and sex abuse scandals and the revelations of savagery by religious to children as unwelcome, complicating factors. But it will not have deflected them from their objective of re-establishing Church authority over the people. On the contrary, it is more likely to have hardened their determination to get back to the basics of order, discipline and obedience.

This is not speculative analysis. It's to put succinctly and in a certain context what the Church leaders themselves say they are at. The vague hopes often expressed by Catholic liberals of 'repentance followed by renewal', and of the Church transforming itself, by 'listening', into a 'church of the people', are the product of light minds, and lacking in substance.

The authentic voice of the contemporary Catholic Church comes through in an interview in the current edition of the Redemptorist magazine *Reality* with Southern Irish Church chief Desmond Connell, Archbishop of Dublin. The problem of Catholics refusing to take Church leadership on trust is 'very serious', he admits. There has been 'a kind of politicisation of the Church', he complains, with some of its members coming to believe in the possibility of a 'loyal opposition' to the Pope and the bishops.

This, he argues, is to misunderstand the fundamental nature of the Church as a 'mystery of life', embodying unquestionable truths to be defined only by 'the successor of Peter'.

What this means in practice is evident in developments in the 'universal Church' which might at first sight seem unconnected to experience in Ireland. During his visit last month to Latin America, John Paul told journalists travelling with him of his satisfaction that 'liberation theology was no longer seen as a problem... Following the fall of Communism, liberation theology has fallen a little, too. The bishops confirm that ideologies are no longer a force or a problem.'

When the Brazilian Franciscan Leonardo Boff, one of the talismanic leaders of the 'Church Of The Poor' in the region, protested that the ideas of liberation theology could be contained within Catholic orthodoxy, the Vatican's chief doctrinal spokesman, Joaquin

Navarro Valls, slapped him down. Whatever Boff might mean by liberation theology, 'Priests in politics and a Marxist basis for analysis, these two things are over.'

John Paul was welcomed on arrival in San Salvador by the successor to Archbishop Oscar Romero, the outspoken prelate assassinated by a military death-squad on the altar of the city's cathedral in 1980. The new Archbishop of San Salvador is Fernando Saenz Lacale, appointed by John Paul last year. He is a member of the far-right group Opus Dei. His previous posting but one was as head chaplain to the Salvadorean military.

Five days before the Pope arrived, Saenz had sacked the Rector of the San Salvador diocesan seminary, Luis Coto, known as a rather mild, academic supporter of liberation theology. Thus, John Paul did not have to endure the embarrassment of being greeted by Fr Coto when he called at the seminary: the Vatican now literally won't touch ideas which were regarded as debatable, at least, just a decade ago.

There are other straws in the unsettling wind. Robert Nugent and Jeannine Gramick have just been ordered by the Vatican to submit written accounts of the beliefs underlying their longtime ministry to gays in the US. Nugent is a priest in the Salvadorean order, Gramick a nun with the Notre Dame sisters. They have been conducting a 'Catholic ministry to homosexuals' for 24 years, giving workshops and seminars on the problems encountered by both gay and straight Catholics in handling issues of sexual orientation within the Church. Their ministry has mainly been carried out at the invitation and under the supervision of individual dioceses.

But not for much longer.

Two years ago the Vatican established a commission under Detroit Cardinal Adam Maida to look into Nugent and Gramick's activities. The commission held three lengthy meetings with the two religious and their provincial supervisors and, in February last year, submitted a report to Rome. Now Maida has been in touch with Nugent and Gramick again to relay an instruction from the Congregation for Institutes of Consecrated Life and Societies of Apostolic Life (the body which controls religious orders), telling them to set out in writing their views on two questions to do with homosexual activity and one to do with homosexual orientation.

In the Instruction, the Congregation tells the two that the views attributed to them 'may have created an ambiguity which has caused confusion in the minds of some people'. Connoisseurs of Vatican-speak will be in little doubt from this what's to happen next: Nugent and Gramick will be required to recant their views and desist from their ministry, or be silenced.

These are not isolated occurrences. A trawl through the Catholic press any week now reveals an enormous concentration on the ne-cessity of authority and the impermissibility of dissent. The letters page of the *Catholic Times* has recently featured regular dire warnings that hellfire awaits Catholics who challenge papal authority. The once-restrained *Universe* can now (18 February), without any ap-pearance of irony, splash a headline on the front page urging, 'Ban All Talk Of Women Priests'. (The story underneath begins: 'Primary school teachers who publicly promote the ordination of women could face official sanction from the Church'.)

The *Irish Catholic* (22 February) pours a torrent of contemptuous abuse on a book of essays, *Authority In The Church*, edited by the vet-eran Catholic commentator Sean MacReamoin. A contribution by Professor Mary McAleese, pro-chancellor of Queen's University, Belfast, a mainstream Catholic and an adviser to the hierarchy at the Forum For A New Ireland, is splattered with scorn. To Professor McAleese's contention that a Catholic can raise questions about Church teaching and still remain in good standing, the *Irish Catholic* responds with New Testament texts: 'Anyone who preaches to you a gospel other than you were first given is to be under God's curse… Hand such a man over to Satan to be destroyed as far as natural life is concerned.' (Again, it's maybe worth saying that there's no hint this stuff is intended to be taken with a pinch of irony.)

In his own column, the editor of the *Irish Catholic*, David Quinn, provides weekly evidence of the Catholic Church retreating behind a circle of certainty from which it proposes to issue forth and re-establish its unique right to control the ideological destinies of the land. A certain mild persecution mania emerges as Quinn crouches down behind defensive dogma for protection from the slings and arrows of the erroneous elements whooping anti-Catholicism all around.

'What adds up to anti-Catholicism?' he asks. And answers: 'I would have to say that if you don't believe in objective right and wrong then you're well on your way. If you don't believe in hierarchies, then you're gone a considerable step further. If you don't believe in the priesthood further still…'

(This is so lacking in logic and suggestive of paranoia that it's tempting to dismiss Quinn as of no account. Certainly, he is not a deep thinker. But he was appointed editor of the *Irish Catholic* late last year following the sacking of Brigid Ann Ryan specifically because the most influential of the hierarchy, particularly Desmond Connell, wanted somebody to steer the paper steadily in the direction the 'official' Church wanted.)

Given his distinctive definition of the term, it's not surprising that Quinn sees 'anti-Catholicism' everywhere. The only newspaper in Britain or Ireland which he seems able to identify as definitely not anti-Catholic is the *Daily Telegraph*. As for Ireland… 'The newspaper etc in question could be sensationally anti-Catholic, for example the *Sunday Independent*, or sophisticatedly so, for example the *Irish Times*… The *Irish Times* is more anti-Catholic than the *Sunday Indo*. Its ideology is set foursquare against it. Failure to recognise our media as in the main anti-Catholic stems from the fact that its anti-Catholicism is so all-pervading, we are inured against it.'

This is the mind-set of the Catholic Church at the moment, and not just in Ireland. Far from being humbled by its recent experiences, it bristles with arrogant certainty as it rises above the material world to escape the sins it is besieged by, retreating deeper into its own councils away from the sight of scandal, all the while toughening up its ideas and renovating its machinery for the requirements of the future.

The aspiration of Irish liberals has never been to extirpate the Catholic Church and end its influence. What they've always wanted is a new accommodation with the Church. But all the indications are that this is no go. The furtive cabal which descended on Dundrum is not talking terms.

Sooner or later we'll have to have it out with them.

. . . .

Hot Press—26 June 1996

I wrote in the last issue about Labour Education Minister Niamh Breathnach proposing to establish for the first time a legal basis for the infliction of a 'religious ethos' on primary schools in the South. It would be a mistake to imagine that things are better in the North.

In the run-up to Gay Pride Week, a number of activists voiced the unremarkable plea that schoolchildren should not be taught to see gay people as depraved or gay relationships as abominable.

This prompted a long letter in the *Belfast Telegraph* from three primary school head teachers—Billy McIlwaine of Lisnagelvin, David Canning of Strabane and William McElhinney of Ashlea—declaring that, 'We accept the Bible as our authoritative standard in matters of faith and practice.' They went on to quote Romans, Leviticus, Corinthians, Genesis and Jude to the effect that homosexuality is unnatural, depraved, abominable and 'certain to bring upon itself the crushing judgement of the Almighty'.

The three were nothing if not forthright in explaining how they applied these personal beliefs to their positions as educators of children. On the 'authority of the Bible', children were to be instructed that homosexuality was 'not only a deviant form of behaviour but utterly depraved'. Presenting a non-judgmental account of human sexuality in the classroom would amount to 'subjecting...children to instruction on sodomy'.

This sad trio is, of course, entitled to its loopy opinions. But the schools they run are State schools. And there is no legal basis for their use of the State system to inculcate their opinions into impressionable children. If head teachers of equivalent schools in England were publicly to issue such a brazen account of their classroom priorities, even the far-right of the Tory Party would be hard-pressed to defend them.

But here in the North there hasn't been a cheep. It is with a sense of weariness that I wonder whether the Old Testament is also used in these schools as a textbook for instruction on other aspects of life. Genesis, after all, presents an account of the emergence of humankind in direct contradiction of all scientific knowledge and basic rationality. Other Old Testament passages give sanction for slavery, the extermination of 'enemy' peoples, the torture and ritual sacrifice of women. Is that part of the deal, too?

Here in Derry in the past year, there has been a spate of attacks on gay people in the streets—commonly on their way home from a gay disco in the city centre and from functions at Magee College. The spotty thugs involved in this bigoted violence are expressing in their own way the classroom notion that gay people are unnatural, depraved, abominable. They are boot boys for the bible, with good reason to think themselves sanctioned by respectable society.

All around us, we see the results of narrowed minds, hatred towards people perceived as different from ourselves, fear of ways of life that we have been led to see as strange. Sometimes we wonder aloud where all this unnatural hatred comes from. But we know, in reality, that, North and South, much of it comes still from the classrooms.

The State funds it in both jurisdictions. And those who are prominent and influential in the politics of the State either ignore it, or enact new laws to reinforce it.

. . . .

Hot Press—11 December 1996

Any notion that the days were done when Irish politicians were hand-in-glove with the Catholic Church should have been dispelled a few weeks back when the education minister, Niamh Breathnach, led an 11-strong parliamentary delegation to Rome for the beatification of Edmund Ignatius Rice, the founder of the Christian Brothers.

The delegation included members of all parties represented in Leinster House. The trip was entirely state-funded. No TD or senator spoke against it, nor has any newspaper raised a fuss. The trip to the Vatican is not to be recorded as an occasion of controversy.

Edmund Ignatius Rice was a controversial choice for beatification, even among dutiful Catholics. It is possible to argue that the Brothers played a positive role in the education of an unmonied layer of young Catholic males in the past. But it is also now generally acknowledged that the Brothers attracted many damaged young men with a penchant for violence, and that brutality in many of their schools reached levels which should have been unacceptable then and would certainly be held indefensible now.

It has also emerged that in a significant number of cases boys in the care of the Brothers were sexually as well as physically violated.

In Australia, the Order faces ruin as hundreds, literally, of former pupils come forward to testify to the savagery inflicted on them by Rice's followers.

All this was widely reported before Rice's beatification was formally proposed, and led to questioning by Catholics of the advisability of his 'promotion'. But the tax-funded Oireachtas delegation to Rome has signalled that the State has no reservations in the matter.

The Minister and her fellow-parliamentarians joined thousands of other Irish in St Peter's for the ceremony: that is, the Irish State joined in a controversial Catholic pilgrimage, without, as far as we can see, rippling the surface of political life.

This hints at something which is also detectable in two recent policy announcements by Labour ministers—the decisions of Ms Breathnach to copperfasten Church control of much of the State's educational system, and the associated decision of Equality Minister Mervyn Taylor to exempt Catholic schools from key provisions of new anti-discrimination law.

There were clues to what's afoot during the closing stages of the divorce referendum campaign, in which all of the Leinster House parties officially urged a 'Yes' vote. It was argued then by the anti-divorce side that the legalisation of divorce would lead on to further 'liberal' reforms, that the introduction of civil divorce would prove a staging-post on the road to a fully secular society.

Instead of joining battle on this basis and arguing in favour of a fully secular society, the parties urging a 'Yes' vote challenged the delineation of the battle-line and denied that any further reform was contemplated.

Health Minister Michael Noonan was forthright before the vote and on RTE's 'results' programme afterwards that this was the last item on the government's 'liberal agenda'.

Give us this and we'll call it quits, ran the message. We have no further demands.

These assurances must have come as a considerable relief to leaders of the Catholic Church, following the seismic disturbances arising from the various scandals and revelations of recent times.

It's commonly observed that the authority of the institutional Church is at its lowest ebb since the foundation of the State. And yet it's now that politicians, including those of the 'Left', have backed off from further confrontation.

And not just politicians. I recently chanced on a radio discussion of the *Faith Of Our Fathers* album and heard Nuala O Faolain suggest that the tone of the hymn-fest was in tune with the placid atmosphere in the land these days, now that the issues of divorce and abortion 'have been disposed of'.

But the abortion issue has not been disposed of. Abortion in the circumstances of the 'X' case has been made legal through a referendum vote of the people. But no provision has been made for legal abortion actually to take place. Every week, women travel to Britain for abortions, not because it would be illegal for the abortion to be carried out in Ireland, but because, although legal, it's not allowed. The issue is surely more tangled and less satisfactory than ever. And yet a commentator as closely associated with feminism as Ms O Faolain argues that there's no need to grapple with it any longer. What's going on?

Unease at the collapse of Catholic Church authority has by no means been confined to the Church. Facing a future fraught with political and economic uncertainty, and with no coherent ideological system of their own, many who might have little time for the Church in their personal lives have felt a frisson of alarm at the fraying of the main source of moral authority within the State.

They looked into a future in which secular authority alone would be available, and shrank back in fear.

It wasn't just run-of-the-mill Labour cowardice which led Breathnach and Taylor to renew the bishop's franchise for controlling the State's schools: it's a confession of their own ideological bankruptcy.

Breathnach's leadership of a State contingent on the Edmund Rice pilgrimage was a signal to the Church, and to society at large, that notwithstanding the unease of a large number of citizens at many aspects of the Church's role in education through the years, the State was resolved to make no issue of it.

What we are witnessing is not a continuing process of separation of Church and State, but the making of a new concordat between Church and State, on terms highly favourable to the Church in its present condition and indicative of weakness on the part of the State.

. . . .

Hot Press—September 1995

The nervous agitation of the liberals is fun to behold as they explain that they are in favour of divorce—but not in such a way as to offend anybody.

Clifford, the RC Bishop of Cashel, is given acres of space in newspapers and on news bulletins to advance his theory that divorced people are more likely than others to smoke heavily, commit suicide, crash cars and much else.

Meanwhile, Comiskey from Ferns warns that if more politicians don't start speaking up for Catholic bigotry, the bigots, 'alienated', might form militia-type organisations along the lines of the group favoured by Irish-American Timothy McVeigh, who is alleged to have blown up the Federal Building in Oklahoma City in April.

Such dementia drivels forth from the anti-divorce faction day and

Daly. But instead of roasting them for their lack of reason, the liberals offer apologies for presuming to disagree.

Although all parties in Leinster House are formally committed to ending the ban on divorce, there's no clear call from them for people to be allowed to make their own decisions about what relationships they want to enter into or make their exit from. Reluctant to have it out head-on with the bigots they come across as unconvinced and unconvincing.

Listen to this from Vincent Browne:

'Is it not the case that, in our culture, marriage has assumed a status of such proportions that it is impossible to separate our personalities from it? That we see ourselves integrally as married or as not married to a particular person; married in many senses but, critically, also in the sense of official legal recognition, quite separate from the legal entitlements?

'And that given the embeddedness of this view of marriage in our sense of personal identity, one can indeed talk of divorce in terms of a right, a right founded on personal identity and therefore of a character that trumps considerations of the common good.'

This, in case you are wondering, is an argument for divorce.

Then Vincent goes on to point out: 'The language of rights is dangerous because of the profusion of rights claims without regard to how rights fit together or how conflicts between them are resolved.'

Oh indeed.

Can't imagine why the anti-divorce crowd bother campaigning at all when, left to themselves, the liberals could be counted on to agonise their way to yet another defeat.

. . . .

Hot Press—7 August 1996

Too much has been made of the Catholic bishops' seemingly positive reaction to the proposal to make religious education an exam subject in the South.

Headlines such as 'Bishops Welcome Religious Education' greeted the plan for a Leaving Certificate course which would include a section on 'world religions' and which would encourage students 'to identify how understandings of God, religious tradition, have contributed to the culture in which we live'.

This is an advance on rote-learning of the catechism and drumming Catholic doctrine into little children's heads, it's suggested. It's further argued that the fact that the Irish Bishops' Conference formally welcomed the proposal at its last meeting in Maynooth indicated a move by the church itself away from old, entrenched attitudes.

This is too optimistic a view. What we should be paying attention to is the way the bishops are adapting to a changing situation while keeping their focus fixed on how to maintain as much of their power as possible. Their real attitude to Church influence in education is like an unreconstructed Provo's to the semtex stash. Not an ounce, if we can help it.

There were specific reasons that the bishops gave the proposed course a general welcome. One was that its inclusion in the syllabus alongside maths, languages, history etc, might lend religion a credibility which, increasingly, it cannot command on its own account. 'With examination pressure in schools, those subjects not studied for examination purposes can seem to pupils to be of less value,' their lordships observe shrewdly.

And anyway the Leaving Certificate course won't have quite the ecumenical range some commentators seem to imagine. The bishops' representative on the relevant committee of the National Council for Curriculum and Assessment (NCCA), Fr Dermot Lane, has assured Catholics that, because Christianity has contributed more than any other religion to 'the culture in which we live', the RE course will not ask students to believe that 'Hinduism, Buddhism, Islam etc are of equal value'.

But there's a gap in Fr Lane's logic. It's true, of course, that, of all religions, Christianity has had greatest influence on Irish life. But it cannot simply be assumed that this influence has been for good. It's at least as arguable, in the light of experience of this influence, that Christianity has been of less value in Ireland than other religions, and that students should be explicitly invited to consider this view.

There's a second reason for the bishops' relatively positive reaction. The new course will mark the first time the Irish State has directly undertaken religious education. In the past, the State has—to a degree that went to the limits of its own constitution—sanctioned and subsidised the teaching of Catholicism in the schools by representatives of the Catholic Church. Now it is itself taking on religious education—and undertaking in so doing to present religion in partisan fashion.

In relation to no other examination subject would the Department of Education openly eschew objectivity and proclaim an ideological bias in favour of one particular, and contentious, view. And yet, far from this approach plunging the minister and members of the NCCA into controversy, the main reaction has been of surprised gratification that the Catholic bishops haven't been more suspicious of it all.

The real surprise is that their lordships didn't turn cartwheels in their cassocks on the lawn in Maynooth once they realised what had been handed to them.

Still, it might seem to some that, since it's Christianity and not Catholicism which is to be promoted in the new course, the approach is at least 'ecumenical' in the restricted sense in which the word is commonly used in this country. But not necessarily so.

The bulk of the course will be set by the NCCA—on which the Catholic hierarchy, as we've seen, is directly represented. The remainder of the course, and here's an interesting phrase, will be 'partially determined according to the denominational preference of each school'. In plain English, this means that bishops or school managers will be able to slot elements of the old Catholic indoctrination into the new syllabus.

And if all that is not enough, the bishops can continue to include full blooded old-time indoctrination sessions in the timetable, alongside the new Leaving Cert course. That is to say, students who choose RE as a Leaving Cert subject might be required also take a parallel course in Catholic teaching. An editorial in the *Irish Catholic* puts it plain: 'If not, what guarantee is there that these pupils will receive a solid grounding in their own faith?' (ie in the faith which the *Irish Catholic* demands they be indoctrinated to accept as their own).

Irish society is becoming steadily more secular, right enough. But any notion that the Catholic hierarchy is going along with the change gently, or at all, is misplaced. They grudge every reluctant inch they are forced to yield. And in all the circumstances, they must be happy enough at how things have gone thus far. When they are together in private they must chuckle throatily at how readily their bona fides are accepted even now.

. . . .

Hot Press—12 June 1996

Our children and our children's children are to be put at the mercy of monks, and it's the Labour Party's fault. That's the bleak conclusion from the latest betrayal by Labour in government—Niamh Breathnach's proposal to confirm clerical control of primary schools.

The news will have perplexed many, after the grim succession of stories seeping out from institutions where the state had consigned children to the care of the Catholic Church.

It will have been widely believed that the State would be somewhat circumspect these days about giving clerics a free hand with children. It may even have been assumed that the Catholic Church, for its part, might have developed a modest degree of humility about its supposed rights in this area.

But not at all. After intense lobbying by the hierarchy, new guidelines drawn up for the Department of Education will, for the first time, make the maintenance of the 'religious ethos' a legal requirement in primary schools. The Church authorities will have effective control over the day-to-day running of the schools and the hiring and firing of teachers.

In language which will strike many as passing strange, the bishops are to be given a legal guarantee that Catholic primary schools will be 'managed in accordance with the doctrines, practices and traditions of the Roman Catholic Church as stated by the Irish Episcopal Conference and interpreted by the Patron of the school'. (The Episcopal Conference is simply the bishops meeting in conclave. The 'Patron'— what a wealth of weaselling there is in the capital P—is the local bishop.)

Some might recall Eileen Flynn. She was a teacher in New Ross in the '80s when she became pregnant. Far from plying her with congratulations and making arrangements for a substitute teacher to take her class during maternity leave, the Church sacked her. She was single. In a notorious judgement, in the face of an argument based on Ms Flynn's individual rights under the constitution, the High Court upheld the sacking on the ground that the Church had a right to impose its 'moral ethos' on the school.

The Flynn case was a cause célèbre in its time. It was widely understood as an echo from a long-gone era. A common reaction was of surprise that such an issue could arise in the '80s. Newspaper editorials, trade unions, most TDs who commented publicly, particularly women TDs, were at one: the law should be changed to ensure it couldn't happen again. And that, in a way, is what's come about, although not in a way anybody envisaged.

An Eileen Flynn case in the future would be unlikely to reach the courts—because the Church authorities would have no case to answer.

Their 'right' to impose their 'ethos' will now be spelled out in law.

This change is being brought about under the Labour education minister Breathnach.

Or consider the novelist John McGahern. He was sacked from teaching in the '60s for 'moral turpitude'—living with a woman he wasn't married to.

The McGahern case is commonly included with the 'Rose Tattoo' incident, the 'Mayo Librarian Sacking', the 'Fethard-On-Sea Boycott' and so on (ask me some other time) as an embarrassing example of ignorant repression in the Ireland of days gone by.

But a legal basis for future McGahern cases is now being put in place.

There are three reasons for this turnabout. The first has to do with the traditional cowardice of Leinster House politicians when confronted with the bishops in determined array.

Much has changed since the time when cabinet ministers would literally bend the knee to bishops at state functions. In relation to contraception and divorce, even politicians from frankly conservative parties now give the pleas of the hierarchy short shrift. But that's not the whole story.

Take the divorce referendum last year. The main parties managed almost to snatch defeat from the jaws of victory. The main thrust of the official 'Yes' campaign featured televised assurances from men in suits that divorce would mean fewer married couples splitting up. They contrived to reduce the pro-divorce majority from 25 percent just four months before the poll, to a fraction of 1 percent on polling day.

Having run scared before the vote, they ran for cover afterwards. 'Phew!' they gasped, wiping their glistened brows. 'That was close.' Nervously claiming credit for having taken on the bishops, they promised not to be so impertinent again.

The second reason for the bishops' victory on schools is that education is more important to them than divorce, contraception, abortion, homosexuality, or indeed any of the usual 'moral' issues.

Control of the schools is life-or-death for the bishops. In a society which is less deferential by the day, control of the shaping of unformed minds is more vital than ever if the social power of the hierarchy is to be sustained.

Despite the blows they have taken, their attitude to schooling has changed little since 1925 when the Jesuit Edward Cahill defined the circumstances in which the State must give way to the Church. 'As

the Church is the authentic and divinely appointed teacher and judge
of moral obligation and duty...it is clear that the rulers of the State
must, in the ultimate resort, abide by the decision of the Church...
The civil power may be said to be subject to the Church, even in
matters that do not appertain directly or solely to the sphere of religion or morals. Examples of this kind would be education; the ap-
pointing of public holidays...'

Nota Bene: Education first.

The third reason for Breathnach backing off underpins the other
two. The government has apparently been advised by the Attorney
General's office (although why they place such store in an opinion
from that quarter is a mystery) that it would require a constitutional
referendum to prise primary schools free from the bishops' grip.

Knowing the ferocity with which the bishops would mobilise their
forces for this battle, and remembering their close call last time out,
the government (including and especially the Labour component of
it) has fled the field for the fox holes.

And so another generation of children is to be handed over to an
institution which in another society might be banned from contact
with children of any kind.

That's if we allow it to happen. A survey of teachers by the INTO
earlier this year revealed that:

* More than half don't believe they should be forced to teach primary
school children religion.
* More than half are themselves teaching religion unwillingly.
* Only 3 percent of those who do not want to teach religion have told
the school authorities.
* Two thirds believe that the State, not the Church, should own the
schools.
* 70 percent believe that the Church should not control boards of
management.

Reflecting on these views, the general secretary of the INTO, Joe
O'Toole, has declared that, notwithstanding Ms Breathnach's new
guidelines, 'we will not have teachers threatened with dismissal on
the basis of private life issues.'

Sooner or later, some school manager or 'Patron' is going to try it
on, against some individual with more backbone than the Labour

Party, and then we'll have it out.

But if parties like Labour possessed a half-ounce of principle we wouldn't have to wait.

. . . .

Hot Press—23 October 1997

The inner life of the alienated Catholic intellectual is something else again. Take the late Monsignor de Brun of Maynooth College, a Limerick man, as you might say.

Snatches from an unpublished poem of the monsignor's say more than any official history about the turmoil and tension which characterised life in Maynooth just a generation ago, and helped shape the minds of the men running Catholicism in Ireland today.

The piece was written in the late '50s or early '60s and comprises 26 verses, each offering an observation on one of the 26 Irish bishops of the time.

Past pupils testify that de Brun was brilliant, moody and, in the right company, startlingly outspoken. Like all teachers of Catholic doctrine, he had taken the oath against 'modernism'—belief in the scientific method of intellectual investigation—declared anathema by Pius IX. Nevertheless, all who knew him say that he was decidedly in the modernist camp.

The fact that he could treat the defining oath of Church orthodoxy as an empty formula gives some indication of the depth of de Brun's disillusion with the institutional Church. There is some reason to believe that in his heart he was agnostic.

He was regarded by the college authorities and the hierarchy with wary suspicion. However, they were reluctant to move against him. The reticence wasn't based on respect for his status as a teacher and thinker but on reverence for his status as Catholic 'gentry'—from one of the landed families whose presence in Ireland pre-dated the Elizabethan settlement and who had held fast to Catholicism through the Reformation. That is, he was an 'Old Catholic'.

Despite this background and his seeming eccentricity, de Brun may have been a more representative figure than is apparent on first inspection. Anyone who attended a Catholic diocesan college in the period will have known priests of quiet, daunting mien, who ever had the air of the outsider about them. They'd walk the grounds engrossed in a book, and were frequently full of sighs. Perhaps they drank in secret. All, including other priests, were in awe of them, but everybody knew they'd never be promoted to college president or become a bishop. If you got to know them, they might want to talk politics, or about a recent movie, or about some row that had broken out concerning the Kennedys.

Perhaps they had been put towards the priesthood and had discovered all avenues of escape cut off by the time they realised how empty was the life that stretched before them.

The piece of verse of de Brun's which I have in mind was called 'The Congress of the Potentates'. Over the years, it has been more talked about than quoted from. As far as I know, it's never been published. Indeed, it's not certain de Brun ever wrote it down. But from time to time he'd recite selections from the 26 stanzas, each in the style of a limerick, to certain groups of students. There were other students in whose presence he never let a line pass his lips.

It's a listing of the bishops attending their annual gathering at Maynooth, when they'd assess the state of the Church at home and internationally and form their perspectives for the coming year. Whimsically patterned after Irish epics like 'The Parliament of Clann Thomais', the poem depicts each bishop speaking in turn to the assembly of their fellows.

The bishops are given nicknames or identified by reference to particular characteristics. The priest friend who recited them to me recalls these two stanzas in particular because he retains in his mind's eye a vivid picture of de Brun declaiming the words while watching through a window with a small cluster of students as the two featured bishops strolled in the manicured grounds of the college.

The late Bishop of Galway, Michael Browne, is 'the hairy mahout', while Dublin Archbishop John Charles McQuaid is 'the King of Siam':

> Then up spake the hairy mahout:
> 'What's all this pother about?
> You may think it odd of me,
> But I prefer sodomy.'
> Cries of 'Shame', 'Kick his arse', 'Throw him out'!

> Then upspake the King of Siam:
> 'For fucking I don't give a damn.
> I find my joy
> In the arse of a boy.
> You may call me a bugger. I am!'

These are the words of a man who regarded the intellectual basis and norms of the institution he was trapped in with bitter derision. His evident relish for the ribaldry of the language suggests deep frustration with the waxen solemnity around him. The hearty obscenity of his references to gay sex and paedophilia directly contradicts the prim evasions which men like Browne and McQuaid would publicly have resorted to in real life.

Intriguing stuff, to say the least of it, and surely telling about the intellectual life of the Church, and of the internal build-up of pressure towards the tail-end of its era of seemingly untroubled supremacy.

If there's anybody out there can supply further fragments of 'The Congress of Potentates', get in touch. Publication and anonymity guaranteed.

. . . .

Hot Press—2 September 1999

An increasing number of Irish people take the same view of god as they do of the Loch Ness Monster.

If it exists, that's OK. And if it doesn't exist, that's OK, too.

People of this sensible strain of thought won't worry over-much about religion. What they should worry about is whether crooked talk by the Churches becomes generally accepted. Because when it's generally accepted it affects us all.

In Dublin magazine has been banned by a Censorship Board which some of us had half-forgotten still existed. Attempts are under way to use the Blasphemy Act of 1868 against productions which diss superstition. Three Independent TDs unfeasibly mounted on the same high horse are demanding, and will very likely be given, another referendum on abortion.

Something is happening and we know what it is, don't we, Archbishop Connell?

The question becomes clearer when we ask if the Catholic Church is now talking straight about child-abuse.

Over the past ten years, I've been suggesting in this space that the bishops' expressions of concern for children violated by clerics have been motivated mainly by self-interest. They'd say what was required to placate an angry public. But when and if anger subsided, they'd switch tactics and try to recover lost ground.

Regular references to the pain and distress of cardinals and bishops at the terrible revelations tumbling out cast the Church as the victim, not the villain, of the piece.

Over time, some unexpected people, even a few with a Loch Ness perspective on life, took up and amplified the Church's defence case. Maybe the bishops behaved badly. Shifty at the outset, on the defensive thereafter, they made a hames of the messy affair. But, be fair, they weren't cynically amoral or deliberately dishonest.

The volume of expression of this sort of sentiment will have been weighed in the balance as the Church considered the timing of the launch of its backlash—which a chill blast of putrid air now confirms is well under way.

Last month came news of legal action against journalist Bruce Arnold over references to a number of bishops in an article in the *Irish Independent*. If the case comes to court, it will play to full houses. A 'first' in Church-media relations, it's already being talked of in colourful terms—the bishops, emboldened, finally coming out to fight back.

We've had a sudden stream of letters-to-the-editor from the likes of Fr John Dardis, director of communications for the Dublin archdiocese, taking RTE to task for its restrained series on children held in Church 'homes', *States of Fear*.

It also emerged last month that secret (as always) meetings of the bishops had decided to take a generally more aggressive role in countering what one report described as 'ongoing innuendo' in relation to clerical sex abuse. The boss of the Christian Brothers has likewise let it be known that he's mad as hell at the media and not going to take it any more.

A significant boost to the bishops' self-confidence came with the collapse of the case against former nun Nora Wall, wrongly convicted of rape in the 'home' in the south east which she'd been running. Her experience was trumpeted as evidence of persecution of the Church. Things gone too far, one injustice replaced by another. The usual suspect commentators took up the cry.

The effrontery has been bare-faced and breathtaking.

The notion that the bishops had been ignorant of the abuse of children until the revelations of recent years is the opposite of the truth. No group of people in the land knew more. And no group did less with the knowledge which they had.

And far from the Church having been given a rough time in the press, it's been treated with soft soap and kid-gloves.

To cite the prosecution of Nora Wall as evidence of the Church wronged is like arguing from the Birmingham Six case that the IRA never planted a bomb in England—with this significant difference: that not a scintilla of evidence has been produced to suggest that anti-Catholic sentiment played any part whatsoever in the decision to prosecute Nora Wall or in the court's arrival at a 'guilty' verdict. The significance of the case lay in what it told us—which wasn't telling us anything new—about the farcical ineptitude of the office of the Director of Public Prosecutions.

It's not the Church which is being treated unfairly, but the victims of the Church, huge numbers of whom are traumatised still, offered neither compensation nor counselling, nor even, in many cases, acknowledgment that they'd gone through the bleak experience which continues to darken their lives.

If the bishops were genuine in the remorse which they advertise, even now they'd take the obvious course, frequently mentioned here but rarely referred to anywhere else. They'd open the archives which their Church meticulously keeps so we could measure the extent of what happened and pin-point what Church leaders knew and when they knew it. In other words, they'd tell the truth.

This isn't a complicated matter. Scores of children treated abominably in 'homes' in Derry in the '40s and '50s were eventually shipped off to Australia where their suffering continued and, if anything, increased. How many children, exactly? Who were they? Children who 'wouldn't be missed', perhaps? Who devised this policy and why, and who supervised its implementation?

Some of the answers are assuredly to be found in records of the Derry diocese. The Bishop of Derry through the relevant period was Neil Farren. His biography, with the imprimatur of the Church, was published in 1993. It describes Farren's admiration for the regime at one of the 'homes' where the children were held in the diocese. It makes clear that he ruled his diocese with a rod of iron. He will have personally attended to the export of the children. But there isn't a mention of the episode in the book.

Nineteen ninety three isn't the dim and distant past. Already, the scandal of the maltreatment of children in Church-run 'homes' was in the public arena. But in 1993 the abused children of Derry were still being written out of Church history. It was as if they'd never existed.

That tells us more about the real thinking of the Church than the bawling of the bishops about being given a bad press.

They don't tell the truth because their priority is not to right the wrongs, but to cover up the crimes.

The Church should consider itself thrice-blessed in its coverage. Given the reversal of roles which the spin-doctors of divinity are currently attempting to contrive, it's worth pondering again what reaction might have been were it not the Catholic Church but some other institution which had been involved in this litany of suffering.

If we'd discovered dozens of cases involving hundreds of victims of officials of a sports association, or a political party, or of a trade union, and we knew that relevant records had been retained, and if the organisation, far from following a policy of openness, were to sit tight and sing dumb and change the locks on the filing cupboards, wouldn't we stir up a political storm?

But far from the Catholic Church being put under this sort of pressure, its leaders seem confident they have brazened it out, that their crooked talk has become generally accepted.

The fact that, as they see it, they've gotten away with the child abuse scandal has emboldened them across a wide range of issues. Herein lies the connection with the new push by the 'pro-lifers', the thought-police operation against *In Dublin*, the resurrection of the Blasphemy Act and so on.

It's the same as it ever was, and as important as ever to bring the bishops to book.

Chapter 5

It's alright ma (I'm only bleeding)

Padre Pio and Mother Teresa have featured regularly in my writing for anumber of years. Viewed in one perspective, they were both darkly humorous figures—the oafish man with the wounds of Christ who could be in two places at the one time, the woman who prattled endlessly about compassion and the poor while hob-nobbing with the cruel and parasitical. But there's a serious side to the likes of them, too. As the *Hot Press* piece on Pio's beatification shows, there's always a political aspect to these people.

In Ireland, Pio and Teresa have been among the most venerated icons of Catholicism. Both are associated with the rancid 'pro-life' movement. Pio has embodied the nonsensical notion behind 'miracles', that the laws of nature operate at the whim of an Almighty, rendering all science pointless and all effort to control nature futile. Teresa was a great one for lying to desperate people that god would look out for them if they agreed not to complain about whatever it was had made them desperate.

The fawning of Irish media folk and politicians on 'Mother' Teresa in the years prior to the death she ought logically to be have been looking forward to has been at once depressing and hilarious.

Most of the other saints mentioned here are also funny ha-ha as well as, of course, funny peculiar.

. . . .

***In Dublin*—7 December 1989**
Say what you like about John Paul II, his timing's good: 12 November he canonised another St Agnes.

Another Agnes being sainted was hardly big news in the West— I could find no mention of it in any of the Dublin dailies—but it was a major event—prominent on national TV news, for example—in Czechoslovakia.

The new St Agnes is Agnes of Prague, born 1205, died 1282, sister of 'Good King' Wenceslas, the chap who gave his name to the square where huge pro-democracy demonstrations have recently gathered.

Tradition has it that Wenceslas himself was a martyr both for the

Christian religion and in the cause of national independence: he was reputedly murdered by his brother, Boleslav, who wanted to bring Bohemia into the German Empire. In modern Czechoslovakia—which incorporates the territory and rich culture of Bohemia—Wenceslas is both national hero and patron saint.

There is a powerful symbolism about Agnes, too. She was betrothed at the age of three to Bolesias of Silesia, at the instigation of officials who wanted the two territories merged. However, before she reached the age when marriage could decently be contemplated, Bolesias died of a fever.

She was betrothed to Henry, son and heir of the Emperor Frederick of Germany, the notion being that she'd bring Bohemia with her. But Henry, in his turn, was accused of scheming against his father, was thrown into prison, and died. Frederick himself and Henry III of England then competed for her hand, each anxious to bring Bohemia within his own sphere of interest.

It was around this point, in 1231, that Agnes, now 26, sent envoys to Rome with a letter asking Pope Gregory IX to dispatch squads of monks and nuns to run the Church in Bohemia. This would ensure that Bohemian Christianity would be answerable directly to Rome while, as a quid pro quo, Rome would become a guarantor of Bohemian independence.

The arrangement was to be copperfastened by Agnes herself taking vows and becoming head of the Poor Clare nuns in Bohemia.

Agnes professed her vows at a magnificent ceremony presided over by the Pope's personal representative in Prague Cathedral on Pentecost Sunday in 1234, attended by scores of bishops from across Europe, representatives of all the great European powers and, according to one contemporary chronicle, 'an uncountable multitude of both sexes from different nations'.

Thus was an inextricable link between Agnes's heroic virtue and Bohemian national independence publicly proclaimed under the auspices of Rome.

Seven hundred and seven years after Agnes's death the Pope decides to acknowledge her heroic virtue and to make her a saint.

The date of the canonisation is set many months in advance.

It turns out to be the very day of the first in the series of demonstrations in Wenceslas Square which finally brought down the oppressive, foreign regime...

If I were doing PR for religion, I'd concentrate on that sort of thing. So much more impressive than transubstantiation, miracle cures and threats of hellfire for a friendly shag.

. . . .

In Dublin—20 July 1989

A slight fuss was occasioned around 8 July by the thirteen hundredth anniversary of the martyrdom of St Kilian. Cardinal O Fiaich travelled to Wurzburg in Germany when he was chief celebrant of a High Mass and delivered a sermon in which he called for 'a revival of the spirit of Kilian' in order to combat abortion, euthanasia, pornography, shops opening on Sundays and 'the modern tendency to use bad language in the sports stadium'.

A number of newspapers carried features on the life and times of Kilian and the links he is said to have forged between Ireland and Germany—where, so the story goes, he performed mighty missionary work before perishing in Wurzburg. The *Irish Times* of 8 July devoted a full half page, so to speak, to Kilian.

One problem with all this is that there is no evidence whatever that Kilian ever existed. No contemporary reference to him has ever been discovered. No person of that name has ever been canonised. Kilian is not included in any authoritative list of or dictionary of saints. There is no mention of him in Butler's *Lives of the Saints,* for example.

More important is the fact that by allocating 8 July to the supposed Kilian as a feast day a singular disservice is done to the great Procopius, who certainly did exist (the historian Eusebius writes about him at length) and who just as certainly has legitimate title to the 8 July feast day.

Procopius, a Palestinian, was arrested in the early years of the 4th century and taken in chains to Caesarea where the governor, Flavian, engaged him in long philosophical argument interspersed with bouts of horrendous torture. At one point Procopius escaped, picked up a crucifix which happened to be handy and beat a sizeable number of soldiers to death with it. This feat so impressed onlookers that scores of them converted to Christianity on the spot.

Sadly, Procopius was later recaptured, taken before Flavian and sentenced to death. His head was chopped off. This happened on 8 July, in the year AD 303.

He sounds a most impressive character and it is surely intolerable that Cardinal O Fiaich and the editor of the *Irish Times* should conspire to deprive him of his feast day and give it to an Irishman who didn't exist. I dare say Procopius would be rather more effective, too, in discouraging bad language in the sports stadium.

. . . .

In Dublin—27 March 1991
Lipocalcinogranulomatosis!

Lipocalcinogranulomatosis is a desperate disease involving painful and unsightly tumours. There is no known cure. Which is not to say that no sufferer has ever been cured. Take Sister Concepcion Boullon, a Carmelite based in the convent of St Laurence near Madrid. She suffered from 'lipocalcinogranulomatosis with numerous widespread painful and debilitating deposits, the largest one in the left shoulder being the size of an orange. She was extremely wasted, and had a gastric ulcer and hiatus hernia with a severe iron deficiency anaemia.'

The quote is from the Medical Consultants to the Congregation of The Causes Of The Saints. They'd been called in to advise the Vatican on whether Sr Boullon's sudden cure from the disease one night in June 1976 should be regarded as a miracle. A Vatican announcement last month confirmed the consultants' opinion that the cure could not be explained by natural causes.

A team of consultant theologians had then carried the investigation further: they have now concluded that, although Sr Boullon prayed daily (as nuns do) to a large number of saints, and directly to God Himself, the miraculous disappearance of the affliction could be attributed solely to the intervention of none other than Josemaria Escriva, the founder of the semi-secret Opus Dei organisation which provided spiritual sustenance to so many members of the late General Franco's administration in Spain, and which has recently found much favour with Pope John Paul II.

Sceptical sorts on the fringe of Vatican circles have expressed wonderment that Sr Boullon would have been praying to Josemaria Escriva in June 1976—less than a year after his death, many years before the possibility of his sainthood was first mooted, and during the papal reign of Paul VI, who was rather less enamoured of Opus Dei than is the present Pontiff.

Strangely, the miracle lipocalcinogranulomatosis cure was not formally reported to the Church for six years after it happened until 1982, by which time the Throne of Peter was occupied by John Paul

II, who immediately after his coronation had signalled the high regard in which he held Opus Dei by going in procession to pray at Escriva's tomb. Nothing of the sort had ever happened before.

The *Irish Catholic* recently remarked that: 'Opus Dei's founder is now seen as a very important figure in the Church, not only because of his message that all Christians are called to be saints, but also because of the extraordinary spread of his reputation for holiness.'

It has been extraordinary indeed. And it can be attributed almost entirely to the energetic promotion by John Paul of Escriva as a figure to be emulated and revered by all believing Catholics. The lending of the authority of the Vatican to the miraculous cure of Sr Boullon's disease (a disease which is mentioned in none of three medical dictionaries which I have consulted) is a continuation, indeed an escalation, of this campaign of the Pope's.

Is it necessary to point out that the Franco regime of which Escriva was a committed and not unimportant supporter was fascist, and that the propaganda campaign being waged by the Pope is intended to make Catholics see a man who was friendly to fascism as a saint?

. . . .

Hot Press—24 February 1993

I see that not a single member of Dublin City Council has had the gumption to speak out against the proposal to give 'Mother Teresa of Calcutta' the Freedom of the City. Instead, representatives of all parties from the right to the fake left have stumbled over one another in an unseemly scramble to praise the old crone as 'a saint'.

Announcements of the plan have repeated the line that 'Mother Teresa' has devoted her life to the alleviation of the suffering of the poor, particularly in India. There is no truth in this.

For many years 'Mother Teresa' herself has been perfectly prepared to tell anyone who'd listen that her main mission in life has little to do with easing the physical plight of anyone on earth but a lot to do with ensuring that as many 'souls' as possible are properly shined up so as to be admitted into 'heaven' once the no-account physical body has snuffed it.

Logically enough, then, her 'caring' operations, including in Calcutta, are on a very tiny scale, although it might be stretching cynicism, slightly, to dismiss them completely as a front.

What we can say is that 'Mother Teresa's' main impact on the life of the poor, in India and elsewhere, has resulted not from tender, loving care of racked and ravaged bodies but from vigorous campaigns against family-planning education, the provision of contraceptives, the availability of abortion, and so on. Not only has she fought tooth and nail against programmes to help women avoid unwanted pregnancy, she has campaigned relentlessly for society to see women primarily as breeding machines. She endlessly urges women to see themselves in this role.

For more than two years now, 'Mother Teresa' has had no involvement at all in 'caring'. She publicly retired from that minor aspect of her activities in 1990, precisely to devote her energies fulltime to opposing contraception etc. Her campaigns have been effective because they have enjoyed the enthusiastic endorsement of the moral mafioso in the Vatican.

A sizable number of Third World governments have an exaggerated view of the influence of the Vatican and as a result pay more heed to 'Mother Teresa' than they likely need to. The consequence, in Africa, Asia and Latin America, is an increase in hunger, disease, infant mortality and the oppression of women.

She will use her visit to Dublin in May to contribute as effectively as she can to the oppression of women in Ireland. Anybody who thinks that she will take poverty in the world, or in Ireland, as her main theme has misunderstood what she's about—probably as a result of reading the newspapers.

She will speak out against every recent advance in the areas of contraception, divorce and abortion. She will go particularly apeshit over abortion. She will associate publicly and confer what status and authority she can on groups of far-right crazies and women-hating fanatics.

And yet, despite all the talk about what a new, modern, totally refurbished little Euro-country we have here, not a single member of the council of the capital city has the nerve or neck to protest against this woman being honoured in the name of all its citizens.

. . . .

In Dublin—28 July 1993

I'd quite forgotten that there was a first Mother Teresa—on whom the world's most famous Albanian based her career—until I spotted a paragraph in the religious trade press about John Paul II's recent jaunt to Spain, in the course of which he apparently urged Spaniards to show greater devotion to Teresa of Avila, foundress of the order of discalced Carmelites.

'Discalced' means barefooted: one of Teresa's reasons for establishing a new Carmelite Order was that the 'official' Order, which she had joined as a teenager, eventually seemed to her to be 'too much in love with things of the flesh', like shoes.

Mother Teresa (1515-1582) was a learned woman who could hold discourse with the great seers and sages of the time. Attwater's *Dictionary of Saints* suggests that she would long ago have been recognised as a Doctor of the Church and put on a par with Aquinas and Scotus had it not been that she was a woman and therefore couldn't really have been as smart as she was.

She was, as well, something of a mystic in the intensity of her devotion to Jesus, and it was that aspect of her holiness that John Paul was anxious to emphasise in Spain. The original Mother Teresa, like her contemporary successor, had no time for fancy theories about the Church finding its validation in the service of actual living people.

She argued instead that love of god requires not just a personal renunciation of riches but also a disengagement from the material world generally—a perspective which, then as now, tended to find favour with those who reckon that the material world is pretty satisfactorily organised as it is.

Mother Teresa's reveries and mystical visions of Jesus and of various angels and saints are recorded in her ecstatic reverie, *The Interior Castle*. Here, just by way of a flavour, is Teresa describing a spiritual encounter with a 'most beautiful angel...in bodily form...his face burning':

'I saw in his hand a long spear of gold, and at the iron's point there seemed to be a little fire. He appeared to me to be at times thrusting it into my heart, and to pierce my very entrails; when he drew it out he seemed to draw them out also, and to leave me all on fire with a great love of God. The pain was so great that it made me moan; and yet so surpassing was the sweetness of this excessive pain that I could not wish to be rid of it.'

A seriously interesting woman, the first Mother Teresa.

. . . .

Hot Press—20 October 1993
Any day now a hombre called Padre Alession Parente will arrive on these shores to whip up support for the canonisation of the Italian madman 'Padre Pio'.

Pio who died 25 years ago last month, is at the centre of a right-wing cult within the Catholic Church. Devotees of the cult tend also to be associated with the 'Our Lady of Medjugorje' hoax organised by Croatian fascists. The semi-clandestine Opus Dei organisation is heavily into both operations.

Tens of thousands of Irish people are involved in these scams, whether out of conviction or because they have been hoodwinked. The Medjugorje fraudsters are particularly active in organisations which advertise themselves as bringing humanitarian relief to Bosnia but which are in fact support-groups for far-right Roman Catholic paramilitary outfits in western Bosnia-Hercegovina, particularly in the vicinity of Mostar.

The Pio cult runs Padre Pio centres in a number of towns. Some of these act as agents for specialist travel firms which coin a profit organising pilgrimages to the southern Italian village of San Giovanni Rotondo, where Pio operated as a priest for the last 40 years of his life.

San Giovanni was a quiet mountain village of some 3,000 people before the Pio project got under way. By the time Pio died in 1968 it had been transformed into a bustling town of 30,000 with lavish hotels, guest houses and scores of restaurants, and, scattered over the adjacent hills, the villas of newly-enriched entrepreneurs.

My own closest encounter with the Pio cult came when somebody I had never met arrived at the front door one night a couple of years back and held out a tattered thick-woollen glove of sorts, suggesting that I should rub this rag over the body of a child in the house who was seriously ill. 'It's Padre Pio's Mitt,' I was informed in a reverential whisper.

Pio was a 'stigmatist.' That is, he claimed that 'the wounds of Christ' were on his body: holes through his hands and feet where the nails pinned Christ to the cross and a bigger hole in his side where a Roman soldier pierced him with a spear to finish him off.

Pio always wore mittens on his hands and thick socks on his feet to soak up the miraculous blood which oozed continuously from the wounds. (Nothing which I have read on Pio's life explains what happened to the blood from the presumably more spectacular side-wound.)

Howandever: this mitt is supposedly impregnated with the blood from Pio's Christ-wounds and was being offered as a miraculous curative. I was subsequently to discover that it had been circulating in the Derry area for years, being passed from sick person to sick person, I also learned—upon taking a quizzative interest in the matter—that there are other Padre Pio's Mitts in Ireland. There's a Limerick and a Dublin Padre Pio's Mitt, one in the Connemara Gaeltacht, and quite likely others that I don't know of.

These must be among the most dangerously disease-soaked pieces of fabric in the land, slithery with germs, bacteria, bodily fluids and snot. A more inappropriate item to rub on the body of a child already weakened by illness would be hard to imagine. But when I explained this to the zealot on the doorstep the reaction was one of horrified disbelief: it was 'bad luck' to reject the Mitt. Touchy fuckers, these dead stigmatists.

I have no way of knowing how many people have died needlessly from diseases caught from Padre Pio's Mitts, but it must be substantial.

The stigmata apart, there were other miraculous things about Pio, according to the cultists, the most dramatic of which was his power of bi-location—the ability to be in two places at the same time.

All of these holy bi-locationists seem to have specialised in being simultaneously in two places which were out of sight of one another. You'd see them here and then discover afterwards that they've been seen somewhere else at the same moment. But you never saw them at this side of the room and at the other side of the room at the same time. Nobody has ever been able to say, 'Wow! Look! That guy over there and over there is in two places at the same time!'

Pio was never observed starting to give out communion from both ends of the altar rail and meeting himself in the middle. He never played himself at tennis. He never impersonated the Everly Brothers.

Then there was Pio's miraculously perfumed body odour. When he sweated he smelled of 'violets and sweet tobacco'.

He could also foretell the future.

Two things need saying about all this. One, that every time we are tempted to jeer at the likes of David Icke, every time we wonder among ourselves how anybody could be so daft as to sign up with the Koresh chap whose followers were slaughtered at Waco on the orders of the kill-crazy US Attorney General, Janet Reno, every time we chortle at the antics of poor fools who seriously believe that Elvis is alive and well and playing rhythm guitar with Brian Coll and the Buccaroos, every time we think on such things we should remember that none of these delusions is remotely as ridiculous as claims made on behalf of 'Padre Pio'.

There are people in influential positions—at least one former Supreme Court judge, a number of members of the Dublin parliament—who believe in this stuff with the calm fervour of the genuine fanatic.

The second thing which needs saying is that the Pio people have a political agenda which we would do well to take seriously.

It isn't an accident that the Pio cult is energetically promoted by the 'pro-life' crowd, or that the more ominous of his pronouncements are advanced in the Youth Defence comic, the *Irish Democrat*, as rules of right living. 'Love and fear must always be together...', readers were recently advised in large print. 'Love without fear becomes presumption. Where there is no obedience there is no virtue...'

The wounds were assuredly a fraud. But the sick mind was real enough.

The campaign for Pio's canonisation is political, too. Naturally, it enjoys the full support of John Paul II, who regularly highlights Pio's calls for young people to join the 'Blue Army' of 'Our Lady of Fatima' and to combat communism, contraceptives, freedom and fun.

. . . .

Hot Press—5 October 1994

Mother Teresa: have you no old age home to go to?

Urging the recent Cairo conference on world population to reject contraception and abortion, the Albanian prune 'Mother Teresa' alleged that: 'Every child is a gift from God. If you have a child you think is unwanted, give that child to me. I will find it a loving home where it will be cherished as a blessing...' It isn't the first time she's spewed out this sort of bilge.

Forty thousand children under the age of 12 die every day from malnutrition or preventable diseases. Why does nobody ever ask Mother Teresa for the addresses of the millions of homes where these children will be cherished?

But of course she doesn't mean a word of it. We are not meant to take it seriously. There is no practical intention behind her words. They emerge from and float out into a spiritual never-never land which has no intersection with the material reality of human existence.

Nevertheless, her words do have an influence on actual human existence. Their effect is to create more misery in this world, particularly for women. If she is capable of rational thought, she knows this, and is a criminal. If not, she's an ignoramus and a dangerous lunatic. Either way, isn't it time she was locked up?

Hot Press—17 April 1996

That's an interesting spot of bother 'Mother Teresa' has gotten herself into over welcoming the break-up of the marriage of Charles and Diana.

In an article in this month's edition of *Ladies Home Journal*, the writer Daphne Barak describes how, in the course of an interview with Teresa, the talk turned to the laughably dysfunctional royal family. Barak had landed the interview by agreeing to spend time working with a flock of Teresa's nuns on some project or other.

She quotes the daft wrinkly: 'You see? You are here for a reason—to help me. That's why Jesus sent you. I don't just see anybody. Princess Diana had to wait a few days to see me when she was here.' You wouldn't have had to be in journalism more than a wet weekend to know where to steer the conversation next. What, Ms Barak wondered, now that her name had come up, had Teresa made of Princess Diana?

'Oh, she's like a daughter to me,' blabbed the shameless old liar, and went on to ask: 'What is really going on there? Is the marriage over?'

On being told that 'it certainly appears to be', the Tirana sourpuss cackled some empathy into the tape machine: 'I think it is a sad story. Diana is such a sad soul. She gives so much love, but she needs to get it back. You know what? It is good that it is over. Nobody was happy anyhow. I know I should preach for family love and unity, but in their case...' And her voice, according to Ms Barak, 'trailed off'.

The quote caused an almighty rumpus when the piece was published in the US. Mother Teresa may be a wizened midget to many but she's huge in the US, which seems to specialise in wacky far-right celebs. Her 'regional supervisor' in New York, a Sister Sylvia, felt compelled to circulate a letter to all US bishops asking them to defend her boss against the charge of having 'undermined the Catholic Church's teaching on marriage'.

'Many people have already contacted us to verify the quote or to complain against Mother,' says Sylvia sadly. 'Worse still are the millions who will read the quote, believe that Mother really said it, and use it to support divorce.'

There have been occasions in the past when it's been impossible to recall word for word exactly what Sylvia's Mother said. But this time it was on record. And there was no way of interpreting it other than as support for the break-up of the royal marriage.

In other words, the quote can quite properly be used in support of divorce—and of the proposition that the so-called Mother Teresa is, additionally to other character defects, a hypocrite.

What she was saying was that, while she stood by Catholic teaching on the indissolubility of marriage, she made an exception 'in their case'. Since there's nothing exceptional about Charles and Diana personally, but everything exceptional about their position in society, it was clearly this—their riches and royalty—which made them so special in the eye of the old nun and led her to exempt them from the laws ordinary Catholics have to live under.

Of course, the fabulously wealthy and princelings of one kind and another have always been able to obtain nullity decrees, dispensations, indulgences and so forth when they needed them. Didn't one of the Monaco crowd who had been married by a cardinal get the Pope to cancel the marriage when she found somebody else she preferred screwing?

Somebody remarked recently that Mother Teresa seems to be getting smaller every time we see her, and put this down to do with a shrivelling process to do with old age. But I reckon it's just that she's being consumed by corruption from the inside.

Sylvia should think about packing her things, start a new life, maybe marry some fella down Galveston way. Sorry.

. . . .

Hot Press—18 September 1996

At the time of writing, the famous nun, Mother Teresa (86) is in a hospital in Calcutta being treated for heart problems, lung problems and malaria. A few days ago her condition was describes as 'critical', but Dr S Sen now says that she is 'a shade better'. We shall see.

Dr Sen emphasised that 'all possible medical care' is being provided for Mother Teresa. She is being fed intravenously and is hooked up to a heart monitor and a respirator. According to Reuters news agency, 'a panel of six specialists' is keeping a round-the-clock vigil at her bedside in 'an extraordinary' effort to prolong her life.

The dominant note in the extensive reporting of this story has been of fervent hope that the extraordinary effort will succeed. As the Irish News headline objectively put it, 'World Unites In Prayer For "Living Saint".'

Do you not get a niggling feeling there's something vaguely discrepant going on here? Insofar as Mother Teresa is a saint, how can it matter whether she recovers or not? As a saint, she is not going to die. On the contrary, it is only at the point of her mortal death that she will, so to speak, come into her own. So what's the problem? Why the long faces?

The effort to keep Mother Teresa alive is especially extraordinary by the standards which apply in her own institutions in India and elsewhere. What makes the care provided in the hostels and hospices of the Missionaries of Charity distinctive is precisely the emphasis on the spiritual rather than the physical salvation of the poverty-stricken old and infirm. Mother Teresa herself has been forthrightly explicit about this, arguing that eternal salvation is, literally infinitely, more important than prolonging physical life. She has argued robustly for the morality of this approach in the 'Third World' in particular, where medical and other vital resources are ordinarily not available.

It is here that the relevance of the concept of 'extraordinary means' is at its most sharp.

One element in the theological justification for Mother Teresa's approach is contained in an argument that while, as a general principle, 'all human life is sacred', there is no moral imperative to use 'extraordinary means' to prolong it. This is the distinction which governs Catholic teaching on euthanasia. Well, why doesn't it apply to Mother Teresa? Why are extraordinary means adopted to keep her alive, especially when she has constantly protested that she wants to live as the poor she works among. Or, to be more accurate, the poor the PR operation suggests she works among: for many years now, Mother Teresa has spent little time among the poor in Calcutta or anywhere else, but a great deal of time jet-setting between the accommodations provided for her by rich, powerful representatives of the ruling class responsible in the first place for the intolerable poverty in which so many millions in the Third World are mired.

Could it be that in dying so differently from the poor she has made her name from, she's simply dying as she lived?...

. . . .

Hot Press—29 April 1999

Padre Pio is to be declared blessed this Sunday. What fun.

As a musical-hall turn, Pio could have been one of the all-time greats. But he was part con-man, part deluded obsessive, and as a priest he was shite. Not that I'd worry about that. But priests should.

The Pope himself has described the 'stigmatist' as 'a model of the priesthood for our times'. He didn't mean that priests should pretend or psych themselves into believing they have the stigmata or develop the wide range of magical accomplishments which made Pio a cult figure.

He meant that priests, as personifiers of the Church, should be figures of mystery and impenetrable authority, such as plain people might be in awe of. He has some chance.

Still, it promises to be a big day out. Three quarters of a million pilgrims are expected to throng the centre of Rome to express their devotion to the mystery man from San Giovanni. He will be the eight hundred and twentieth person declared 'blessed' by John Paul—more than a third of all beatifications since the procedure was initiated in 1588.

John Paul has also canonised 280 saints—compared with 303 by all his predecessors since 1588 combined.

This unprecedented rate of production isn't down to personal obsession. The Pope has organised the gush of saints for mainly political reasons.

Thus, seven priests and a lay brother beatified in March had been put before firing squads by the Republican side in the Spanish Civil War. Franco had god on his side, was the message to Spaniards.

The Croatian Cardinal Stepinac, canonised last year, had been fairly convicted under Tito of collaboration with the wartime Nazi regime of Ante Pavelic. The Nazis weren't pure evil—the anti-Nazis were no saints, the Vatican is saying to Croatians today.

A strong lobby has formed for the beatification of Cardinal Cooke of New York, who died in 1983. His lifetime's achievement was hugely to enlarge the political role of the Catholic Church in the US, particularly in relation to abortion and Church 'rights' in State schools.

Then there was the founder of the Christian Brothers, Edmund Rice. To say nothing of the Albanian wretch, Teresa.

Pio didn't have the sharp-edged political profile of the rest of that crew. But he's been a controversial figure in the Catholic Church for decades. This has not been on account of the 'stigmata'—although relatively rational Catholics find the business embarrassing—nor because of the plausible but as yet unproven allegations of sexual misconduct with penitents in the confession box, but because of the acrid arrogance of his attitudes and contempt for the great majority of his fellow priests. In a polemic regularly quoted in Pio cult publications, he claimed that Jesus periodically visited him in person to complain about priests who conducted 'sacrilegious' communions, showed indifference towards the 'Blessed Sacrament' and treated churches as 'amusement centres'.

Pio confirmed that Jesus, on the other hand, regarded him, Pio, as the right kind of priest. And others agree. An *Irish Catholic* article extolling Pio last year concluded that: 'The basic reason for the confusion in the ministry of Christ in the last few decades has been the identification of the priesthood with liturgy and ceremony instead of with holiness, and the identification of victimhood with social action rather than with human guilt.'

It's original sin, not the evils of society, which it is the business of the Church to oppose, and it's time priests got that straight. Priests out there who want to root the Church in the world rather than retreat into a netherworld have reason to be fearful of the raising-up of the Capuchin hoaxter.

Their problem, of course. The rest of us need note only that while the political message of Pio's beatification is more subtle than was carried in the elevation of the pro-Nazi Stepinac, it's none the less real and substantial.

At another and more attractive level, it's all wholly ridiculous. Pio's admirers say he was on close personal terms with his guardian angel, with whom he discussed all manner of topics, including the weather. He was regularly visited by folk on day-release from purgatory, many of whom wanted to thank all who remembered the Holy Souls in their prayers. On a number of occasions he was physically assaulted—flung across the room once—by Satan himself. But Satan never got the better of him. He had the power to cure illnesses, could be in two places at the one time and exuded a delicate perfume. Plus there were the stigmata.

The stigmata have been his main claim to fame. Few ever set eyes on the actual wounds, since he wore mitts at all times. There are scores of Pio's old mitts currrently in circulation, some in Ireland, stained not so much with blood as with germ-rich mucus from the countless diseased (at least they were afterwards) bodies on which the putrid fabric was piously rubbed.

During his life, Pio never permitted medical examination of the 'wounds'—which he claimed bled continuously, particularly profusely on Fridays, for 50 years. When the mitts and bandages were removed following his death 30 years ago, no trace of wounds was found. As his followers immediately noted, this was a miracle.

Last year, 6,500,000 people visited the village of San Giovanni Retondo, scenically perched on a mountainside near Foggia in Southern Italy. A new church with a seating capacity of 10,000 is nearing construction. The village boasts the largest and most modern hospital south of Rome (although why they should need a hospital when they have the spirit of the man with the miracle mitts in their midst is a mystery).

A 2,500-bed 'pilgrim facility' built by the local Capuchins is also nearing completion. The friars deny that the competition will hit local hotels. 'The big rise in pilgrims which we can expect after the beatification will mean that no one loses out. Dear Padre Pio has been a benefactor of the area in so many ways. We are not interested in money.'

Religion. One way and another, I'm going to miss it when it's gone.

. . . .

Hot Press—15 January 1997

I see that Mother Teresa is coming to Ireland again, and I wonder if there's any chance she might be arrested and put in jail.

I raise the possibility after speaking with the office of an LA lawman, the Deputy District Attorney of Los Angeles, Paul Turley, which I phoned to check whether he'd made progress in his efforts to recover stolen money from the Albanian nun.

The money had been filched from the pockets of pensioners and small savers by one of the biggest fraudsters of the get-rich-quick '80s, Charles Keating. His front operation, Lincoln Savings & Loan, had conned a total of $225 million from thousands of victims before it collapsed towards the end of the decade. When the investigators combed through the Lincoln accounts they discovered that Keating had passed on more than a million dollars of the stolen money to the Tirana charlatan.

The self-styled Mother Teresa wrote to the judge pleading for leniency during Keating's trial. Had she not, perhaps he would now be serving more than his ten years in the State Penitentiary. On the wall of his cell he has a crucifix personally blessed by Pope John Paul and sent to him by Teresa. No doubt it's a source of comfort.

There's less comfort available to the hapless patsies Keating ruined, some of them elderly people now living in poverty and despair, the money they'd frugally put by for their sunset years gone—and the limited state assistance they were entitled to under threat from the far-right associates of Mother Teresa now in office across the US.

During Keating's 1992 trial, Deputy DA Turley wrote in restrained terms to Teresa asking her to give back the stolen money. An organisation representing Keating's victims had been set up with a view to recovering what little of their savings was left and distributing it as fairly as possible. 'If you contact me I will put you in direct contact with the rightful owners of the property now in your possession,' Turley appealed to the nun.

In his book on Teresa, *The Missionary Position*, Christopher Hitchens reported that the old zealot had ignored Turley's plea. But that was 1994. Maybe there'd been developments since. Hence my phone call to LA last week. But no. 'She has ignored us,' I was told.

The DA's office had established that Teresa had received their communication and was fully aware of the position: she had received more than a million dollars stolen mostly from poor people and was being asked politely to give it back.

'We have honestly given up on this,' I was told. 'It's obvious she is determined to keep it.'

Receiving stolen property is of course a criminal offence, as many a one caught in possession of, say, a dodgy car radio could confirm. It is also, I imagine, an extraditable offence. Should not this woman be arrested at the airport if she does indeed arrive in Ireland this year and be subjected to severe questioning about her role in the multi-million dollar robbery?

Chapter 6

London calling

The fact that about 6,000 women from the South and 2,000 from the North travel to England every year for abortions is among the most depressing illustrations of the backwardness of official Irish society.

This incidence of abortion is broadly in line with the rate in Britain more than 30 years after the UK 1967 Abortion Act. But no mainstream party in Ireland, North or South, argues for the law here to be brought into alignment. Again, politicians lag behind the people when it comes to issues which it suits the Churches to define as 'moral'.

In the North, many Nationalist and Unionist politicians say privately that they are in favour of reform, but argue that this is not the time: the peace process takes precedence. That is, we must first sort out the Catholic-Protestant division.

The abortion issue divides people, not according to religion, but according to whether they want to leave repression in the past and move towards a freer, more tolerant future. Campaigning for the extension of the 1967 Act brings to the fore those aspects of our social being which are shared across the divide. It strengthens the peace—whatever about the 'process'.

Nationalist politicians in the South, to their shame, depend on the safety-valve of abortion in England to prevent the pressure for real change building up. The sort of 'Irish dimension' which socialists want to see would be prefigured in an all-Ireland campaign for a woman's right to choose.

. . . .

Hot Press—April 1992
Phyllis Bowman, Director of the Society for the Protection of the Unborn Child in Britain, was 'outraged'. More than that, she 'had never felt such shame'.

The cause of her outrage and shame, she told the *Universe*, the modestly-named Catholic weekly newspaper (29 March), was the failure of the Catholic hierarchy of England and Wales to intervene more decisively to make abortion an issue in the UK general election.

The Catholic bishops had endorsed a 'voter's shopping list' issued by the ecumenical Council of Churches. This document did support the 'right to life'—but included under this heading not only the unborn but 'the handicapped, the sick and the elderly'.

That, said Ms Bowman, 'so watered down the fundamental importance of the right to life as to be futile.'

She went on to castigate a statement signed by Cardinal Hume of Westminster and Archbishop Worlock of Liverpool which had associated 'defence of human life and that of the unborn child' with 'the defence of decent living and working conditions'. 'One should not go without the other,' declared the two prelates.

Linking these two issues, retorted Ms Bowman, rendered the commitment to the unborn 'utterly empty'.

Only 'party politicians who voted for abortion up to birth' could have been gratified by the bishops' performance, she concluded.

As an example of extravagant overreaction, this outburst of Ms Bowman's takes both the kimberly and the mikado, not to mention the coconut cream. But what was more interesting about it was that the Catholic bishops across the water, far from dismissing her diatribe as the product of deep-seated hysteria, ran immediately for cover.

Spokespersons for the hierarchy explained that, while the bishops supported the statement from the Council of Churches as far as it went, the Catholic Church's own position was near-enough identical with Ms Bowman's.

In Scotland, the bishops went further. An editorial in the official journal of the archdiocese of Glasgow, *Flourish*, directly attacked the Labour Party for its stand on abortion, while a leaflet produced by the Scottish Bishops' Conference and distributed at all masses told Catholics to make 'the right to life' the decisive issue in the poll.

The Scots bishops will have been relieved to learn that Ms Bowman was very content with their approach to the issue.

All of this raises a question which is at least as relevant here as across the water: why are all these people so ferocious in their opposition to abortion?

Why do they bring to this issue a fervour altogether different in its intensity to the feeling they bring to any other matter whatsoever? Why is it impossible to conduct a rational argument with the average 'pro-life' campaigner?

During the 1983 abortion referendum I spoke at more than 40

meetings, from Tralee to Letterkenny, appealing for the rejection of the Eighth Amendment. At many of these I became involved in vigorous exchanges with 'pro-lifers'.

As well, I wrote extensively about the campaign, and was rewarded, if that's the word, with scores of letters denouncing my views and inviting me to ponder the prospect of hellfire for all eternity.

This experience brought it home to me long before polling day that the 'other side' had no interest in actual debate. Their position was rooted, not in reason, but in faith. And faith, of its very nature, is not open to rational refutation.

Abortion is murder in the eyes of god, they'd say. And that's that.

Pro-lifers do, as they must, join in discussion of the issue from other angles. But at the core of their argument lies a glittering certainty which has nothing to do with logic or rational calculation, but rather with a transcendent and incommunicable apprehension of god's will.

Essentially they are arguing for the primacy of religion over politics.

What is at issue is whether human society is to be shaped according to the edicts and strictures of a divine being, or according to the needs and conscious desires of human beings themselves.

Specifically, at present, the Catholic Church, with SPUC in the vanguard, wants to maintain the whole area of birth and sexuality as the exclusive preserve of religion. Their reasons have to do with the role of religion itself.

Religion arose as an expression of human helplessness in the face both of the natural elements and of the societies in which people lived.

The wind, the waves, earthquakes and eruptions, thunder, storm, drought and deluge, plague and pestilence—human beings were utterly at the mercy of them all, unable to understand, much less control, them. So they attributed all this awesome power to 'gods', whom they sought to placate by means of ritual and sacrifice.

Naturally, in accordance with the law of supply and demand, specialists in placating and interpreting the whims and wishes of the 'gods' soon emerged: priests.

The social order, too, whether feudalism, slavery, military dictatorship, whatever, seemed all-powerful and unchallengeable to primitive people. So it, too, was imagined as the work of an almighty being. Rulers ruled 'by the grace of God'.

It is for this reason that religion—for our purposes, Christianity—has resisted every advance in human understanding, or human beings' ability to shape and control their own lives. Religion depends on ignorance and powerlessness.

Of course, there is a contradiction here, out of which the Reformation arose. In order to progress, and to stay abreast of advances elsewhere, societies needed to make scientific advances. So the frontiers of religion were inexorably pushed back.

The power of the elements was studied, understood, reproduced and harnessed. Bacteria replaced demons as the cause of severe illness. Vaccines took over from magical ritual as the cure.

Increasingly, religion was forced back into what the socialist writer John Molyneux has called its 'specialist areas'—morality, birth and death.

And it now had to secure this last redoubt as the exclusive preserve of religion, to be defended at all costs from human intervention and control.

Thus the 'pro-life' crowd show not the slightest interest in reducing the demand for abortion by encouraging the prevention of unwanted pregnancy. On the contrary, they want barriers erected around the entire area of contraception, gestation and birth, and all human intervention outlawed.

That is to say, they want this area, of overwhelming importance to the ability of women to control their own bodies to the same extent as men, to be designated officially as beyond the permissible range of human control.

They do not take this stand out of concern for the life of the unborn. (I have never met nor heard of a single 'pro-lifer' who followed through the logic of the 'pro-life' position. Catholics among them, if they really believed that a fertilised egg is a fully human person, would baptise late periods, which they don't.)

They take this stand out of concern for the life of religion—and particularly the Catholic religion which for hundreds of years has been the dominant tendency in the more backward areas of Christendom.

I'm happy to follow the logic of the rational position through and to declare that in fighting for every woman's right to choose abortion we are fighting to diminish and eventually to destroy the influence of religion in this country.

Hot Press—2 September 1996

The impossibility of having a rational discussion with fundamentalists emerges clearly from a controversy across the water about the effects of abortion.

Since abortion first became a topic of open discussion in Ireland, the fundamentalists have argued that women who have abortions tend to live in torment afterwards, racked by feelings of guilt and loss and liable to deep depression, commonly having to undergo psychiatric treatment. A number of Catholic-sponsored groups advertise care and 'counselling' services for those said to suffer in such a way, and cite this activity as evidence of their compassionate approach.

It does seem obvious that a woman with a pregnancy so unwanted she opts to end it won't feel chipper about the situation she's in, before or afterwards. Common sense suggests that this will be particularly true in a society with a strong and vociferous group constantly proclaiming that 'abortion is murder'. To some extent, the fundamentalists are responsible for the problems they point to as proof of their case.

In all the circumstances, what's remarkable about the Irish women I know who have had abortions is how untraumatised they say they are. Now there is objective evidence that this is by no means untypical.

The *British Journal Of Psychiatry* has published the results of a study conducted over two decades of the experiences of 13,261 women who have had abortions. The conclusion is that they have been no more likely to suffer depression or psychiatric disorder than women who choose to carry their pregnancies to full term.

The director of the Birth Control Trust, Ann Furedi, comments: 'Contrary to claims by anti-choice organisations that women who have had an abortion suffer from "post-abortion trauma" and regret their decision, this research, funded by the [British] Department of Health, confirms that where abortion is legal and relatively freely available there is no evidence of significant psychiatric after-effects.'

It is in the 'pro-life' tendency's formal response to the study that their irrationality is evident. Under the headline 'Trust Claims "Outrageous"', the *Catholic Times* (3 September) reports the view of Peter Doherty, editor of the *Catholic Medical Quarterly* and author-editor of what is regarded by British 'pro-lifers' as the definitive statement of their position, *Post-Abortion Syndrome—Its Wide Ramifications*.

Mr Doherty accepts that the study shows that women who have

had abortions do not experience 'psychiatric morbidity' to any greater extent than women who have given birth. But, he goes on, it is well-established that 'mental problems can occur after childbirth'. So the fact that the experience of women who have had abortions doesn't differ significantly from the experience of women who have given birth shows that 'post-abortion syndrome' does exist.

Perhaps Mr Doherty's line of reasoning is less than clear. Perhaps an analogy will help:

* Smoking cannabis makes people into killers?
* Studies show that people who smoke cannabis are no more or less likely to commit murder than the generality of the population.
* But it's well-established that some members of the general public commit murder.
* Therefore smoking cannabis makes people into killers.

Oi!

. . . .

Hot Press—4 September 1996
IT'S BLACKMAIL. A woman gets pregnant with twins, announces she's going to have one of them aborted because she can't afford two babies, and, in a twinkling, the pro-life crowd are onto the tabloids appealing for the necessary readies.

'Send 50 grand or the foetus gets it!'

Has it not occurred to the pro-life crowd that they are conceding the economic argument for abortion here? The way to reduce the incidence of abortion is to make the choice of having a baby as un-problematic as can be, to ensure that as much as possible of the burden will be lifted from parents and children.

The pro-life crowd howl loudest about a 'holocaust' of the handicapped. But isn't it obvious that only if parents of handicapped children enjoyed as of right all the support that can be provided, if they knew they could depend on speech therapy, physiotherapy, respite care, financial support and all the facilities that modern technology and medicine make possible, and if the educational system was structured so as to welcome handicapped children and to give them every chance of realising all the possibilities within them, and if dignified employment was then open to them, isn't it obvious that only then will it be possible for women to make the decision to have a handicapped child in a positive frame of mind?

But all of these things would require the sort of reordering of economic priorities which the pro-life crowd, almost to a man and woman, can be counted on to oppose. The pro-lifers have never been less interested in seeing their issue in humanitarian terms. They are aglow with abstract, moralistic self-righteousness, thrilled to bits by what they reckon is a propaganda bonanza arising from the controversy about the 'selective' abortion of twins. Not to mention the publicity which surrounded Ms Mandy Allwood as she decided what to do about being pregnant with octuplets. They have taken it all, so to speak, as a heaven-sent opportunity.

The conservative commentator Bruce Anderson mused a couple of weeks back that 'the anti-abortion groups have had their most successful week in decades'. But in the end, the pro-lifers won't win. When emotion subsides and facts have to be faced, even leaving the social context aside and taking their case on its own terms, their argument just doesn't hold water.

Once it's accepted that abortion is permissible in any circumstances, the only function of the law and of social morality can be to define and codify what these circumstances are. And with the issue of principle disposed of, the case for allowing women to determine the circumstances for themselves becomes, eventually, irresistible.

The only securely defensible anti-choice position is to oppose all abortions, disregarding entirely the wishes of, and implications for, the women directly affected. And this argument can be founded only on the contention that every fertilised ovum has a soul and on that account must be accorded the same rights as the adult who carries it. But that's a matter of faith, not of fact. Many of us regard it as self-evidently nonsensical, but for the moment, no matter. The point is, its truth or otherwise cannot be established by majority vote. Because it is a position which, of its nature, cannot be grounded in rationality. It cannot be grounded in democracy either.

While the general climate of opinion might change from time to time, the trajectory of development for the future, in Ireland as elsewhere, is clear enough, and it is not in the direction of the pro-lifers. The pro-life crowd cannot win other than by destroying democracy. Which many of them, of course, wouldn't balk at.

. . . .

Hot Press—18 September 1996

The reaction of Catholic fundamentalists to the disposal in Britain last month of up to 6,000 frozen embryos whose 'parents' could not be traced has been impressive in its continuing intensity. The 'trade press'—the *Universe*, the *Catholic Times*, etc—is still full of it. On this side of the water, the *Irish Catholic* went ballistic at reports (inaccurate, as it turns out) that an Irish clinic offering fertility services was planning to freeze embryos here, too.

The usual spokespersons have been on a permanent red alert for media opportunities to preach the 'pro-life' message. William Binchy, Niamh Nic Mhathuna, Mary Kenny and Paul Johnston have been full of fire and well to the fore. 'The best opportunity in years to force an amendment to the Abortion Act', declared Phyllis Bowman, the national director of SPUC in Britain, seeming to savour the situation even as she evinced horror at its implications. Here, Binchy, a professor of law, no less, blithely ignoring his disastrous track record in interpreting previous constitutional measures, has been demanding another referendum to 'protect the unborn'.

But while the morale of the 'pro-lifers' might seem high at first sight, there is a deep fear underlying their fervour—that the Catholic Church itself may no longer have the ideological self-confidence or fixity of purpose to hold the line on 'the right to life'. They are summoning up all the energies because they are alarmed that the men supposedly leading their side may not have the stomach for a fight to the finish. They are fighting, then, as they would see it, not so much in the name of the official Church, but in its place, because the official Church may no longer be wholly committed to the cause. One of the most interesting comments on the frozen embryo affair came from Cardinal Basil Hume of Westminster, who, having deplored the publicity surrounding the issue, went on to offer two solutions which, he said, would be in keeping with Catholic doctrine: to allow the embryos to 'die with dignity', or to have them adopted.

What's fascinating about this is that the first option certainly (and the second possibly: it's far from clear what it means) is not in accordance with Catholic teaching at all. As mentioned here last issue, the fundamental basis of the 'pro-life' case is that a soul enters 'the body' at the instant of conception. It is this which makes the embryo 'fully human', even at the point when it consists of only two cells and is of such a size that scores clustered together could be contained within the full stop which follows. But if this is so, allowing the embryos to 'die with dignity' is the exact moral equivalent of euthanasia. Indeed, it is euthanasia—a mortal sin. The fact that the most senior official of the Catholic Church in Britain could advance such a proposition testifies to the extent of doctrinal disarray at the highest levels in the Church as it struggles to get to grips with a changing world. Writing in the *Universe*, the Roman theologian Bruno Quintavalle took the logic of Catholic teaching to its rigorous conclusion when he recommended the 'option ...to keep [the embryos] frozen until such time as their parents can be located or artificial wombs developed to host them'. He pointed out that 'embryos can, in fact, be kept frozen at home in a thermos flask topped up every week with liquid nitrogen, which costs about the same price as fresh milk. Compared with the £1,000 per day and continuous medical supervision needed to run an incubator for premature babies cryopreservation is medical technology at its simplest.' Even if the embryos were allowed to thaw out, he argued, the moral imperative to keep them alive for as long as possible would remain. 'Embryos can be kept alive for up to 17 days in a culture dish—again a very inexpensive straightforward procedure. Having thawed the embryos one could not simply sit back and watch them starve to death.'

I suspect that the reason Cardinal Hume didn't mention these options is that they are simply grotesque—repellent to common sense and human sensitivity. But they do follow on inevitably and inescapably from the core doctrine of the Catholic Church on human life. Herein lies the dilemma which can easily become obscured by the pro-lifers' frenzied emotionalism. Nor is this the end of it. No Catholic writer or pro-life spokesperson that I'm aware of has suggested that each of the embryos should have been baptised before being allowed to melt away. But why not? Were they not as entitled to the sacramental grace of the baptismal ceremony as any other human being? The chairman of the Catholic anti-choice lobby, Lifer Jack Scarisbrick, did criticise the British health authorities for failing to 'show the minimum respect for these human beings by insisting that they be reverently buried'. But he balked at advocating baptism. This was to evade the implications of his own most loudly-proclaimed fundamental principle. Why, for that matter, are arrangements not made as a matter of course for the baptism of fertilised ova which are naturally discarded from women's bodies? The pro-choice parliamentarian Lord Winston was deluged in angry condemnation from Life, SPUC and the rest of them last month when he suggested, sarcastically, that 'candlelit vigils should be held every time a Catholic woman menstruates'. This was a crude and inapposite formulation, but it did highlight the fact that a majority of human beings (on the 'pro-lifer' definition) never make it to birth, indeed never make it to implantation in the womb. Why should they be discriminated against on this account? Don't they have 'souls', too? Isn't the case for baptising these little ones exactly the same and exactly as strong as the case for baptising anybody else?

Lord Winston might have been on stronger ground had he confined himself to advocating vigils for late periods. But it would still have been a piece of sarcasm. For a number of reasons—the insolent invasion of a woman's private space, the grotesque absurdity of the procedure necessarily involved—no one, as far as I know, has ever suggested baptising menstrual blood in any circumstances. The point is the 'pro-lifers' would advocate the practice if they were true to what they say they believe is the fundamental point of human existence. They'd insist on it. They don't because, deep down, they know it doesn't make sense. The tiny, fundamental point at the core of the heart of their argument is a self-evidently fantastical notion which in practice they don't even believe in themselves.

. . . .

Hot Press—23 April 1998

It will be 30 years ago next Monday since the day abortion became legally available in Britain. But not, of course, in Ireland. An aspect of discrimination and second-class citizenship which was been strangely ignored in the planning application for paradise drawn up at Stormont a fortnight ago.

We are told that women in the North cannot have equal rights with women across the water because the fervent believers in the bible who infest our public life wouldn't allow it. But, as a matter of fact, nowhere in the bible does it say that abortion is wrong. Abortion is mentioned—in Exodus 21:22 for example—but not denounced. Wifely disobedience, gay sex, tax fraud, bestiality, all these are declared abominable in the eyes of the Lord. But not abortion.

If the termination of pregnancy really was a sin which cries out to heaven for vengeance, you'd think god would at least have hinted at this in his book. But no. Not a dicky bird.

Here's another thing. The bible doesn't say that life begins at conception. The bible says that life begins at birth. Most readers will, I imagine, have total recall of Ezekiel, 37:5-6. 'Behold I shall cause breath to enter you, and you shall live. I will lay sinews upon you, and cause flesh to come upon you, and put breath in you, and you shall live, and shall know that I am the Lord.'

The sequence is clear. First the physical body is formed, then it breathes, and only then does it live in the eyes of the Lord.

Some might still doubt. Almost any proposition can be proven by cunning selection of biblical quote. But god was mindful of this danger when laying down the law about life. The key book here is, of course, Genesis—god's own account of the beginning of human life. Chapter 2:7: 'And the Lord God formed man of the dust of the ground, and breathed into his nostrils the breath of life, and man became a living soul.'

Hard to see how ambiguity might infiltrate that passage.

Of course, there's more evidence for Santa Claus than for the existence of a soul. But if there is a soul, the bible says it enters the body, not at conception, but at birth.

That's that cleared up. So will some party out there say in its manifesto that it will move in the new Assembly to give women here the same right to choose as their sisters across the water have had for the last 30 years?

. . . .

Belfast Telegraph—19 August 1998
On RTE's *Questions and Answers* on Monday night Mary Holland of the *Observer* asked Steven King of the Ulster Unionists whether he reckoned there was a chance of the new Assembly bringing the law on abortion here into line with the 1967 British Act.

Did Mr King, the Southern media's latest very favourite Unionist, bristle with righteous indignation and make with the mantra about abortion being a crime which cries out to heaven for vengeance?

No, he did not. He shrugged, and mentioned opinion poll evidence suggesting that a majority of Northern voters may well be in favour of the extension of the 1967 Act. Nobody else picked up on the exchange, and the panel moved on, or back, to discussion of the subtle and perfect lineaments of both the Stormont Agreement and all who assisted in its construction.

But the brief interchange said a lot about some of the shifts beneath the surface which generated the Agreement.

The split within Unionism is not just between hard-liners and soft-liners, but between those for whom Unionism has both a political and religious resonance and those who, consciously or casually, are ready to slough off the religious raiment.

This is to over-simplify, and it is by no means the whole story. Nevertheless, there is a perspective in which the division within the UUP over the Agreement can be seen as reflecting a widening split between secular and scriptural versions of Unionism.

The religious basis of anti-Agreement Unionism is seen in the person of Ian Paisley, who now offers a single transferable speech from platform and pulpit, alternately damning the Agreement as surrender to Dublin and sell-out to Rome. Paisley's anti-Talks rally at Kilkeel a fortnight ago opened with a prayer: television footage showed the audience/congregation with bowed heads as the DUP leader/Free Presbyterian Moderator clenched his eyes and called on god to come to the aid of Protestant Ulster.

This identification of the cause of 'Ulster' with Protestant fundamentalism makes less and less sense to more and more people who see themselves still as Unionists.

The scriptural/secular division is seen not just between Unionist parties but within parties, and within Loyalist paramilitarism. It is not an accident that Willie Thompson of East Tyrone, the UUP man most fervently opposed to Unionists entering the Talks at all, is also the most frank of the UUP MPs about grounding his politics in religious conviction.

Neither is it coincidence that the Loyalist Volunteer Force is distinguished from other paramilitary groups on the Unionist side not only in its opposition to the Agreement and the associated ceasefires, but also by its claim of religious motivation. This is spelled out in the remarkable pamphlet *Is there a Place in Heaven for Billy Wright?* It is also the real basis of the LVF's stated admiration of the Rev Paisley.

The specifically religious component of not-an-inch Unionism is rarely highlighted in political analyses, perhaps out of uneasiness about badmouthing anything biblical. But it is real and relevant, and raised by the issue of abortion.

When the last Northern Assembly debated abortion in 1982, the longest, strongest speech against choice came from Willie Thompson. Evidently, Mr King now takes a different line.

This difference is as relevant to the drift within Unionism as difference over the Agreement. Which is to say that by and large it's the same difference.

Hot Press—18 March 1999

I see that the Archbishop of Glasgow, Cardinal Thomas Winning, has been subjected to harsh criticism for announcing that his diocese will offer any woman who decides to have a baby rather than an abortion £5,000. I cannot imagine why. This is a splendid idea, uncannily reminiscent of a scheme devised by my good self in this very space no very long ago.

All contentedly pregnant *Hot Press* readers should immediately contact the Cardinal and ask for their money by return of post.

My old slogan, 'Five grand or the foetus gets it', should put the message effectively across.

. . . .

It's easy to assume that attitudes in the North never change, but the 'pro-lifers' don't think so, and they're right.

A couple of weeks ago, each of the three main Catholic newspapers in these islands, the *Universe*, the *Catholic Times* and the *Irish Catholic*, carried a full-page advertisement headed, 'Without Your Help The Bloodshed Will Begin Again In Northern Ireland'.

This wasn't a plea to David Trimble to stop fucking about with the peace process but a pitch for money for 'Precious Life', one of the myriad 'pro-life' organisations infesting the land.

The British Government, warns the advert, plans to impose abortion on the North. Tony Blair, Mo Mowlam and 64 Labour MPs are 'determined' and 'downright militant' on the issue. 'If they succeed, thousands of Irish babies from both Northern Ireland and Ireland will endure horrible deaths in the years ahead.'

But if readers send their spare dosh to 'Precious Life', 'We will save the babies of Northern Ireland'.

In fact, the abortion rate in Northern Ireland is in line with the rate in the South which is in line with the rate in Britain. There is no reason to suppose that the extension to the North of the UK 1967 Abortion Act—the key demand of campaigners for choice—would significantly alter these figures. The most likely effect would be to reduce the incidence of late Northern Ireland abortions—significantly higher for Irish women than for British women because of the hassle they have to go through, the need to raise money, arrange travel, devise a cover-story and so forth.

So, even if the crazies' campaign was successful and women in the North remained disadvantaged in relation to women in the rest of the

UK, it is unlikely that any 'babies' would be 'saved'.

The notion that Tony Blair and Mo Mowlam are gung-ho for the extension of the Abortion Act is just as far from the truth. Both have voted for extension in the past. But positions adopted in the past have proven a very poor guide to New Labour action in government.

Mowlam has been a disgrace on the abortion issue, not only in refusing to act but in suggesting that Labour MPs who raise the issue are somehow putting peace at risk.

What may have unnerved 'Precious Life' and other advocates of compulsory motherhood is the evidence of a shift in Northern opinion following the pattern of change which has been charted in the South.

On 17 February, the British paper the *Independent* carried a 'readers' interview' with Gerry Adams. Responding to an e-mailed query from a London woman, 'Which women's issues do you support?', Adams volunteered a view on abortion.

'A woman's "right to choose" is an important matter with serious implications for Ireland. Every year…at least 5,000 Irish women travel to Britain for abortions. While not supportive of abortion on demand, our party policy on this issue recognises a range of social and medical circumstances which can give rise to women having abortions, such as where a woman's mental and physical well-being of life is at risk, on in grave danger.'

This isn't a clear and detailed policy statement, but the reference to 'a range of social and medical circumstances' and risks to 'mental and physical well-being' define in broad terms the provisions of the 1967 Act. Put alongside the Progressive Unionist Party's commitment to the extension of the Act, Adams' statement points towards the real reason for the 'pro-lifers'' alarm.

Adams wouldn't have said what he did in the *Independent* were he not content that he was broadly reflecting the thinking of Sinn Fein voters.

The reason 'pro-lifers' pretend that British politicians plan to 'impose' the 1967 Act on the North is that they know the direct opposite is the truth.

British politicians are resisting the demands for abortion reform which are coming from within Northern society and which, increasingly, are reflected in the pronouncements of politicians.

Contrary to Mowlam's claim, a no-holds-barred debate on abortion would be good for the North. It would be divisive, certainly. However, the division would run, not along the line of communal allegiance, but according to whether we want to enter a new millennium as a modern society shrugging off the old shibboleths, or as a backwater still burdened down with superstition and bigotry and corralling its women in continued oppression.

Chapter 7

Rock of ages ago

The remit of religion, and therefore of anti-religion, is as wide as the world. It's possible to write about anything under the guise of writing about religion. How else to get to the ontological significance of Scottish football?

Organised religion has always paid close attention to popular culture. Jazz, the blues and rock and rock and roll were all denounced as the devil's music, and sometimes still are. In Britain and Ireland in the second half of the last century, as trade union pressure won the five and a half day week and working men filled the fresh-air freedom of Saturday afternoon with football, Christian ministers of all denominations ranted about the evils of such misplaced passion. The sounds of the city have never been in harmony with the music of the celestial spheres.

My own interest in the area was sparked by a Fr Flanagan, spiritual director of St Columb's College in Derry in the late '50s, who once assured a packed chapel of senior boys that Elvis Presley had just been unmasked by properly qualified theologians as an agent of the devil, and that we'd all have to make a choice between Elvis and Jesus Christ. This didn't present some of us with a huge dilemma. *Jailhouse Rock* was on at the Rialto.

The incident allowed me to see that there can be great depths in popular culture, and great shallows in organised religion. I have written about religion in pop-music and sports columns and vice versa ever since. Mostly, it's for fun. But, as always with religion, there are dark shadows, too.

· ·

***Hot Press*—28 January 1988**
Tomorrow (16 January) is the feast-day of St Fursey. The best known of the early Irish monastic missionaries, Fursey went to England in 630 or thereabouts. The Venerable Bede recounts that Fursey would frequently fall into a trance in which state he would see visions of 'the fires of falsehood, covetousness, discord and injustice lying in wait to consume the world'.

Fursey would then wake up and compose sacred songs based on the visions he had experienced. Many troubled people found the songs soothing of the spirit. Fursey was quite famous for this. Some say the influence of his songs is detectable in Dante's *Divine Comedy*.

Fursey was attached to the court of King Sigebert of the East Angles. Sigebert ante-ed up the readies for the monastery Fursey founded near Yarmouth. This monastery was called Burgh Monastery. Later it became Burgh Castle. The noble family eventually based there was called 'de Burgh'. Thus Chris de Burgh.

Blame Fursey.

. . . .

***Hot Press*—24 August 1989**
Three o'clock on Saturday afternoon will be the Mo-ment of Truth.

That's when Maurice Johnston, a Catholic, will trot out onto the Parkhead pitch for the first Celtic-Rangers clash since he signed for the Blues.

Some have said that Mo won't make it through the next 90 minutes, so deep-seated are the hatreds now focused on him. Others hold out hope that his signing signals the beginning of the end of sectarianism in Scottish soccer.

In the midst of this speculation and controversy, little mention has been made of the terrible dilemma on the horns of which non-sectarian Celtic fans are presently impaled.

That is to say, Celtic fans, to be true to the way they have traditionally portrayed themselves, may have to hope that Rangers triumph in the tussle at Parkhead.

This will not be easy. Mo's dramatic defection to the hated Huns has inevitably induced a sour sense of betrayal.

And there's more. Mo, by joining Rangers, has threatened to deprive Celtic fans of one of their most treasured possessions: the glittering sense of moral superiority which they have always been able to feel over Rangers.

Although Celtic is a 'Catholic' club and Rangers 'Protestant', Celtic has never had any inhibition about signing Protestants—whereas 'No Catholics need apply' remained inscribed over the entrance to Ibrox until the mo-mentous developments of last month.

It's never been possible to support Celtic on the basis of all Protestants being bastards, but possible to follow Rangers on a vice versa basis. This distinction is reflected in the rhetoric and rhyme and in the general ideological atmosphere surrounding each club.

After the end of the cup final in May, which Celtic shaded one-nil, thousands of Rangers fans stood their ground defiantly singing in tones of serious rage for 15 minutes at least, until lines of police pushed and shoved them up the terracing and towards the exits. The song they sang, over and over again, was 'The Billy Boys':

> We are! We are! We are! We are the Billy Boys
> We are! We are! We are the Billy Boys
> We're up to our necks in Fenian blood
> Surrender or you die…

The song refers not, as is commonly supposed, to King Billy, but to a cut-throat from Greenock, Billy Fullerton, who in the '20s and '30s led a fascist outfit about 300 strong which, when it wasn't urging support for Oswald Mosley as British Führer, accoutered itself with knives, hatchets and Rangers regalia and specialised in terrorising Catholics.

There are sectarian songs on the other side too. As the famous victory was celebrated in Celtic pubs in Pollockshiels on cup final night, one specifically Catholic song featured prominently among the Republican ballads:

> Roamin' in the gloamin' with a shamrock in my hand
> Roamin' in the gloamin' with St Patrick's Fenian band
> And when the music stops
> It's fuck King Billy and John Knox
> Oh, it's great to be a roamin' Catholic.

Which is never going to be adopted as an ecumenical anthem. But the irreverence and wit of the words drains almost all of the nastiness out of the sentiment. It's the sort of song people smile when they're singing.

The contrasting attitudes implied here in verse help explain one of the most intriguing phenomena associated with soccer sectarianism in Glasgow—the ex-Rangers followers who now follow Celtic.

I know a number of these folk who wear their coats inside out. For the most part, they are people born into Rangers but who, as they grew into adulthood and political wisdom, found it impossible to fit the jagged sectarianism associated with Rangers into any sensible view of the world.

Go among any sizeable gathering of the Celtic fraternity in Glasgow and eventually you'll be introduced to somebody who'll give witness to once having lived in sinful support of the Hun.

Thus do Celtic fans proclaim their virtuousness vis-à-vis the enemy. It's this sense of moral superiority which is now put at risk by the arrival of Catholic Mo at Ibrox. And so to the terrible dilemma: if Celtic fans are genuinely unbigoted, they must logically welcome the withering of bigotry at Ibrox.

And there's nothng would help rid Rangers of sectarian hate like a Scots Catholic as key to success. Serious anti-sectarians have to hope that Mo has a stormer of a season.

Maybe we always knew deep down it could come to this. That sooner or later we'd be called to make the Ultimate Sacrifice.

. . . .

Hot Press—12 April 1990

Record companies in the US are no longer laughing off the campaign to portray much of modern rock music as satanic, pornographic, anti-Christian.

Last month's decision by Cardinal John O'Connor of New York to throw his weight behind the campaign has made a significant difference. Hitherto, the operation had been the 'property' of small groups of Protestant evangelicals who had some support in the Congress but, being widely recognised as long time residents of Paranoia Gulch, no hope of building an effective, broad-based coalition.

The backing of America's most senior Catholic prelate changes all that. The *New York Times* now reports plans for a campaign which would parallel the movement against pornography which has had some success in winning anti-porn 'ordinances' in a number of major cities. The anti-porn movement has brought together mainstream Catholics, fundamentalist Protestants and a section of the women's movement.

Although there is—as yet anyway—no sign that a feminist element would weigh in against allegedly corrupting rock, companies like CBS are taking seriously the possibility that albums and concerts might eventually be banned in certain areas or certified as suitable only for particular age groups.

Even the latter, limited possibility would have repercussions for an industry heavily dependent on the youngest identifiable section of the consumer market.

This represents a considerable achievement for the tiny group of bible-belt crusaders who set out in the early '80s to make their long-standing concern about 'the devil's music' into a mainstream political issue. And it's worth noting that this core group regards the restrictions presently envisaged as merely the beginning.

What they want, eventually, is all forms of pop music banned outright. The biblical basis for this ambition has been set out in a document currently being circulated among members of State legislatures across the US.

This draws attention to the significant fact that, of the 500 or so mentions of music in the bible, only around 30 occur in the New Testament. And of these, only ten have to do with Christians here on earth: the others refer to the heavenly harmonies of the hosts of the Revelation.

Of the ten, two are direct quotations from the Old Testament.

Of the other eight, six simply tell that music was played or songs sung on particular occasions.

Which leaves two passages in the New Testament in which any instruction is given in the matter of music. And both of these—Ephesians 5:19 and Colossians 3:16—give exactly the same instruction: that psalms, hymns, and spiritual songs are occasionally to be sung in thanksgiving to God.

From this it is deduced that no other form of music has biblical sanction, which in this context is synonymous with saying that all other forms of music are forbidden by the bible.

Today, Megadeath. Tomorrow, Daniel O'Donnell.

. . . .

Hot Press—8 September 1993

I know how Ireland could win more gold medals at athletics.

The thought struck me as I watched the wondrous performances of the Kenyan squad at Stuttgart, and recalled both the role played in Kenyan athletic success by the Irish Catholic clergy and the rather different role played at home by the Christian Brothers.

The golden age of Kenyan athletics dates back to the late '60s when a group of Patrician Brothers at St Patrick's High School at Iten noted the immense potential of many of their pupils and resolved to give sport in general and athletics in particular a new and much higher priority.

Iten is 7,900 feet above sea level, built on the Elgeyo Escarpment, 2,000 feet above the great Rift Valley. Its people undergo 'altitude training' every time they run for a bus. They would also appear to be brilliant 'natural' athletes. Very quickly after the Patricians made sport an important element in the curriculum, St Patrick's pupils came to dominate competition in Kenya.

In 1972 St Patrick's made its first mark on the international scene when Mike Boit finished third in the 800 metres and fourth in the 1,500 at Munich. His success spurred the enthusiasm of other St Pat's pupils—although the effect of this was not apparent to the outside world on account of a series of boycotts which kept Kenya out of the Olympics for 12 years.

So it wasn't until the Seoul Games of 1988 that the rest of the world really took notice of the phenomenal achievements of St Pat's. Peter Rono became the youngest man ever to lift the 1,500 metres title, and told reporters at the trackside that he owed it all to 'Brother Colm'. This turned out to be a reference to Colm O'Connell, who had travelled out to Iten from Tullow in the '70s, and who, as reporters quickly discovered, had also coached eight other members of the small Kenyan squad.

St Pat's has since produced the likes of world steeplechase recordbreaker Peter Koech, Ibrahim Hussein, winner of three Boston marathons, William Koskei, steeplechase gold medallist at Barcelona, and many more. Colin Welland, who wrote *Chariots of Fire*, is working on the screenplay of the movie.

Could not the Catholic clergy, who control the education of so many thousands of young people at home, not emulate the success of the Patricians in Kenya, I wondered?

Of course, Ireland isn't Kenya. Nobody here lives at 'altitude'. We seem, for whatever reason, to produce far fewer 'natural' athletes. Traditions are different. Most importantly, the teaching Orders here appear to see their relationship with the young people in their care very differently.

But that, I thought, could be the key to it. Perhaps what we have to do is to use that different relationship in a creative way, so as to reproduce the effect on athletic performances achieved by the Patricians in Kenya.

My proposal is that every male Irish competitor in a major international race should be allocated a Christian Brother to run after him. Thousands would run far faster than anybody, including them-selves, thought possible if there were Christian Brothers pelting down the track behind them, swiping at their flimsy-clad bums with a rod or strap and shouting encouragement along the lines of, 'C'mere t'me, ya bowya!'

You got a better idea?

. . . .

Hot Press—23 November 1996

How amazing that it should have been on 5 November that a spokesper-son for Enigma Productions announced that the album *Faith Of Our Fathers* had 'begun to take off' in England.

The fifth of November! Bonfire night in Britland! And the night on *Brookside* when Jules confronted Gnat and George about them shagging one another!

Stay tuned.

It has been widely acknowledged that the commercial success of Enigma's collection of 'classic religious anthems of Ireland' is down to a yearning for innocent days gone by when children with shiny eyes would queue all the way down the centre aisle for the Bishop to lay hands on them while parents watched with moist-eyed joy.

Ah yes, I remember it well.

Here are the songs the choirs sang out as innocence shuffled toward a rendezvous with religion. 'Holy God We Praise Thy Name', 'Soul Of My Saviour', 'Sweetheart Of Jesus', 'To Jesus, Heart All Burning', 'I'll Sing A Hymn To Mary', 'Oh, Sacrament Most Holy', 'Jesus, My Lord, My God, My All', 'Hail! Queen Of Heaven', 'We Stand For God'. Nothing like songs to evoke the spirit of an age, especially when sung in the style of the age, as here by Frank Patterson, 'Ireland's ambassador of song', Regina Nathan, 'much sought after soprano', Ros Ni Dhubhain, winner of the Gay Byrne 'Young Voice of Ireland' competition (1995), Mark Duff, boy soprano, and the Gregorian chancers of Glenstal Abbey.

Benedictines, they are. Isn't that a thing?

I was a boy soprano, once, singing out from the choir loft at St Eugene's at the top of William Street at high masses, holy week, Xmas, and the weddings and funerals of quality folk. You could psych yourself into soft thoughts of sheer goodness as the sharp, clean voices filled the vast cavern.

All a load of crackpot whimsy, of course, as we well know now and knew at some level even then. Along the street, there was poverty and madness, spiritual blight and the fear of being forced to face uncongenial truth. What's really conjured up by this album, then, what's hoisted it to the top of the charts, are its misty water-coloured memories of the way we were not.

For which there's a big market, and not just in Ireland. Across the water, politics has entered into one of its periodic fits of morality. Blair and Major, for want of wit or solid belief, now read from the same book of revelation, announcing in disharmonic stereo that they were both propelled into politics by a passion for Christian belief. The speechwriters fashion phrases for them to envision an ersatz yesteryear, where the young were neat and clean and well-advised and Christian morals provided a secure and certain framework for body and soul alike.

The Catholic Church across the water has acquired a sudden relevance as a result. Taking Blair at his moralising word, Tom Winning, Archbishop of Glasgow, recalled the Labour leader's claim that, while he was personally opposed to abortion, he supported party policy on the maintenance of the 1967 Abortion Act, not wishing to impose his own moral beliefs on others.

But if his politics were based on his morality, Winning wondered, should not his political and moral stance be one and the same? A good question, and brings us back to the long-playing *Faith Of Our Fathers*.

The reason the album's title track is no longer sung every year before the All-Ireland football final is that the GAA learned the truth: that it's not, after all, about the ancient Irish struggle for the freedom to be Catholic but is, on the contrary, a call for the reconversion of England.

The key verse goes: 'Faith of our Fathers, Mary's prayers / Shall win our country back to thee / And with the Truth that comes from God / England shall then, indeed, be free.'

'Faith Of Our Fathers' harks back to the 16th century, when Europe was ravaged by a war fought in the name of religion.

The new Protestant ideology of self-reliance and individual relationship with the Almighty reflected the mind-set and interests of the rising merchant class which had become dominant in what is now Holland and Belgium and in the trading cities of Germany. The feudal regimes of Spain and France, in contrast, continued to espouse centralised, authoritarian Catholicism.

The war came home to England in 1603 when James I acceded to the throne and came under pressure from the merchant classes, many of them members of a new radical group, the Puritans. They wanted rid of the remnants of the old Catholic order who were holding England back as continental regimes forged ahead.

James enacted a series of 'Penal Laws', which led to repression of Catholics and to the public execution in 1604 and 1605 of a number of Catholic priests. At this, a group of Catholic gentry decided to fight back and hired a Yorkshire convert to Catholicism who had served in the Spanish army against the Dutch Republic to lead them.

This was Guido Fawkes. He hatched a plan to blow up the king and his entire court and their ladies and advisers at the State Opening of Parliament in 1605—which is how come 'Guy' Fawkes is still burned every year on the anniversary of the failed 'Gunpowder Plot'—5 November.

And on this very day, more than three and a half centuries later, it is announced that 'Faith Of Our Fathers' has 'begun to take off' in England!

Cardinal winning, right enough.

I was so a-tingle at thought of this wondrous 'coincidence' as I prepared for *Brookside* the same night, that I had to slip the disc onto the player, for the Gregorian chant of the Glenstal Benedictines to soothe the fever in my mind.

Gnat and George, brother and sister, have been shagging in Brookside for almost a year now. Gnat, gnatch, did a runner from Jules within hours of their summertime marriage. Now Jules had them rumbled—5 November saw the confrontation.

The founder of the Benedictines was born in Norcia in Umbria in 480 AD. Sent to Rome to study, he was 'disturbed' by the life of the city and 'fled to become a solitary at Subiaco' (I quote from the *Dialogues* of St Gregory the Great). He founded a monastery at Monte Cassino, and wrote the 'Holy Rule', a reasonable document in many ways, outlining a monastic regime considerably less insane than some others. Rule One calls for 'a School of the Lord's service, in which we hope to order nothing harsh or rigorous'.

Benedict had a sister, Scholastica. Some say they were twins.

Scholastica left home some time after Benedict and settled down close to Monte Cassino, whether alone or in a community it is difficult to determine. We do know that she and Benedict met regularly. Sometimes Benedict would stay over. Sometimes he had no choice.

Take his last-ever visit. Here's the account of the leading Catholic hagiologist, Dr Donald Attwater:

'Scholastica implored her brother to stay the night, 'so that we may go on talking 'til morning about the joys of Heaven'. Benedict would not. Whereupon Scholastica fell to prayer, and so fierce a storm suddenly arose that departure was impossible, and she had her way.

'Three days later, Scholastica died. St Benedict was buried in the same grave with his sister, "so death did not separate the bodies of these two, whose minds had ever been united…"'

Attwater's quotes, too, are from St Gregory. He of the Gregorian Chant.

Remember, remember.

Brookside Close. Benedict and Scholastica close. Gnat and George, and Guido close.

We will be true to thee till death.

Chapter 8

Child cares

Since the begining of the '90s Catholic Ireland has been shuddering at revelations of sexual abuse of children by Catholic clerics.

The Church could have gotten away with the scandals surrounding Bishop Eamon Casey and others. Only human, after all. Always suspected he was a bit of a boyo... But the torrent of pain which gushed out once the wall of silence surrounding child abuse was breached was something else entirely. Faithful Catholics of 30 or 40 years standing weren't saddened or disappointed but deeply angered at the grotesque contradiction between the gentle values their Church had pretended to stand for and the savagery to children it had tolerated in its midst.

Yet, far from the Church expressing abject remorse and seeking forgiveness, it first tried to brazen things out, then brush it under the carpet, and has more recently been acting as if none of it had ever happened. They genuinely just don't get it.

The vast majority of the children violated in Church 'care' had been given into Church custody by the State. This is the main reason the State hasn't pursued the Church on the issue.

A couple of the pieces included here hardly make a 'good read' but do, I hope, illustrate the way Church leaders reacted, or contrived not to react, to the scandal as it unfolded.

. . . .

In Dublin—2 March 1989
Additional evidence of a major child abuse scandal just beneath the surface of Irish society came in two recent pieces in national newspapers which should have curdled any complacency among readers.

Deirdre Purcell in the *Sunday Tribune* (12 February) and Nuala O Faolain in the *Irish Times* (20 February) told of the effects on two families of the discovery that children had been sexually abused. In one case the abuse was within the family; in the other the abuser was a family friend. What shone through both stories with horrible clarity was the helplessness and bewilderment of the victims, the utter devastation of the happiness of other members of the families when the truth finally faced them, the permanency of the damage and the absence of any support or solace from the official agencies of society.

I wouldn't doubt that many thousands of readers reacted to these stories with pity and rage and a feeling that surely there's something which can be done. But almost certainly, in the short and medium term anyway, nothing practical actually will be done. The scandal of child sex abuse tends to surface occasionally, and then to submerge from view as tranquil assumptions close in again.

Catholic Ireland is far less likely than secular Britain to sanction the profaning of 'the family', without which it is impossible to acknowledge how twisted, sour and stunted inner-family relationships quite commonly are.

Which is not to deny the usefulness of breaking the taboo on talking about the subject.

It will be recalled from about three years ago, around the time of the Self Aid fiasco, that Bob Geldof jolted an audience of rock hacks at RTE with a polemic about the incidence of child sex abuse. He suggested as a statistical likelihood that at least one of the listening journos was an abuser. He was interpreted as meaning that child-abuse would be the subject of his next campaign/crusade.

As I understand it, Mr Geldof is scheduled to be awarded the title Freeman of Dublin in the near future, an occasion which will doubtless be attended by pomp, ceremony and television cameras. It would be no bad thing if he were to use the occasion to deliver himself again of his thoughts on this matter.

. . . .

Hot Press—Xmas 1992

A teacher who had been sexually harassing schoolboys for more than 25 years has gone missing following his suspension from work at St Columb's College in Derry.

The suspension followed complaints to the college authorities from the parents of a 14-year-old, who alleged that he had been intimately fondled when he bent over while getting onto a school bus. One of the 14-year-old's uncles had himself been sexually harassed by the teacher at St Columb's.

The case has been the talk of Catholic Derry for a number of weeks as former pupils recall their own experiences of sexual harassment and physical assault by both clerical and lay teachers.

Catholic Derry is steeped in the influence of St Columb's. A majority of the town's Catholic solicitors, doctors, journalists, teachers, accountants etc are ex-St Columb's boys, as well as a high proportion of white-collar workers of all sorts. In these circles, the reaction has been that there was nothing unusual about the incident which led to the suspension: the particular teacher has been notorious for behaviour like this since the '60s; and he wasn't the only one.

'It was just taken for granted that we'd be touched up as well as beaten up,' recalls a local solicitor. Since the experience, although common, has rarely been examined or discussed in public until now, we can only speculate about the effect it has had in shaping the psyche of Catholic maledom in Derry.

I attended St Columb's from the mid-'50s to the early '60s and, while there were good times, certainly, there also were days full of dread, when you walked to school knowing that at some point during classes you would likely be subjected to severe physical assault, and possibly to mild sexual assault.

Physical assaults could be 'provoked' by a wide range of 'offences'; mistakes in homework, giving a wrong answer, lateness, real or imagined rudeness, running, not running fast enough, looking untidy, neglecting to call a teacher 'sir', forgetting to close a door, closing a door too loudly. During six years at St Columb's I was assaulted for all of these and other 'reasons', as were all of my contemporaries.

'Assault' here covers not only raps on the knuckles or slaps on the hand, but beatings with fists, sticks, straps, wooden instruments of one kind and another, and, on occasion, boots. I was beaten unconscious with his fists by a priest when I was around 13, for 'rudeness'.

Serious violence of this sort was by no means an everyday occurrence, but it was an everyday possibility. And sometimes, when a particular teacher was 'on the rip', for boys in his classes it could be taken as a near certainty.

There were a number of teachers who regularly beat pupils for no reason at all, and who didn't pretend a reason. One priest used regularly to pick somebody out, beat him with a strap on the hand and/or with his own hands on the head and face and then explain to the class that 'that's just to let yeez know...'

Of course, there isn't or ought not to be, anything shocking in this. I've no reason to suppose St Columb's was a more vicious institution than any other Catholic secondary school at the time. And I imagine the same goes for the sexual harassment we encountered.

We are dealing here not with rape and buggery—if that happened I didn't know about it—but 'peeping tom' perusal of boys' genitals, stroking thighs, touching buttocks and genitals, general 'groping'. We had a teacher of Irish who spent considerable time looking up small boys' short trousers, breathing gradually more rapidly as he did so and becoming slightly glassy-eyed. To manoeuvre his subject into position he would instruct him—in Irish, by way of testing comprehension—to stand on a table in front of him, or to put his feet up on a desk.

Looking back, I can see now that he was a sad, lonely man, and can feel pity for him. And I find it hard to estimate what lasting damage, if any, the experience did to the 'victims'. But I can also recall the mixture of emotions which swirled around the class as we watched this uneasy ritual virtually every day—naturally experienced all the more intensely when one was that day's 'victim'; guilt, fear, confusion, ignorance, anger. Mainly guilt, maybe.

Any boy whose trousers bulged with an erection during the experience would be ribbed unmercifully afterwards as a 'fruit' or a 'nancyboy'. Among my own most excruciating memories of St Columb's is of the desperate effort not to have an erection when this happened to me, and of the even greater desperation and feelings of helplessness, self-loathing and panic when I failed. Some of us blustered our way out of it afterwards; some of us collapsed in tears; some of us reacted in both of these ways, in succession. The teacher in the current case supervised gaelic football training, and had it as a strict rule that no underpants were to be worn under football shorts. He would line boys up, pull out their shorts and look down to check that no 'sissy' was wearing the forbidden garment. In class he was known to all pupils as a 'groper', and would caress inner thighs, stroke buttocks and so on.

It never occurred to any of us to ask parents to intervene to put a stop to either the physical or sexual attentions of the teachers. And even today there's no shortage of ex-St Columb's men in Derry to snort with derision at any suggestion that there was, and is, a cause for concern here. Among those who take this line most firmly are those who themselves became teachers in the all-Catholic, all-male schools of the Derry diocese.

It is hard to quantify the damage done, to estimate with any confidence how much of the sourness and ugliness which we have to fight to overcome within us might fairly be put down to the way our souls were bruised by having been in the power at that time of people who were themselves products of the same self-generating system, some of whom had been 'selected' for the avowedly celibate priesthood when they had been mere adolescents. We can only refer to what we remember as fact.

We did learn that people in Catholic positions of power would routinely assault us and humiliate us, put us in pain and fear, and induce guilt and apprehension with regard to our unformed sexuality. We understood that, although all of us, and presumably therefore many others as well, knew of these things happening, it wasn't to be talked about, other than among ourselves in tones of furtive salaciousness.

We were given to understand, or to feel, that there was something darkly secret and shameful about sex, and that the authority which imposed this perspective on us was maintained by arbitrary violence. I think that did a lot of us a lot of damage, and that I can feel the damage still.

The good news is that these days 14-year-olds don't stand for it any more.

. . . .

Hot Press—3 November 1993

The Catholic hierarchy won't get away for much longer with its lack of response to the rush of revelations about physical, sexual and psychological abuse done to children placed in its care.

We are dealing here with the most serious scandal to emerge in Southern Ireland for many years, more important for what it tells us about the nature of Catholic Irish society than the business shenanigans which gave rise to the Beef Tribunal, or the Nicky Kelly affair, Eamon Casey's affair, or any of the other causes célèbres which litter the history of the last couple of decades.

It is a measure of the lingering arrogance of the chiefs of the Catholic Church, and of their isolation from the thinking of the people around them, that they seem to assume they can continue to sit tight and sing dumb.

Last year, Julian Vignoles' RTE Radio documentary on the Magdalen Laundries brought to the surface a sudden stream from Ireland's vast reservoir of hidden misery. Since then, a number of publications— most prominently the *Sunday Tribune*, the *Irish Times*, and *Hot Press*— have carried series of articles detailing the abominable treatment over many years of thousands of Irish children in schools, orphanages and other Catholic Church-run institutions.

The reaction of the Catholic authorities came through harsh and clear in Gerry McGovern's recent heart-wrenching summation of the Magdalen story so far. He had spoken with members of the Magdalen Memorial Committee—the group set up to lobby for some official acknowledgement of the wrong done to women incarcerated as slaves under the Sisters of Charity for having broken some of Catholic Ireland's brutal rules as to how women ought to behave.

The MMC was established after it emerged that the bodies of 132 of the Magdalen women were to be dug up from their graves at High Park convent in Drumcondra and cremated and reburied in Glasnevin Cemetery so that their original resting place could be sold off by the nuns for property development. None of the relatives of the women was told what was happening or invited to the mass re-burial.

The MMC wrote to the Archbishop of Dublin, Desmond Connell, making three requests: that a public funeral for the women be held; that the burial ground be used as a garden or shrubbery, not sold off as a building site; and that the Church help fund a memorial which would act as a reminder of this sort of injustice.

The dignified restraint of the Memorial Committee was evident from the nature of these proposals. But Connell didn't deign to respond to them directly. Instead, the answer came from a Catholic Church press officer in an RTE exchange with a member of the committee. The answer was: No, no, no.

This is in line with the Church response to a story I wrote in the *Tribune* in July about the transportation to Australia of hundreds of 'orphan' Irish children between the late '30s and the early '60s. I put 'orphan' in inverted commas because many of the children, although living for various reasons in Church institutions, had families still alive and well in Ireland.

The families were not told that the children were being shipped to the other side of the world. On their arrival in Australia many of the children were given new names, then allowed no contact with their relatives back home. They were dispersed around Western Australia to be brutalised and exploited—some were literally worked to death—in 'homes' and work-camps run by mainly-Irish Christian Brothers. Their story is now a major scandal in Australia, where the Catholic Church, and the Christian Brothers in particular, have been forced to acknowledge and apologise publicly for their crimes.

After the *Tribune* piece was published I wrote to a former Australian

Minister for Immigration, Al Grassby, who when he came into office in the '60s had put a stop to the mass importation of children by the Catholic Church. I asked him how it had come about that the practice had been tolerated in the first place.

How come children as young as five and six had been admitted as immigrants without their families in Ireland being aware that this was happening? How come many of the children, when they grew up and set about trying to find their own identities, discovered that the civil authorities held no papers relating to them?

Mr Grassby has now written back explaining that a succession of Australian Federal Governments had, in effect, subcontracted control over aspects of immigration to 'trusted' institutions—like the Catholic Church. The government wanted healthy, white children from English-speaking backgrounds to people and develop the country. The Catholic Church wanted to boost the numbers of Catholics in the country so as to secure its influence for the future. So the Catholic Church was licensed to import orphans from Ireland and Britain, no questions asked.

Scores of compensation cases are being prepared in Australia. Argument continues about whether the State as well as the Church should contribute to the damages which will eventually, assuredly, be awarded. The identities of some of the senior Christian Brothers and of others implicated in the scandal are being unearthed and publicised by journalists and campaigners.

But the Church here in Ireland, which organised the other phase of the operation, selecting and processing the children for shipment, appears to feel no pressure at all to explain itself in public, much less apologise. It's regarded as having all been par-for-the-course, run-of-the-mill, not worth bothering about.

One reason Church chiefs feel no need to respond is, maybe, that they are perplexed by the furore. After all, none of it will have come as a surprise to them: they've known all along.

Up to a point, we've all known all along. When I was growing up in the Bogside people talked in whispers about the suffering of the 'home boys'—the 'orphans' held in St Joseph's Home, Termonbacca, overlooking the Brandywell—and of the savagery being meted out to them day in and day out by the Christian Brothers. I remember a decade of the rosary being offered up in our house in Rossville Street for god 'to take pity on the home boys'.

This must have been true all over Ireland. People knew, sort of, what was happening, but also knew that it would be impermissible to make a public issue of it. The prevailing atmosphere would have choked controversy off in an instant.

That's what's changed. For the first time in a century it is possible to talk freely and in public in Ireland about the real role of the Catholic Church.

The economic changes of the last three decades, and the consequent ideological transformation, have provided a context in which the suppressed memories of masses of people can at last be freed for expression. It is for this reason that, almost every week now, somebody else stands forward to tell a terrible story.

Once you write about this area of Irish life you hear from others anxious to release their own experiences. Some say that things weren't as bad as all that. Others complain that you haven't told the half of it. We all remember things differently. But there's no denying the vivid reality of the stories which tumble out.

In the past few weeks I have listened to a woman who had been taken as an unmarried teenager into a 'home' run by nuns in the '50s when it was discovered she was pregnant. She recalled how, as she screamed in agony feeling herself being ripped asunder as she gave birth, a nun stood at the side of the bed cackling, 'Now you feel the pain of your sin, go on, scream with your pain...'

I have spoken with a woman who remembers with a shudder being punished in an orphanage for having sicked up her dinner. A nun stood over her and forced her repeatedly to spoon the vomit back into her mouth and swallow it, and keep it down.

On the phone to Australia I have listened to a man in his 50s taken from this country as a small child, the sobs overwhelming him as he tried to explain the bleakness which has hollowed him out from inside as he has tried and, so far, failed to find out who his parents were, and whether they are alive, and if he has any brothers or sisters.

Add to all that the various casual cruelties which were part of the pattern of life in scores of Catholic institutions for generations and we have some measure of the vast criminality of the Church in its treatment of children.

What has been happening in recent months is that some of this evil has begun to ooze up through cracks and fissures caused by deep shifts in Irish society. I'm an optimist despite all, and believe that soon enough will come the earthquake.

. . . .

Hot Press—9 February 1994

Controversy rages about whether the papers should have published the story about Fr Michael Cleary being a da. What fun. Some say *The Phoenix* was way out of line printing the yarn when his corpse wasn't cold in the grave. Others engage in earnest disputation as to whether the story is actually true.

As we go to press it's suggested that maybe DNA tests will resolve the issue once and for all. We shall see. But why bother? There's another point of view—that the papers were right to go with the yarn whether it's true or not.

Consider all the things which have no more basis in fact than the tale of the tooth fairy but which are proclaimed on-air and in print day in day out by the outfit Michael Cleary represented.

What about Adam and Eve, Noah and the 40 soft days, the biog of Abraham, the Xmas story, the 'Ascension,' the 'ensoulment' of foetuses, etc, etc, and so on and so forth? And why are there no dinosaurs in the bible?

You make this sort of point to any sky-pilot still extant and you will very likely be told that none of it matters because even if these stories aren't actually true they symbolise or illustrate much greater and more profound Truths than can be located in mere physical fact.

Fair enough, so. But equally and by the same token, then, irrespective of whether Cleary was actually screwing around, the story that he was, and that he fathered a child (or even children) in the process, symbolises and illustrates an important profound Truth about the RC Church in our time. Which is that the celibacy rule has acted as a cover for widespread sexual activity by priests and other religious, much of this activity taking the form of the sexual abuse of children placed in the care of the Church.

Given the numbers of priests and religious involved, it is beyond argument that the Church authorities have known about it for yonks and have schemed to keep it from the laity. The sleazy secret has been carefully sealed inside the institutional Church which meantime presented a gleaming pure facade to the world as it denounced, anathematised and damned any who transgressed its strictures on the permissible expression of human sexuality.

Whether or not it's the literal truth, the image of Cleary mounting the pulpit to rant against sex outside marriage and then mounting a member of the congregation symbolises a Truth about the Catholic Church which it is important we should all be aware of.

Consider: The *Universe* reports that the archdiocese of Santa Fe, New Mexico, faces bankruptcy and the seizure of all its assets because of lawsuits related to sex abuse by priests. Archbishop Michael Sheehan has told local media that the diocese faces demands of almost £33 million.

Just along the Rio Grande in Albuquerque, the USA's first Hispanic Catholic Archbishop has resigned after revelations that priests in the diocese have for years been sexually abusing small boys while the Archbishop himself has had affairs with five women.

That excellent little magazine *The Freethinker* reports that in the last eight years the US Church has stumped up more than $400 million dollars in compensation and legal fees arising out of allegations of sex abuse by clergy.

Up in Canada, more than 100 priests and brothers have been charged with sexual assault and the sexual abuse of children, while 4,000 people alleging physical and sexual abuse by nuns are claiming £640 million in damages.

A year after it was set up in response to widespread horror among local lay-people, an 'internal' Church inquiry into the case of the Birmingham, England, priest Fr Samuel Penny has still not published its findings. Penny's sex-abuse victims included five children from one family: the parents were devout and energetic lay-workers in the diocese and had trusted Penny implicitly. It emerged after they had gone public with their allegations that Penny had been sexually abusing children for 20 years and that the diocesan authorities had known this for at least six years and had done nothing about it.

The Independent on Sunday reports that Penny was by no means the only priest in the diocese involved in child sex-abuse, while the *Guardian* tells of priests elsewhere in Britain being transferred to 'retreats' after allegations of sexual misconduct.

The cases of thousands of children sexually abused by priests and brothers in Australia meanwhile wend their way through the legal process. In Western Australia more than 300 former inmates of Church institutions called one phone-in radio programme last year alleging sexual abuse by priests, brothers and nuns. They named a total of 29 clergy as paedophiles.

Across the continent in New South Wales more than 250 writs alleging sexual abuse by clergy have been lodged in the Supreme Court in what promises to be the biggest class action in Australian legal history.

We could ramble if we liked around the shenanigans and scandals presently enraging and entertaining the peoples of Latin America, the Philippines, Western Europe and so on, but the picture is clear enough already.

Everywhere the word is out. The Catholic clergy is at it, in numbers which the faithful are finding it difficult to believe, but which they are increasingly being forced to accept.

There's nothing new in any of this. Since the first, unsuccessful effort to impose celibacy on the clergy (at the Council of Nicea in 325 AD), sex has given the priesthood no end of headaches, and pains elsewhere as well.

Celibacy engendered a fear of sexual pleasure which has stunted and twisted psyches through the ages. Expressing their sexuality in furtive secrecy, the clergy tended towards abuse of the most vulnerable. After celibacy became the rule in the 12th century, the sexual activity of the clergy, particularly at the highest levels, was marked by a perverse intensity. When gentle sexual pleasure is deemed utterly abominable, orgiastic excess can't seem entirely inappropriate.

The most extravagant example was probably the first John XXIII (1410-15), described by Peter de Rosa in *Vicars Of Christ* as a 'former pirate, pope-poisoner, mass-murderer, mass-fornicator with a partiality for nuns, adulterer on a scale unknown outside fables, simoniac par excellence, blackmailer, pimp, master of dirty tricks.' (De Rosa is, I believe, here detailing the list of charges which led to John's downfall at the Council of Constance in 1415, so it's worth nothing Edward Gibbon's suggestion that 'the more serious charges were omitted'.)

None of this means that all Catholic priests, nuns and brothers are or ever have been sexually active or involved in sexual abuse, nor is it to presume the guilt of those currently facing allegations.

In the nature of the thing, nobody can say for certain what percentage of Catholic clergy live lives which generally contradict Church teaching on sexual morality. From the US again, we read of surveys seeming to show that, while thousands have left the clergy because they couldn't hack the celibacy, around 40 percent of those who remain are not celibate either.

There is a profound Truth here which the stories about Michael Cleary symbolise and illustrate, whether there's a literal word of truth in them or not.

. . . .

Hot Press—Xmas 1994

On the morning of the 18th of last month, a Friday, I phoned and then faxed a series of questions about alleged child sex-abuse by a priest in Derry to the Catholic Press and Information Office (CPIO) in Dublin.

I'd contacted the CPIO after being advised by the Bishop's residence in Derry that this was the appropriate path to the people I wanted to speak with: the diocese couldn't deal with the queries; that's what the CPIO was for.

My enquiries were directed to three Derry bishops—the current incumbent, Seamus Hegarty, the former Bishop Edward Daly and the Auxiliary Bishop, Francis Lagan—and to Cardinal Cathal Daly and to the head of the Church institution where I believed the alleged child-abuser was living. I was hopeful of reasonably speedy replies. Cathal Daly and various bishops had been protesting for weeks that while they may have secreted away such scandals in the past they were now more than willing to face up to the unpalatable facts.

By late afternoon I had had no response. I phoned the CPIO again and spoke with its director, Jim Cantwell. He told me he was sorry, he hadn't been able to contact any of the Church leaders I'd mentioned.

I thought this strange. It had been widely publicised that the Irish bishops were meeting that day at Maynooth: Cathal Daly and Seamus Hegarty at least would have been there and, surely, relatively easy for the CPIO to find?

Jim appeared not to have thought of that. At any rate, he said, the bishops were all now 'scattered'. There was no way of finding them until after the weekend. Which also seemed odd, given that weekends are when Churchmen are most predictably available.

With a deadline to meet, I went to the Bishop's residence in Derry and handed in copies of the questions to the three locally-based men and was assured by a pleasant woman that they would receive them by next morning. The questions to each of the three were along the same lines:

Whether you are aware of allegations by a family from…of sex abuse of a member of the family by Father X? What action is currently being taken by the Church authorities in the diocese in response to these allegations? When was Father X transferred from his parish, and what were the circumstances of his departure? To where was he transferred? What is his status and function within the Church now? And whether, prior to his appointment to Derry, the diocese had had reason for concern about his likely behaviour towards children?

The deadline passed with no response, and I filed no story that weekend. Over the following week, the questions set out above and variations on them were again, repeatedly, conveyed by phone, fax and/or hand-delivered letter to all the men mentioned. None was answered. I knew by this stage that Seamus Hegarty at least had received and read my communications and had discussed them with advisers and with clergy who had been serving in the diocese at the time of the alleged offences. But it proved impossible to obtain even an acknowledgement from his office.

On the 24th, I phoned Jim Cantwell again and protested that this silence sat strangely with the new position of the Church with regard to openness. He replied: 'We can't handle this. It has gone beyond this office now.' Did he mean that there was no point my trying to work through the CPIO any more, that I would have to persist in efforts to make direct contact with men concerned? Yes, he told me. I had been told exactly the opposite at the outset.

On the following day, yet more faxes and telephone messages to the bishops, the Cardinal and the Abbot went unanswered. So I wrote a story about the case for that Sunday, the 27th, necessarily without comment or rebuttal from any Church source. Within hours of publication, Seamus Hegarty had rediscovered his tongue.

He invited a television interview in which he expressed disapproval of any 'cover-up' of allegations of child sex-abuse by priests, claimed that it had been priests who had first informed the RUC about the allegations in the case, and promised full cooperation with any official investigation.

Four days later I contacted Seamus Hegarty yet again, substantially repeating some of the questions previously posed, and asking whether he stood by the claim that priests had informed the RUC about the allegations against their fellow priest. My fax was placed directly into his hands. But again, and by now not unexpectedly, there was no response.

This increasingly tedious pattern of my forwarding phone messages, faxes and hand-delivered letters to Seamus Hegarty et al, and his refusing to respond was repeated the next day. I made a final effort, in a fax timed at 5.15pm, Friday 2 December: 'As you know, I have been trying for a fortnight now to speak directly with you… If it is the case that you have decided not to respond to my questions and that you have decided not to grant me an interview I have repeatedly asked for, I would be grateful if you would make contact and tell me this straight, so that I can proceed on that basis.' He received and read this message. It scarcely needs saying that he didn't reply.

Openness, transparency and accountability are the new buzzwords in both Church and State. But experience suggests to me that, in practice, none of these qualities informs the attitude of the Catholic Church on this particularly fraught issue.

There's a conclusion to be drawn, too, from the response of Hegarty on the one detail of the case which, eventually, he chose to pick up on—his claim on 27 November that it had been priests of the local parish who had informed the RUC of the alleged child sex-abuse.

This version of events is contradicted by the priest of the parish who had been in closest contact with the victim and her family at the relevant time. I interviewed him on 3 December. He told me that the victim had named Fr X to him as her abuser and that he had advised her family to contact the RUC and had assured them that he would cooperate personally in any RUC investigation which followed. He did not claim that he or any other priest had themselves informed or made contact with the RUC.

The matter is further complicated by the fact that the family cannot recall this priest—or any priest—advising them to contact the RUC or offering to cooperate in an RUC investigation. This was, of course, a period of great turmoil for all concerned. Quite possibly, the priest did offer the advice he says he did but the family didn't 'take it in'.

But the priest doesn't claim that he or any other priest took the course Seamus Hegarty says that priests took.

This detail is important because the question of the extent to which the Catholic Church has regarded itself as effectively fenced off from civil law, specifically with regard to cases of child sex-abuse by priests, is at the heart of the present crisis in Catholic Ireland. In giving a version of events which depicts priests acting speedily and of their own volition to involve the civil authorities, Hegarty was contributing to the Church's defence against the key charge which has been laid.

It was a politically significant claim and, I believe, false.

If I am wrong, Dr Hegarty should have no difficulty putting me right. One of the questions I tried repeatedly to put to him was: Who were the priests who reported this matter to the RUC and when did they report it? The question must be very easy to answer. No priest would likely forget phoning or writing or calling to the RUC to make a complaint of this nature against a fellow priest.

If Seamus Hegarty has a version of events which differs from mine, he should produce it in public. If he hasn't, he should resign.

. . . .

Hot Press—6 August 1997
For sheer gall, you can't beat cardinals.

At All Hallows College on 4 July Cathal Daly delivered a long address on 'The Media And The Church', in the course of which he said: 'We in the Church should ourselves be active in making our institutions and our activities such as to have nothing to fear and nothing to hide from competent media enquiry. I am on record as stating that the media have done a service to the Church in Ireland in regard to scandals which have occurred… The media have discharged their rightful function in reporting these scandals… In regard to the horror of child sexual abuse, for example, the Catholic Church authorities in Ireland now have in place clear and public guidelines for dealing with complaints made against priests or religious.'

Dr Daly's own handling of allegations of child sexual abuse by priests is at variance with these sentiments.

Dr Daly will be aware of the case of the child rapist, Fr Gerard McCallion, currently in prison in the North. He will, I think, recall the many efforts I made more than three years ago to speak with him about the allegations, as they then were. He will recall some at least from a letter, a series of telephone messages and a number of faxes I sent to him.

He may also have been made aware by the Catholic Press and Information Office of my attempts to solicit their help to persuade him to talk to me.

Dr Daly knew something of the case already. A relative of one child raped by Fr McCallion had sent him a copy of a letter to the Bishop of the diocese in which the crime had taken place. Dr Daly's office had acknowledged receipt of the letter.

I wanted to talk to him about his response. Had he, for example, informed the civil authorities of the allegation against Fr McCallion?

I also wanted to ask him about the circumstances in which Fr Mc-Callion had come to be serving in the parish where this attack took place.

I had been told by a priest that, on the day before Fr McCallion had arrived in the parish, he had been asked to 'keep an eye on him'. I was aware that another priest had tracked Fr McCallion as he called to homes in the parish and advised parents not to allow him in if he called again.

This suggested a truly remarkable state of affairs. But Dr Daly refused to discuss it. Even now, with McCallion convicted and behind bars, his lips stay sealed.

In his All Hallows address, Dr Daly repeated the weary mantra of the Catholic Church being treated unfairly in media coverage of child sex scandals: the Church was among the victims, the media accused of villainy.

The same moral inversion is to be encountered in the publishers' blurb for *Goldenbridge—A View From Valparaiso* by former nun Teresita Durkan. The book is a rejoinder to Louis Lentin's February 1996 RTE documentary which told of a daughter's search for the mother who had 'abandoned' her as a baby, and described the horrific treatment of children in the Goldenbridge Industrial School in west Dublin.

Durkan's line is that, while 'the place had its flaws', Goldenbridge was 'also a warm, struggling and compassionate community, and it served the people of West Dublin with dedication and generosity for nearly 150 years.'

With an insouciance which in another context might be accounted admirable, Durkan dedicates the book to 'children who suffer and those who try to love and help them'!

The media, she complains, traduced Goldenbridge in the wake of Lentin's programme. She felt compelled to counter the 'adverse judgement' passed on the place.

Far from facing the dark truth recently revealed, the Catholic Church's first instinct was to admit nothing. Then it strove to limit the damage. Now it's fighting back.

How can we forgive them their crimes against children when there is no sign of true repentance, nor of a firm purpose of amendment?

Hot Press—20 July 1994

Listen to this: 'It is now claimed that his generosity led him to a relationship with a woman resulting in offspring.'

That's from an editorial in the *Irish Catholic* about Micheal Cleary. It was his generosity which led him to con a vulnerable young woman into his avowedly celibate bed...

Would she have gone to bed at all with someone so physically unappealing if he hadn't been a priest and able to fashion a load of lies about 'Jesus' wanting them to get it together? I'm surprised nobody has mentioned the possibility that Cleary only became a priest because he reckoned this was the only way he'd ever get to have sex with a woman without paying for it.

The *Irish Catholic* also says that 'in his life Fr Cleary had helped countless people by his example, by his kindness, frequently by putting his hand in his pocket.' Bollocks. I've met people, fools the lot of them, who handed over honestly-earned money to Cleary. He seems to have spent it on cigarettes, drink and gambling. But who did he ever help? Apart from himself to innocent females. As for putting his hand in his pocket, he was probably getting his todger ready.

Then there's this. 'Last week in the midst of great personal distress and anxiety following the dreadful events of the Fr Curran case, Cardinal Cathal Daly...' etc, etc, blah, blah, blah. That's from somebody called Fr Paul Clayton-Lea in the *Catholic Times*.

Not a word in the rest of the piece about anybody else suffering personal distress or anxiety as a result of the Fr Curran case. Only Daly. Our sympathy is expected to gush out towards him.

I've seen no evidence of Daly suffering distress or anxiety over what Curran or any other of his priests have done to children. He does seem distressed that his Church has been found out. But if he and his bishops had honest compassion for the children whose lives have been shredded by paedophile priests they'd have come clean by now about the way they covered up in the past.

All of Daly's pledges about 'openness', and promises that there will be no hiding places provided in the Church for abusers, have been expressed in the present or future tense. There has been no acknowledgement of the cover-ups in the past. But why should we believe what they say about the future when they won't tell the truth about the past?

Remember the scandal of the Magdalene Homes, where hundreds

of decent young women were locked away and held in miserable life-long slavery by agents of the Catholic Church, in many instances because of transgressions of the Church's irrational moral code which were very minor when compared with the hideous sins of Smyth, Curran, Cleary and a long list of others whose names you will soon know?

You'd think, would you not, that even the bureaucrats who run the Catholic Church would be a mite circumspect about allowing any of their underlings to try that sort of stunt again. You'd think they would at least be chary about using the word 'Magdalene' in the context of 'saving' 'fallen women'. You'd think the Good Shepherd nuns who cruelly exploited women in their laundries for decades would steer clear of this area for a century or two.

But some of these people just don't give a shit.

A full page ad in the 2 July edition of the *Catholic Times* solicits money for the 'Magdalene Rescue and Rehabilitation Fund' which will 'rescue innocent children from sex slavery'. An 'international network of pro-life missionaries…under the direction of the Good Shepherd Sisters' is apparently already at work in the Philippines and Thailand snatching victims.

The guy who signs the ad is Fr Paul Marx. He's the sick fuck who a couple of years back toured Irish schools getting his rocks off showing little girls a foetus in a jar. If you send him £767.78 he promises to 'provide everything' for two small children a year.

Contrition? They don't even feel shame.

. . . .

Hot Press—28 June 1995

One in five priests is sexually involved with a woman, one in ten with a man. One in 50 is a paedophile. Fewer than half have stayed celibate.

So says former priest Richard Sipe in his book, *Sex, Priests and Power—Anatomy Of A Crisis*. His research was conducted mainly in the United States, where he interviewed more than 1,500 clergy.

The statistics may be different in Ireland. Maybe the figures are lower. Or higher. Who's to say? At any rate, one truth underlined in the book is that clerical sex abuse, far from being a peculiarly Irish phenomenon, is part of a general pattern in the Catholic Church worldwide, and more deeply ingrained than many of us had imagined. Despite this, the Catholic Church worldwide shows no sign of facing up to the fact.

The Swiss Bishop Hansjoerg Vogel has resigned after his girl-friend became pregnant. His colleagues have pleaded with Swiss Catholics to 'show compassion', pointing out by way of excuse or explanation that he had turned to the woman concerned for 'warmth and comfort' in the onerous, isolated position he had attained. At a human level, we can all well understand. Most of us, too, turn to our partners-in-sex for warmth and comfort in the cold world we live in. But this understanding is nowhere reciprocated.

Last week, the Vatican Congregation for Catholic Education published a booklet announcing an overhaul of the training of priests to deal with matters concerning 'the family'. The aim is to equip priests with a 'clear vision' of issues such as abortion, contraception, divorce, artificial insemination, and sex outside marriage. The initiative does not betoken a new liberalism but, on the contrary, a determined retrenchment, a further strengthening of the barriers against 'modernism'.

The 'traditional family', says John Paul II, must be defended at all costs. Priests must denounce all sexual activity outside a family context. Nowhere does he acknowledge the sexual activity of, apparently, a majority of priests, or the fact that all of priests' sexual activity takes place outside 'the family'.

It's like the government discovered that a very high proportion, probably a majority, of drugs officers at our ports were strung out on smack which they were personally importing and decided to say little and do nothing about it but instead issued an instruction that they were to crack down a lot harder on cannabis...

But then the bosses of the Catholic Church have been getting away with hypocrisy on this scale for centuries...

Chapter 9

Black magic woman

There are statues of the Virgin Mary everywhere in Catholic Ireland, the virgin mother being an obvious icon for Catholic attitudes to women, sexuality and motherhood.

Some aspects of the cult of the Virgin are comical, and I hope this comes through here and there. But mostly it's not comical at all. The specific manifestation of the Virgin at Medjugorje in Bosnia-Hercegovina makes this scarifyingly clear. In what context other than of religion would tens of thousands of ordinary Irish people associate themselves with a political conspiracy to rehabilitate one of the remnants of Nazism?

The cult of the Virgin also provides cover for the Vatican regime of John Paul as it wages ideological war against the forces of progress and freedom in Europe. Socialists who dismiss religion as irrelevant would do well to ponder the Vatican's interventions in the Balkans in the '90s, ostensibly to tend to the spiritual needs of its flock, actually to buttress reaction and evil. It was because Our Lady of Medjugorje doesn't exist that they had to invent her.

And, as I've tried to explain, they continue to reinvent her.

In this, as in so much else to do with religion, and especially the Catholic religion, the Mother follows the Son.

. . . .

In Dublin—2 October 1986
Is there nothing can be done about the sad and seemingly inexorable decline in the power of prayer?

Ms Leila Collins, to whom discarded Minister of State Eddie is married, lamented last week that the storm of prayers she'd besieged heaven with on behalf of her husband had fallen on stone-deaf ears.

Ms Collins revealed that during the last election she had offered up no end of novenas (novenas, mind!) for Garret FitzGerald. But Garret rewarded her husband with a mere minister of state-ship while elevating his constituency colleague, Austin Deasy, to a top-table seat in the cabinet itself.

I don't mind telling you that the failure of Ms Collin's novenas to achieve her intended object has been the subject of some anxious discussion among members of our neighbourhood prayer circle. And to be frank, I'm not at all certain that we have managed to still the sense of unease which has been astir in our souls. Theories and explanations aplenty have been mulled over and meditated upon. (A suggestion that we should ourselves pray for enlightenment on the issue was rejected on the ground that this might only complicate matters further.)

Only last night, during a coffee-and-biscuit break between the Joyful and the Sorrowful mysteries (oh yes, we like to enjoy ourselves, we're far from gloomy fanatics, I can tell you) the theory was advanced that perhaps the fault lay not with god, nor even with Garret, but, inadvertently, with Ms Collins herself! Perhaps, Concepta Mulrooney suggested thoughtfully, Ms Collins had targeted her novenas rather carelessly. The evidence for this was that on her own admission Ms Collins had dispatched the novenas heavenwards (spiritually) labelled to indicate that they were designed to encourage divine benignity towards Garret. And Garret had won the election. So Ms Collins' prayers had been answered...

Well, this brightened up the Circle more than somewhat and we were just waiting for young Laurence O'Toole O'Donovan to finish the last coconut cream before making a sortie into the Agony in the Garden when Bernadette Comiskey pursed her lips firmly, shook her head and announced that, no, this wouldn't do.

Bernadette's point was, I thought, a rather interesting one. It may well be, she argued, that Leila Collins had offered up the novenas for Garret. But, clearly, she had taken this course in order that Garret, having won, would make her Eddie a full minister. Which he hadn't. Indeed, continued Bernadette (who has a brother a Jesuit), even if her ambition for Eddie to be a full minister had been buried deep in Leila's subconscious soul, it was, nevertheless, the source of her wish that Garret should win. And since god can see into the farthermost recesses of our beings (there's no arguing about that), it followed that god knew this, and deliberately had not answered her prayers.

Now that caused a commotion and no mistake. Padraig Mac Giolla Phadraig allowed that Bernadette was treading on dangerous ground here. Selfless prayers are always the most acceptable in heaven, he argued, and it was improper to imply, as he alleged Bernadette was implying, that god would look for an ulterior, selfish motive in prayers offered ostensibly for the intentions of others, and if He discerned such a selfish appeal, would be minded to grant it. 'A notion certainly not rooted in Catholic apologetics,' was his final, firm pronouncement.

Well! Bernadette was ablaze at this point and seemed to be experiencing some difficulty getting the words out, so I chipped in in an effort to re-establish harmony and suggested that since the act of offering prayers was spiritually beneficial anyway, no matter for whom they were being offered, was it not possible that someone offering selfless prayers (like Leila Collins' for Garret FitzGerald) might reasonably expect a personal favour from god as well as the granting of the prime object of the prayers... I could tell from the solid silence all around me that this wasn't going down at all well, but I could see no way out except to plunge on and try to lighten the atmosphere somehow...rather like, it suddenly occurred to me, and I encouraged them with a bright smile, the way the seller of the winning ticket in the monthly raffle for the Late Vocations Fund is always given a small prize too...

Of course the minute I finished I knew I'd made a desperate mistake altogether. Bernadette Comiskey and Padraig Mac Giolla Phadraig were now both glaring at me, and over in the corner John Bosco O'Mahoney blessed himself with his rosary beads before kissing the crucifix that has the relic of the True Cross in it, while Xavier Smith began to recite the Act of Contrition in a loud and sort of singsong voice that I hadn't heard him use since the day he had the Experience near the top of Croagh Patrick and Maria Goretti Stokes-Kennedy had taken the Lady of Lourdes statue out of her handbag and was asking it, would it ever intercede with its Son and get me forgiven for being in the Prayer Circle for what I could get out of it?

I was trying to think of something to say that would extricate me from the terrible position I was in when Oliver Plunkett Plunkett came at me sprinkling Knock Water from a blessed flagon and shouting that if I had any religion in me at all it's down on my knees I'd be asking for forgiveness, which I thought was a bit much seeing as how I was already on my knees and still all set for the Sorrowful Mysteries, it having been my turn to give out the decades. Luckily enough (from my point of view) it was then that Laurence O'Toole O'Donovan spoke up and said that what he wanted to know was why, novenas or no novenas, god had given the OK for Garret FitzGerald to win when god must have known that Garret FitzGerald intended to bring in divorce and abortion the first chance he got? How, he wanted to know, could a woman who had prayed for the intentions of a man who had intentions like that expect any luck for herself or her husband or anyone else to do with her? The prayers had, understandably, done the Collins family no good. But even so, the stated purpose of the prayers had been achieved. And it had not been a good purpose.

How, in the context of Catholic teaching, was this to be explained?

We spent a good hour on that one and had to postpone the Sorrowful Mysteries until next week when we'll make an early start and do two sets of Sorrowfuls to make up. I'll update you on developments in the next issue. Bernadette has promised to phone her brother the Jesuit in the meantime. Laurence O'Toole O'Donovan said on the way home that the more he thinks about it the more he reckons it's just another mystery, so why all the puzzlement? And he reminded me that the wives of Fianna Fail men, too, are frequently to be found on their knees praying, but that usually what they are praying for is that their husbands will come home at night.

. . . .

In Dublin—16 October 1986

I've been thrown out of the Prayer Circle and it's all Pat Robertson's fault.

To be honest, I suppose it was partly my own fault as well, seeing as how it was myself brought Robertson into it. But I'd only been trying to help. Things were getting out of hand and Padraig Mac Giolla Phadraig was choking Oliver Plunkett Plunkett with his Green Scapular when I chipped in, 'It looks like Robertson's blown it with the hurricane,' intending it as a harmless little quip that might inject a modicum of levity into the proceedings. But, as per usual, it had the opposite effect. The whole lot of them turned on me for the second week running, led by Bernadette Comiskey (who's never really liked me ever since I gave her a Ballinspittle souvenir Virgin Mary glove-puppet to mark the Feast of Our Lady, Terror of Demons, last year).

The session had started out calmly enough, even if we did rush through the 20 decades (you'll remember we had to do two sets of Sorrowfuls to make up for the time lost in argument the previous week) because everyone wanted to resume the discussion on whether Leila Collins had herself to blame, or Garret FitzGerald, or god, for the fact that her prayers had not resulted in her husband, Eddie, being made a full cabinet minister. Bernadette Comiskey had promised to contact her brother the Jesuit who we all agreed (at least we did at the time!) was a competent authority to pronounce on such a complex conundrum.

We managed to rattle through the rosaries at a fair lick (luckily enough Demetrius O'Leary who always insists on saying a Hail Holy Queen after each rosary instead of a single Hail Holy as a wrap-up at the end, was absent, down in Mullingar with Torquemada O'Boyle planning a campaign for votes for the unborn) and in no time at all we were all sitting around expectantly waiting to hear what the word was from Bernadette's brother. To be fair to Bernadette, she had gone to no end of trouble to contact the brother, who, it turned out, was currently participating in a guerrilla war in Peru.

Now if I were to tell you that the answer that Bernadette read out to us took the breath from the entire company I'd be telling you no word of a lie. In fact, Magdalen Murphy near fainted on the spot and if it hadn't been for Ignatius of Antioch Doherty being right beside her and able to start opening the buttons on her blouse there's no guarantee she'd have made a sudden recovery. Ignatius of Antioch got all his experience in the Knights of Malta.

What Bernadette had to relay was in the form of a 'radiogramme' and as soon as she'd uttered the first word I could tell there was every chance of a commotion. 'Comrades', she began.

I didn't quite catch the entirety of the rest of the message word for word, what with Padraig Mac Giolla Phadraig suddenly throwing himself on his knees in front of the portrait of Our Lady of Perpetual Succour and beginning to ejaculate at the top of his voice. But the gist of it seemed to be that all members of the Fine Gael party were advance-booked into Hell and that if people up in Heaven had any interest in them at all it was only to look forward to eventually gloating at them writhing in agony down below. I'm paraphrasing here of course. There was a lot about Dr FitzGerald's government refusing to vote against Mr Reagan bombing places and paying to have people with no money killed in Nicaragua.

It goes without saying that this was not the class of stuff we had been used to hearing at the Prayer Circle and Bernadette, unusually for her, was faltering in the midst of all the hubbub as she reached the last sentence which was, 'Free the Birmingham Six, Venceremos'.

I won't go into the full details of the way the matter developed after that. Apart from anything else, I was dizzy for a while after the Child of Prague that Ambrose O'Donovan threw at Maria Goretti Mulrooney hit me on the side of the head by mistake. The point was that Oliver Plunkett Plunkett insisted that Garret FitzGerald, as a proven abortionist and pro-divorcer, was doomed to eternal perdition and hellfire and that Bernadette's brother therefore had the right of it, no matter that his argument is founded on a deficient moral base. Padraig Mac Giolla Phadraig rejoined that Oliver was 'indulging in exactly the type of a posteriori reasoning that led directly to the Protestant breakaway'.

You can easily imagine the effect that that had on Oliver Plunkett Plunkett!

Everybody began taking sides with shouts of, 'True for you, Phadraig!', 'Ye have him there, Oliver Plunkett!', 'Aquinas is your only man!' etc, but unfortunately the tone of the exchanges began to deteriorate after Magdalen Murphy made some reference to a niece of Oliver Plunkett Plunkett's who had apparently been seen at a contraceptive meeting in Carndonagh the year before last. It was then that Oliver Plunkett pulled the Green Scapular out from under his shirt and Padraig grabbed at it, swinging him round so that he slammed into Ambrose O'Donovan, causing him to fall on top of Maria Goretti Mulrooney who didn't take kindly to being knocked down by what she called 'a rampant ecumenist', which is why Ambrose tried to hit her with the Child of Prague which hit me instead.

You know me. Always the peacemaker. I was just sitting there once I'd recovered consciousness and it occurred to me that if I could steer the argument towards Pat Robertson we might all find something to agree on.

Pat Robertson is the famous TV preacher in America who says that god has asked him to go forward for the presidency. He was going great guns too until a month ago when he said on television, to illustrate his close relationship with god, that he had talked the Almighty into diverting Hurricane Charlie away from the Mid West region and up toward New England, where Pat has his chapel and TV studios and entire HQ. It seems that a lot of the people who had been backing Pat deserted him after that, since the crowd in the Mid West didn't believe it was him who had steered the Hurricane away, but the crowd in New England did, and what with one thing and another the whole episode did him no good at all.

My point, as I developed it, was that, leaving aside altogether the question of how the incident had affected Pat Robertson's chances of taking over from Mr Reagan at bombing places and killing people with no money, considering the question of the Hurricane being diverted and whether this is credible on its own, and looking at it objectively from the strictly spiritual point of view, wouldn't you have to agree that, since god is infinitely powerful, and since the amount of divine exertion which it would therefore take to divert a Hurricane is exactly the same as the amount required to, for example, help Oliver Plunkett Plunkett's son that has no head for figures through the Maths Inter —which we'd done a round robin rosary-chain for last year and it worked great!—isn't it clear when you think about it that the only proper Catholic position is that Robertson's claim was credible after all?

There was maybe half a second's silence after I'd finished.

'This fellow Robertson', said Padraig Mac Giolla Phadraig, clearing his throat of the Green Scapular. 'This fellow Robertson is not, as I understand it, a Catholic'.

'More', Oliver Plunkett Plunkett nodded in reply, 'a Protestant'.

'A particularly convinced Protestant,' added Maria Goretti Mulrooney.

'That's not my fault,' I protested, in what I suspect came across as a wheedling tone of voice. 'What can I do about that?'

'Ye can depart from us, ye accursed,' Bernadette Comiskey explained, pointing to the door in a serious tone of voice.

And that's how I came to say 'Amen' to prayers.

. . . .

Hot Press—28 September 1989

It is not widely known that the flag of the European Community is based on an apparition of the Blessed Virgin Mary.

The designer of the flag, which features 12 golden stars against a blue background, is reported in a recent edition of the monthly newsletter of the International Secretariat of the World Apostolate of Fatima. He explains that he was inspired by the 12 stars which form a halo around the head of the BVM in the standard representations of the BVM's appearance to St Catherine Laboure in Paris in 1830. This, of course, is the apparition represented on the so-called Miraculous Medal.

Nor is this the only association between the EC and the BVM. Just a few minutes walk from EC HQ at the Berleymont buildings in

Brussels is the Church of Our Lady of Finistere, within which is to be found the Shrine of Our Lady of Good Success. The diocese of Brussels has recently drawn the attention of MEPs and Eurocrats to the availability of Our Lady of Good Success, should they require intercession in respect of problems currently facing the community.

Providentially, there is no representation of the BVM in all Europe more suited by her history to this task. Truly, Our Lady of Good Success is a European BVM.

She was originally Our Lady of Aberdeen, carved by a Spanish artist for Aberdeen Cathedral and erected there in 1436. However, at the time of the Reformation which made Scotland the most Protestant country on earth, it was deemed prudent to remove the statue. In the early 17th century she was spirited to the continent and into the safe keeping of the Archduchess Isabella of Flanders.

Astonishingly, on the very day that the statue arrived in Ostend, Isabella's army inflicted a decisive defeat on a Protestant army from Holland, slaughtering many thousands. Isabella gave Our Lady of Aberdeen full credit for the slaughter: one of the chaplains in her army, an Augustinian priest, carried the statue in triumph the 65 miles along the road from Ostend to Brussels.

On 3 May 1626 the statue, renamed, for obvious reasons, Our Lady of Good Success, was enthroned in an Augustinian church in the city, bedecked in the crown jewels and clad in a robe battened from pure gold. A mass was sung giving thanks for the extermination of the Dutch Protestants.

A century and a half later the statue had to flee again—from supporters of the French Revolution—but was eventually retrieved from obscurity and installed in her present shrine on the Rue Neuve.

Sneer not. Given that the Commission decided on 20 September last that there can be no increase in the overall level of structural funding, and that any increase in one country's allocation must be at the expense of another's, Ireland's only hope of hiking up the £3.02 billion towards the originally sought £3.7 billion may lie in doing down one of the Protestant countries... An obvious precedent beckons.

. . . .

In Dublin—9 July 1992

Did you know that the Virgin Mary changes colour on Sundays? She wears a blue dress during the week, changes into gold on Sunday.

This fascinating fact has been revealed by a performing Croat who was recently on tour around Ireland, entertaining sizeable crowds with tall tales about her frequent meetings with the mother of god.

Ms Marija Pavelic is among the six self-proclaimed 'visionaries' from the village of Medjugorje. The Medjugorje Six claim that the Blessed Virgin Mary began regular visits to them more than ten years ago. And that she's dropped in every day since. This would make her much the most persistent of the scores of Blessed Virgin Marys who have been popping down from paradise over the past couple of hundred years for a chin-wag with whoever's passing by.

Ms Pavelic's tour was organised by Irish devotees of the Medjugorje cult. Thousands flocked to her gigs, to listen to the magical messages which Marija says the BVM has asked her to pass on, and to gaze and gasp in awe when, as can happen if the vibes are right, Marija experiences an apparition of the BVM right before their very eyes. She had a sighting during her performance at the National Stadium last month, although, disappointingly, not on this occasion in full view of the audience.

The lucky ones with backstage passes who were able to accompany Marija to the dressing rooms and who saw the apparition—that is to say, who saw Marija as she saw the apparition—reported that Marija came over all glassy-eyed, and was flushed of face and strangely radiant and quite unable to speak while the apparition was in progress.

(As a matter of fact I have been backstage in the Stadium at a couple of gigs in my time and seen loads of people in exactly that state, but none of them ever claimed to be in direct communication with the Blessed Virgin Mary… Although, now that I recall, a few did make equally outlandish claims, such as they'd just turned down Polydor because they refused to compromise their artistic integrity. But I digress…)

Let's note before we finish that two of the Medjugorje Six spoke recently at a rally in Germany attended by many Croatian exiles. Newspaper reports referred to 'pilgrims' waving Ustashe flags as they prayed to 'Our Lady Of Medjugorje'.

It's easy to laugh, and indeed I do, at this loopy young woman and her demented revelations about the Blessed Virgin Mary's dress sense. But there's something ugly going on here, too, of which the Vatican's speedy recognition of Croatia, the rehabilitation of the Nazi sympathiser Stepinac and the growth of the anti-rational Medjugorje cult are all ominous symptoms.

Hot Press—19 May 1993

Writing in the *Observer* a couple of weeks back, journalist John Sweeney described how he had watched Serbian soldiers checking out a United Nations convoy in Bosnia: 'To watch hairy Chetniks' (an abusive word for Serbs) 'pawing over medical aid, like monkeys inspecting a consignment of bananas, is a deeply depressing sight.'

In both Britain and Ireland heavily opinionated pieces from the former Yugoslavia have been masquerading as new reports on front pages. Polemics against Serbs have won prizes for news coverage. Some, like the *Observer* piece quoted above, haven't bothered to conceal the ferocity of their hatred of Serbs.

For more than a year now, the people of Serbia have been depicted as devils. We have been invited to believe that it is a source of shame on us all that the West didn't weigh in sooner to blast them, home as it were, to hell.

Thus, Margaret Thatcher's call to arms against Serbia last month found an echo in unlikely places. The left-wing magazine *Tribune* declared: 'Mrs Thatcher is right.' British Labour MP's, Ogra Fianna Fail(!), the Council for the Women of Status, to name but a representative selection, have tried to outdo Mrs Thatcher in outrage as they joined in the howling for Serbian blood.

It goes without saying that the multiple rape and 'ethnic cleansing' carried out by Serbian forces is a crime against humanity. The same goes for the rape and ethnic cleansing of Serbs, and Muslims, by Croats. And for the Muslim atrocities visited on Croats and Serbs. All of these are ordinary people like ourselves, and, like us, capable of appalling cruelty when consumed by sectarian fervour.

One faction in the former Yugoslavia is like us Irish in a relevant and significant respect. The Croats are overwhelmingly Catholic. Indeed, Croatian Catholicism has had a 'presence' in Ireland for more than a decade, in the form of the cult of 'Our Lady of Medjugorje'— the worship of a supposed manifestation of the 'Virgin Mary' in a Croatian village in Bosnia-Hercegovina.

Tens of thousands of Irish Catholics have travelled to Bosnia-Hercegovina in the last few years to worship and pray. The leader of the group of Franciscan priests which presides over the cult, a Fr Slavko Barbaric, is a frequent visitor to Ireland where he is ferried around and feted by Irish followers of the Medjugorje 'visionaries'.

This, on its own, provides an 'Irish angle' on the Bosnian war, an obvious hook for Irish editors to hang feature-pieces on. But it's hardly happened. Because it would be hard to focus on Medjugorje without telling some of the truth about the role of the Catholic Church in the region. And no Irish newspaper is willing to do that.

Medjugorje is in the diocese of Mostar, whose Bishop, a decent man called Pavao Zanic, has for years denounced the Medjugorje cult as a politically-motivated conspiracy and dismissed the six alleged visionaries as 'sick in the head'.

He has pleaded in vain with the Vatican to impose discipline on the Franciscans who control the 'visionaries' and orchestrate the worldwide Medjugorje operation—not least because he had understood from the outset that, in the context of the Yugoslavia's disintegration and the unleashing of old ethnic hatreds, the zealots of Medjugorje have been playing with fire.

A few months ago the Pat Kenny programme on RTE Radio One carried daily reports of the progress across Europe of an 'aid convoy' from Ireland to Bosnia. The destination was the diocese of Mostar where distribution of some of the supplies—I have no way of knowing exactly what proportion and I suspect nobody else has either— was undertaken by members of the Franciscan Order.

I doubt if much of this aid went to the Muslim people who once constituted up to 30 percent of the population of the region: over the months, it's been cleansed of Muslims, by Catholic Croatians.

Croatia was fascist during the Second World war, the 'Independent State of Croatia' having been set up in 1941 by the Ustashe movement led by Ante Pavelic. Pavelic was enormously assisted by the endorsement of his movement by the Catholic Archbishop of Zagreb, Alojziji Stepinac, who hailed the establishment of the Nazi regime with: 'It's a long-cherished wish…a work of God that arouses our admiration.'

The official Catholic magazine *Nedelja* rejoiced: 'God, who directs the destiny of nations and controls the hearts of Kings, has given us Ante Pavelic and moved the leader of a friendly and allied people, Adolf Hitler, to use his victorious troops to disperse our oppressors and enable us to create an independent State of Croatia. Glory be to God, our gratitude to Adolf Hitler.'

When the Interior Minister in the Ustashe regime, Andrja Artukovic, introduced 'racial purity' laws, Stepinac wrote to congratulate him, asking only that 'Catholic non-Aryans be treated in a respectful manner'.

After the partisan forces led by Tito drove the Nazis out, Artukovic was smuggled across Europe by Catholic priests to Dublin, where he hid out in a Northside nunnery for more than a year while Catholic clergy schemed to have him admitted to the US. As far as I know, he ended his life in California, no doubt dreaming of the old days, and gas ovens.

No representative of the Catholic Church has ever apologised for this deep involvement in Nazi war-crime or disowned the criminals responsible. We are not talking here of a fringe group of Catholics supporting the Nazis, or of the Church being interpreted as providing ideological support for Nazis, but of the active, practical, official participation of the Church in Nazi mass murder.

Franciscan priests routinely accompanied death-squads which slaughtered Serbs, Muslims, Gypsies and Jews in droves. The clergy of the Serbian Orthodox Church were specifically targeted, so as to break the morale of the Serbian people and make them amenable to 'conversion'.

Communities of Serbs were rounded up, their priests killed off and the people then given the choice of 'conversion' or dispatch to the concentration camps.

'We shall kill one part Serbs, we shall transport another and the rest will be made to embrace the Roman Catholic religion', declared Dr Mile Budak, Minister of Education in the Ustasha regime.

The aim was to make Croatia '100 percent Catholic in ten years', according to Dr Mirke Puk, Minister for Justice and Religion.

After the war Stepinac was sentenced to 16 years in prison. But far from feeling embarrassment at one of its archbishops being jailed for collaboration, the Vatican defended Stepinac vigorously. Removing any doubt, Pius XII promoted him to Cardinal, and ordered a worldwide campaign for his release.

Children in schools throughout Ireland were made to pray for Stepinac, while papers like the *Irish Press* and the *Irish Independent* carried articles presenting him as a victim of 'communist persecution'.

Vatican-orchestrated pressure secured Stepinac's release after only five years.

The reign of terror in Croatia during the Nazi years was one of the key factors shaping the consciousness of the various communities in the region. It is not possible to understand fully what's happening now without reference to what happened then. But we hear scarcely a mention of it.

Those who have campaigned most fervently for Western intervention have a political agenda which has little to do with ending the torment of the people in the region.

The people of the Balkans are intent on tearing one another to pieces. So outside powers must intervene to keep them apart. So runs the refrain.

It's nonsense. The people of the Balkans aren't naturally more inclined to hatred of one another than people anywhere else. Why should they be? In fact, insofar as they do hate one another, it's because of outside intervention.

That comes through with brilliant clarity in Trotsky's writing on the Balkan Wars of 1912/13—still easily the best stuff to read on the region.

Trotsky went there as a journalist and reported first on the poverty and backwardness which he found everywhere, a legacy of centuries of domination by the Ottoman Empire. The Empire was decaying and receding, and Russia, Britain, France and Austria-Hungary, among other powers, were moving in to carve the region up.

There was a great national diversity in the Balkans—Greeks, Turks, Serbs, Romanians, Albanians, Bulgars, Jews, Gypsies, Armenians and many others—the product of repeated migrations and invasions and the creation of a multiplicity of military buffer-zones.

Each of the imperialist countries wanted client states in the region which would be powerless in relation to the Great Powers but strong enough to counter and negate the influence of the clients of rival imperialisms.

In this way, the European powers, as Trotsky put it, 'converted the national diversity of the Balkans into a melee of petty states... None was to develop beyond a certain limit, each separately was entangled in diplomatic and dynastic bonds and counterposed to the rest, and the whole lot were condemned to helplessness in relation to the Great Powers.'

The new frontiers, Trotsky predicted, were fated to become the front lines in new wars.

'The new boundary lines have been drawn across the living bodies of nations that have been lacerated, bled white and exhausted. Not one of these Balkan nations has succeeded in gathering all its scattered fragments. At the same time, every one of the Balkan states now includes within its borders a compact minority that is hostile to it… Such are the results of the work carried out by the capitalist governments and professional diplomats.'

We should remember these words if we are ever tempted to give credence to the oleaginous David Owen who, having devised a new map to further lacerate bleeding Bosnia, has then called on the 'world community' to rain death down on the Serbs for refusing to accept it.

The solution to the Balkans problem lies in bringing people together, not in erecting new borders between them.

'The only way out is a union of all the peoples in a single economic and political entity, on the basis of national autonomy of the constituent parts', wrote Trotsky. And this, he continued, could come about in only one of two ways.

It could come from above, 'by expanding one Balkan state at the expense of the weaker ones—the road of wars of extermination and oppression'.

Or it could come from below, 'through the peoples themselves coming together—the road of revolution that means overthrowing all of the Balkan dynasties and unfurling the banner of a Balkan federal republic'.

That is to say, we should be standing with the many thousands of Serbian trade unionists, students, pacifists, members of women's groups and others who have bravely opposed the Milosevic regime and who last year brought together more than 50,000 people in a brilliant demonstration in Belgrade under a banner telling the regime 'You can't count on us'.

There are thousands of Croatians who regard the Tudjman regime in Zagreb with hatred and contempt. We should be with them.

I know less of the opposition Muslim forces in Bosnia but I haven't a scintilla of doubt that they too are numbered in thousands and hate the war and the atrocities committed in the names of all the peoples of the region.

It's in the overthrow of all of the sectarian leaderships that real hope reposes. There's no hope to be found in an approach which invites the great powers to plunge in to broaden the battlefield and increase the flow of blood.

Above all, we shouldn't listen to the lying media.

. . . .

Hot Press—15 August 1993

The bonfires which will blaze in Catholic areas of the North tonight (15 August) are just one of the many intriguing aspects of today's great liturgical occasion, the Feast Of The Assumption.

The Assumption was chosen by ghetto-Catholics for conflagrationary celebration, not because Northern Nationalists have any special attachment to the doctrine of the Assumption, but because this is the only specifically Catholic feast to fall within the Orange marching season. As a result, it has been adopted as the Catholic-Nationalist answer to the Orangemen's Twelfth. The Ancient Order Of Hibernians will parade in many Catholic districts before bonfire carousing commences at dusk.

Whether smoke-grimed revellers essaying a seventeenth chorus of 'The Men Behind The Wire' is a suitable method of acknowledging the body-and-soul Ascension of god's mother into Paradise is a moot point. As always, I hesitate to pronounce dogmatically on such matters.

As, indeed, for centuries, did popes.

There is no evidence for the Assumption in scripture, and the great teachers of the Church—Augustine, Jerome, Hieronymus, for example—taught that we can know nothing of the fate of Mary's body. It wasn't until the Reform of the Breviary under Pius V in 1568 that bodily assumption was formally advocated—which is not to say that all acrimony on the issue thereby ceased.

In 1688, upwards of a thousand people were killed in Paris in a theological argument following a declaration by part of the Chapter of Notre Dame that Pius V had gotten it all wrong. They took their doctrinal disagreements seriously in those days.

Benedict XVI restored peace in the mid-18th century on the basis of a compromise position which defined the Assumption as 'a pious and probable belief'—but not an article of faith.

And there was the matter rested until recent times—until 1950, to be exact—when Pius XII, who regarded devotion to Mary as an essential bulwark against the encroaching libertinism of the post-war world, declared the Assumption part of the *depositum fidei*.

Rationalists and secularists of one sort and another have since poured scorn on the doctrine—as on the longer-established doctrine of the bodily Ascension of Jesus—pointing out that either body, in order to escape the earth's gravitational pull, would have had to attain Second Cosmic Velocity, roughly 25,000 mph, resulting in friction with the atmosphere which would have charred the flesh off the bones of both Mother and Son.

However, that such considerations will not trouble the minds of those who gather garrulously in the North's ghettoes tonight can be taken as a fair, so to speak, assumption.

. . . .

Hot Press—September 1998

As the Pope prepares to sanctify a Nazi collaborator, the 'Blessed Virgin Mary' has endorsed ethnic cleansing.

At a ceremony in the Vatican attended by John Paul II on 3 July, Cardinal Alojzije Stepinac was formally designated a 'martyr'. This is the last stage prior to canonisation. During a visit to Croatia next month, John Paul will declare Stepinac 'blessed'.

A week earlier, on 27 June, in a village in Bosnia-Hercegovina, a contingent of priests led thousands in prayers asking 'Our Lady of Medjugorje' to intercede on behalf of a number of Croatian men charged with crimes against humanity at the International War Crimes Tribunal at the Hague.

Stepinac was jailed by the government of the former Yugoslavia for collaboration with the regime of Ante Pavelich during World War Two. Pavelich's Ustashe movement had seized power in Croatia in 1941 and brought the country into alliance with Nazi Germany. Stepinac, Bishop of Zagreb, capital of Croatia, was explicit in his support for the regime and for its association with Hitler.

Roman Catholicism was the State religion of Nazi Croatia.

After the war, Stepinac was convicted of collaboration. The reluctance of the regime of Marshal Tito to make an even more implacable enemy of the Vatican—Tito was already at odds with both the US and the USSR—helped save Stepinac from the gallows. Sentenced to 16 years, he served only three before being released into house arrest in his home town of Krasic.

During this time, Stepinac was elevated to the College of Cardinals by Pius XII, who had himself been silently complicit in Nazi crimes. Stepinac died in 1962.

Even some conservative Catholics are distinctly uneasy at the proposed canonisation of the collaborator. Reporting the Vatican ceremony which made him a martyr, the *Irish Catholic* referred to Stepinac as the 'controversial Croatian Cardinal' and enclosed 'martyr' in inverted commas.

During three years of Ustashe rule, Nazi squads were commonly accompanied by clergy as they went about the business of murdering Serbs, Jews, Muslims and Gypsies, or herding them towards the concentration camps, or giving them the option to 'convert' to Catholicism. Franciscan priests played a prominent role.

The Medjugorje 'apparitions' rekindle memory of these terrible events.

The Francisican Church of St James in Medjugiorje had been an Ustashe organising centre during Croatia's Nazi years. Medjugorje is across the border in Bosnia-Hercegovina, but with an overwhelmingly Croatian population. After World War Two, understandably, the Mostar diocesan authorities were anxious that the Medjugorje Franciscans should steer clear of politics.

Church-State relations under Tito (himself a Croat) were, at best, edgy. The balance between the different ethnic 'republics' was delicate. To stir up communal rivalry risked destabilising the State as a whole and bringing the wrath of the federal authorities down on the Church.

The Franciscans, jealous anyway of their relative independence from secular church structures, were continually at daggers drawn with the Mostar diocese.

Thus when, 17 years ago, the Medjugorje Franciscans announced that six Croatian children from the village were speaking every day to the 'Blessed Virgin Mary', the Bishop of Mostar, Dr Pavao Zanic, denounced the affair as a 'hoax', pronounced the children 'sick in the head' and condemned the Franciscans as 'motivated by politics'.

The children responded by reporting that the Blessed Virgin Mary had told them to tell local people to pay the Bishop no heed.

Today, after six years of civil war and the fragmentation of the old federal State, Medjugorje is in now-independent Bosnia-Hercegovina. But the writ of the Sarajevo government doesn't run: instead, armed members of the Croatian paramilitary organisation, the HVO, responsible for the 'cleansing' of thousands of Muslims from the area, 'police' the town. It is the HVO which provides 'security' for the tens of thousands of pilgrims who now converge on the village each year.

A Channel 4 documentary last year offered convincing evidence that aid organised by groups in Britain and Ireland associated with devotion to 'Our Lady of Medjugorje' is, in fact, being distributed by and to the HVO. The 'aid' included fourwheel-drive vehicles, electricity generating equipment and heavy winter clothing.

In Church law it is the bishop of the diocese in the first instance, and the National Conference of Bishops in the second instance, which has authority to pronounce on the authenticity or otherwise of allegedly supernatnural phenomena. In April 1991, the Conference of Bishops of the former Yugoslavia, in the 'Declaration of Zadar', confirmed Dr Zanic's original view: 'It cannot be affirmed that one is dealing with supernatural apparitions and revelations.'

Last year, the present Bishop of Mostar, Dr Joseph Peric, restated the position: 'My conviction is not only "*non constat de supernatural-itaten*" but "*constat de nonsupernaturalitate*" of the apparitions or revelations in Medjugorje.'

Not only is there no reason to believe there's anything supernatural happening in Medjugorje, there's every reason to believe that nothing supernational is happening

But, as the thousands of pilgrims converging on Medjugorje in June showed clearly, the relevant Church authorities have made little impact.

June is a big month in Medjugorje. June the 25th 1981 was, it's said, the date of the first apparition. This year, 145,000 communions were distributed and 3,689 priests concelebrated mass at the Church of St James during the month. Among the highpoints was a parade led by Croatian regular soldiers and members of the HVO, from the church to the 'Hill of the Apparitions' where cult leader Fr Slavko Barbaric led the throng in the rosary. Scores of priests concelebrated mass for the troops, after which the soldiers and paramilitaries paraded with lighted candles back to the church where they knelt to be blessed individually. Ustashe flags and insignia were everywhere.

Another highlight came on 27 June when, according to some of the many magazines associated with the cult, 'thousands' took communion and then processed, led by 'hundreds' of priests, from the church, to light candles at the foot of a huge cross erected at the summit of 'Cross Mountain'. Prayers were said for all who had suffered in the recent wars. The *Medjugorje Herald* adds that among those 'prayed for in a special way' were 'all those Croatians accused in Den Haag'.

The reference is to the handful of Croatians arraigned for war crimes by a tribunal which generally has seemed to target Serbs only.

There is a clear line of connection here, an apostolic line so to speak, between the Croatian fascism of 50 years ago and the cult of the Medjugorje Virgin today.

Catholics throughout the world will be required to revere the Croatian Nazi collaborator when he's canonised next month. Meanwhile, 'Our Lady of Medjugorje' effectively endorses ethnic cleansing in our own time. Wafting across the decades, a stink of roses perfumes the death-stench.

Naturally despite the provisions of its own laws, the Vatican shiftily refuses to support its bishops in Mostar. Its most recent statement, on 28 May last from Cardinal Josef Ratzinger's Congregation for the Doctrine of the Faith, weasels its way around the pertinent point.

The statement expresses 'respect' for the Yugoslav bishops' Declaration of Zadar, but goes on immediately to say: 'Since the division of Yugoslavia into different independent nations, it would now pertain to the members of the Episcopal Conference of Bosnia-Hercegovina to eventually reopen the examination of the case and to make any new pronouncements which might be called for.'

It quotes in full, and with a show of approval, Dr Penc's declaration that nothing supernatural is happening at Medjugorje and then adds that this 'could be considered the expression of the personal conviction of the Bishop'.

Not without justification the newsletters and journals of the cult have taken this as vindication of the Franciscans' repudiation of the diocesean authorities.

The Vatican is saying, too, implicitly, that being hugger-mugger with Hitler can be accounted blessed. And heaven may be stormed with prayers with the intention of ensuring that ethnic cleansers of Muslims escape punishment.

The Medjugorje cult is not a major factor in the region. Neither the western powers nor the ruling groups in the region give it weight when balancing out where their interests lie.

But it's hugely important for the Vatican. Veneration of 'Our Lady of Medjugorje' fills the same role as will that of Stepinac, emphasising the centrality of Catholicism to Croatian nationalism, sharpening differences, enhancing hatred, and all the time confirming the Vatican as an active player in the Balkan power game.

Croatia serves as a Catholic implantation at the intersection of the Balkans with the West, a bridgehead to the East, a wedge into Islam.

Most people who 'believe in' Our Lady of Medjugorje are, no doubt, sad folk with empty lives which they fill with fantastical nonsense. But the Pope, Ratzinger, the coterie of bishops in Ireland who are part of the same 'set', the Franciscans of the Church of St James and the like, they know what evil they are at.

Chapter 10

Home tales

Three children from the Derry diocese recall their childhood days

***Hot Press*—15 November 1995**

Was I stupid or what? Or blinded by the cloth? You'd been warning us. You knew.

That's what keeps coming back to me, late at night when I'm forcing vodka down to try to get sleep. That you knew. And all you did was keep an eye and give us hints.

My mother never says a word. She always had priests in the house. Ours was always the house in the village where there were priests sitting in having a cup of tea. The only reason there was ever brandy in the house—because none of us ever touched it—was a bishop sometimes spending half an evening in the armchair talking and laughing. My mother loved that, a bishop taking his ease in our house.

It must have been some of the other priests who mentioned us to Fr Johnston. He was at the door in his first couple of days. My mother was all over him. A new young priest in the parish, she wanted to bid him welcome.

He was odd, but there was no reason for worry. He was skinny and had a flick of hair that was always falling down across his eye and a thick smile. His eyes were pale blue. Sometimes he looked very young to be a priest. When my mother said the hallway needed doing up, he was round the next day with dungarees and paint and a bucket. There was something peculiar about that, but not so as to make you start worrying.

It was always the females in the house he socialised with, that was noticeable from the beginning, my mother and me and my daughter, Ann Marie. She was seven at that point. He had no time for the fellows. But then, my mother said, they wouldn't give him the time of day. They used to make themselves scarce when he'd come in and sit down.

When he started taking Ann Marie on runs we didn't think anything of it. She'd always dash straight upstairs when they arrived back, and he'd sit on the arm of the armchair for a while, dangling his keys.

My mother took his side when the other priests said we shouldn't have him in the house so much. Fr Grant and Fr Rooney both said we shouldn't encourage him. That's the phrase they used: don't encourage him. Maybe we should have twigged then. Harold said he was probably just not pulling his weight in the parish. My mother thought he was just younger than them and lonely and needed a bit of home life.

She was livid when she heard he was leaving. It was all very sudden. At mass on Sunday, Fr Rooney got up and asked us all to pray for Fr Johnston. Some people said that teachers up in the school had gone and complained about him, that's why he more or less left overnight. But there was no real explanation.

It was a doll's wardrobe that sparked it all off with Ann Marie. He'd bought it for her a while before he left. It had all sorts of outfits for her doll in it, nurse's, a princess' riding outfit. But she wouldn't touch it. I put it into the attic and there it stayed until the next year, when I gave it to my sister for a birthday of one of her kids. And then I took Ann Marie round there the next Sunday, and that's when it all burst out.

As soon as she set eyes on the doll's wardrobe she opened up and screamed and screamed. We knew on the instant it was nothing ordinary. I've lost half the time since then. It was the end of my life that had gone before.

After that for weeks on end she wouldn't go to sleep at night. She wouldn't go upstairs after it was dark, not even to go to the toilet. She became very aggressive to my mother and myself and Maisie, who was living at home then. She'd call us bitches and hoors, and she was only eight. We had to let her stay up all night, until she saw it was daybreak, and then she'd go to sleep for a few hours on the sofa. We kept her off school all the while this was going on. We spent countless nights crying, getting this abuse from her and not being able to help her. She was reared in a home that was just oozing with love and none of us could understand what had happened.

It got to the stage I couldn't look at her. I began to think she must be possessed. I phoned my sister one night at three in the morning and held the phone out and said, 'Listen to this.' And she gasped and said, 'What is that?' I said, 'It's Ann Marie.' She was howling. It wasn't a scream. She was crouched down behind the sofa with my mother and Maisie and me standing around with our hands to our heads. She was howling like an animal. My sister came over and we walked her around the roads all the rest of that night until the dawn came up, the two of us holding on to her. She was sobbing and crying and, when we kept asking her to please tell us what was wrong, she just cried harder.

My mother and Maisie and me started fighting. We had exhausted all our resources and didn't know where to turn. Maisie left home. It was like waiting for a nightmare to happen. Once it got dark, it began. We had to get help for Ann Marie at that stage. We thought she had gone insane. Doctors came to see her but they couldn't pinpoint any problem. We sent for the priest one night when she was in the middle of a tantrum. Fr Rooney came and he was able to calm her a bit, but he couldn't get her to go upstairs. Then one of the doctors said she'd bring a child psychologist to look at her. After he'd had a couple of sessions with Ann Marie, he said she was blocking something out of her mind that we would have to get at. Then one night she was sitting there with me and Fr Rooney. She had gone very quiet. She looked at Fr Rooney and said, 'It was Fr Johnston.' Fr Rooney started crying.

It came out in drips and drabs. There's a lot of it still Ann Marie doesn't know I know. He told her, 'I'm not really a priest, you know. If you tell anybody what happened I'll come back at night and kill you all.' That's the reason she was afraid to go upstairs at night.

The psychiatrist made an appointment for her to see somebody who specialised in abused children, in a hospital in the city. We took her up there and they told us she'd have to stay for a few days for assessment. I stayed with her and then they still wanted her to remain on, so members of the family had to start taking turns to stay over, so that there was always somebody there for her, but it was heartbreaking having to leave her at night.

She was still terrified of the night-time, still howling and sobbing her heart out every day. She wasn't getting any better and I wanted to bring her home with me, but the staff said she wasn't ready. Then they said there would be a meeting with psychiatrists and social workers to determine whether she'd come home. I started to panic. Harold and a few of us just took her the day before the meeting and he brought her outside the jurisdiction in case the meeting went against us. But

the outcome was for her to stay at home. If it had been the other way
I'd have had to move away with her. All the time it was going round
and round in my head. But we didn't do anything wrong—why is all
this still happening when they all know it was Fr Johnston?

The doctors say Ann Marie will have to be treated for years. I'm
in treatment too. She's a lot better. If you didn't know her, 90 percent
of the time you'd swear she was a happy balanced girl, becoming a
young woman. I don't think straight sometimes. I don't know how
much she knows I know. I couldn't ask her. There's nothing I could
do to bring it out in public. I couldn't bear to have people pointing
the finger at her and saying, 'There's the wee girl who was raped by
the priest.'

The day that man molested my child he messed up the lives of
many people. We were ten of a family. It affected all of us very deeply
and in turn affected all of our families. He will never know the distress he caused and he got to walk away from it all. I lay the blame
entirely in the lap of the two bishops who knew about him before he
came here, who were responsible for him coming here.

I wrote to the head of the church house where he was hiding. I got
a letter back saying they were aware there had been incidents but
they hadn't realised it was so serious. They said he was receiving
treatment, and they could vouch and assure me it would never happen
again, and that they'd remember me in their prayers and that they
would show my letter to him. Imagine that. I thought when I read it
it was like something from the script of a comedy show.

I know in my heart that he will stand before God some day and be
judged. But I also want to remind you that there is the law of the
land. You helped a criminal escape from judgement.

But then you know all this already. It gnaws at me inside that you
knew when I didn't—when I was in desperation not knowing what
was wrong, you knew. That's why you had him moved away. You'd
known that there was danger all along. That's why you sent priests to
knock on our door to hint and warn us against him.

I hope when you read this you remember all the times you sat in
your armchair sipping your brandy and talking to me and my mother,
and Ann Marie at your side. Then you let this happen. When we
needed you, you weren't in the armchair. You didn't call or even write
a letter. You don't know how much that would have meant to me. I
can understand why. It must be hard to look someone in the face and

speak to them when you know it was you who brought this torment on them.

Harold wrote to the Cardinal years ago and spelled it all out in detail, and had an acknowledgement back saying how distressed he was. I'm not denying that he probably was. But he says now that years ago nobody knew about priests and child abuse. He knew about Fr Johnston and our Ann Marie. He knew every detail and didn't do anything. I can understand your embarrassment. But I hope you can understand my utter disappointment and disillusionment.

What I am asking of you now is that you stop saying in public that you didn't know, that you've only realised the extent of the pain and the sin in the last two or three years. There must be other people like me out there, probably quite a number who cannot speak up. I still catch my breath sometimes when I look at Ann Marie. When she's going out with her friends I wonder what she's thinking, how much she remembers, how heavy it is on her mind. But I can't ask her. I don't dare. She's the only one I have, and there's a whole part of her closed off from me. To this day when I'm alone I can think of nothing else.

. . . .

Sunday Tribune—18 July 1993
Peggy Gibson still finds it hard to talk of her long search for her only brother, Pat.

'I remember him so well. I remember him looking after me when I was out playing in the street. I remember when I was in the Nazareth House and he was in Termonbacca, the way I would wait for him on Sundays to come and take me out. He would take me on a walk out the Letterkenny Road and lift me up and sit me on a wall, a wall that is there to this day, and we'd laugh together. He had bright red hair.

'And then they took me away and sent me to Australia. They never told me why. They never told me why they took me and not him. All my life ever after I kept it in my mind that I would find him again. I searched and I searched but nobody would tell me where to find him. Nobody would tell me anything.'

Peggy Gibson was born Margaret McFadden. Her mother was also called Margaret. Her father was Patrick McAllister, nicknamed 'Heavy'. Her father and mother never married. She doesn't know why.

She says that 'my early childhood was very happy, as I recall.' She lived with her mother and her mother's parents and Pat, who was four years older, in Quarry Street in the Brandywell. 'It was a real extended family, warm and full of affection. But then I was separated from my family, when I was six.' She was taken to live with the nuns at Nazareth House. Pat, ten, went to the boys' home at Termonbacca. Until last year she believed that this had happened because her mother died.

'Then I found out that I was taken from my family five and a half months before my mother died. Neither my brother nor myself was brought back to the house to see her before she died. Nobody told us.'

They still hadn't told her by the time they sent her to Australia. She doesn't remember the detail of being told where she was going, only about a country where the fruit grew in thick clumps on the trees and the sun always shone. She remembers that on the way out a nun told her that she had no brother.

'We were taken to London and then to Southampton and onto the ship. There were several hundred children on the ship: Irish, English, Scottish, from Catholic homes, Church of England homes, the Salvation Army, from every welfare agency in the UK as far as I could see, all us so-called orphans, except that many of us weren't orphans at all.'

She recalls that almost as soon as they had set sail she was told that she was no longer to call herself 'Peggy', that her name was now 'Margaret Theresa'. No one had ever called her that.

When the ship docked at Freemantle she was taken with the other Catholic girls to the Nazareth House in Geraldton, which she says at least had a bit of a coastline, unlike Tardun where most of the boys from Derry went, which was like a desert. She says that the regime at Geraldton was 'not kind—institutional life had a harshness at that period'.

'I won't say much about the people in charge there. They weren't qualified. They didn't know us. Maybe they could have related to the aged or the infirm. But we were children. What I'll say is that because of the way we were treated we bonded together, and that when I left I never went back.'

She says that, when she was 'tipped out of the orphanage at 16', she had it firmly in mind to start the search for her brother.

'I knew that I was Irish and that I was from Derry and that I had a brother. I wrote to the Children's Welfare Department to ask them to help me find him. I have the answer here. It's all yellow now, with the date on it, 10 August 1956, promising to do all they can to help me find my brother. But that's the only thing they ever did, write that letter.

'I would cry myself to sleep and look forward to dreaming that my brother would come and find me in this foreign country and take me home. It's hard to explain now. But it did take a grip on me. I suppose it was a sort of obsession. It was the main thing I knew about myself, that I wasn't alone, that I had a brother, who had also been taken away from the family at the same time as me, who must be in the same situation with me.'

After leaving the orphanage she was sent to work as a 'domestic' for a prominent Catholic lawyer in Perth. She was expected to work hard for long hours for little pay, and slept in an outhouse. She wanted to get as far away as she could get, and saved all she was paid until she had the boat fare to Melbourne where she has lived ever since. She is married and has two sons.

'But I kept trying. I was speaking to the welfare authorities all the time, trying to get somebody to help me to get answers.'

She began writing to any name she could discover in Derry, asking about her family, mainly about her brother. And as a result, to her great disbelief, she found out in 1978 that her father, who she had long assumed to be dead, was still living in the Long Tower area in Derry. The following year she came back to Derry with her husband, Bill, and met her father for the first time in 32 years.

He hadn't been told where she had been taken, and knew nothing of the whereabouts of Pat. But, being in Derry, Peggy went to the Nazareth House in Bishop Street and rang the bell and asked if they could help her in her search.

'They turned me away. All they told me was, "We have no information to impart".'

She came back to Derry two years later and tried again. 'And they just turned me away for the second time. It was disheartening, but I wasn't going to stop.'

Encouraged by a new stirring of interest through publication of *Lost Children of the Empire* and a documentary based on it, Peggy travelled to Western Australia to a 'Nazareth Girls' reunion, to compare notes, and discovered that the Catholic Welfare Officer in Perth was holding the immigration entry papers of the 1947 emigrants.

'I went there in October 1991, and it was then that somebody put into my hand the papers that I had travelled on, that had brought me here. And there was my birth certificate, and my school records. I was

51, and for the first time had something setting out my identity. I stood there in the office and sobbed and sobbed.'

Buoyed up by the breakthrough, and by the sense that the child migrant scandal was now bursting out into the open and couldn't be covered up much longer, Peggy and her husband scraped enough money together to contact a professional researcher in England and to send him, in March 1992, to Derry armed with the new information. He discovered that, in 1953, her brother Pat had been sent from Termonbacca to work for a farmer called Daly in 'Ballybofey, County Monaghan'.

She wrote to the Church authorities in Derry to ask if now they could help trace him. A few weeks were wasted, then it was realised that 'Ballybofey' referred to Ballybay, County Monaghan. A few weeks after that, Peggy had a letter from Bishop Edward Daly telling her that the brother had died in Ballybay on 14 August 1990. She collapsed in the street from grief and had to be carried by her husband into her home. Pat hadn't really been difficult to find. She knows he could easily have been found sooner.

Peggy was back in Ireland last year, on 14 August, to attend a memorial mass at the Church of the Holy Rosary in Tullycorbett, Ballybay. Pat is buried in the little graveyard outside. He had never married, lived alone and had a reputation of not allowing anybody come close to him emotionally.

'I still find it hard to come to terms with the fact that he is dead. He was very real and alive to me in my sense of loss. I had held onto him because I had no immediate family on my side in Australia to share my sons with. He was their uncle, and a brother-in-law to my husband. The sense of isolation has been tremendous, 12,000 miles away.

'My brother suffered tremendously too. I know he felt the same way about me. People have told me that he mentioned my name frequently. I had all these papers to show him, all the letters I'd written and records of the people I'd spoken to, to try and find him.

'I wanted to be able to show him that I'd never forgotten him. I wanted to be able to say, "Look, see, there, I never gave up on you." He was entitled to know that.'

Peggy Gibson said that she deserves a letter from somebody in the Church, admitting that she was grievously wronged. 'I want some recognition of what I have been made to endure and what I am still suffering. I find the grief I feel for my brother terrible to withstand. I want somebody to tell me why all this happened.'

Sunday Tribune—26 September 1993

As far as I know, I was one of 14 children, nine brothers and five sisters. I know the names of them all now except for one of my brothers. I know that I was born in May 1948 in (a village in Donegal) and that at 14 days old I was put into the Nazareth House in Fahan, Co Donegal.

I got to know my birth father after coming out of the orphanage. I say 'birth father' as opposed to father because he was a despot if ever there was one, a most violent man. If I ever arrived in the village in later years and had money for him I was accepted. But I was never accepted as a son. He never reared any of the 14 children he fathered. They were put into orphanages as they came on stream.

At two years of age I was transferred from Fahan to St Joseph's, Termonbacca, Derry, and put in the baby section. At six years of age I was transferred to Termonbacca proper, where the ages ranged from six to 16. There were 72 boys there. Life was deeply austere. The nun I remember most was Sister J. She had the most violent, vindictive streak. There were plastic tops on the tables with rubber rods along the side which she would extract to come down on the children with if you stepped out of line. You would be beaten on the body, the face, the legs.

Her second mode of attack was her fist. Her knuckles were always cut and scabbed and saturated with iodine from the beatings she handed out. She wore mittens in summer and winter. To hear the roars and screams of the orphans was terrifying. When you got to 14, 15 or 16 you could be appointed a monitor and allowed to keep order, using violence. I remember sitting in the dining hall one day and— maybe I smiled or something—a monitor called Billy L came down on my head with a stick. I remember my head falling on the table and a gurgling sound and the hot blood pumping.

I wet the bed as a kid, very severely, the reason being that I was terrified of the dark. I spent many hours at night in bed, lying awake in saturated urine, in fear of the morning ritual. I'll always remember the remarks of the nuns in the morning—'You dirty tramp, get out.' Then you had to run what was known as "the gauntlet", down a long, long passageway from the dormitory to the toilets, and as you ran and stumbled you'd be thumped anything up to a dozen times by the nun and the monitors, by Sister J in particular, the notorious one.

You couldn't wash your body. You just got into your clothes and went to school with the smell lingering. You were never allowed to forget that you wet the bed.

The worst day was Saturday, because then we had to scrub and polish the orphanage, especially the passageway. We had to get down on our hands and knees and take our shoes and socks off because the toe-caps would have been destroyed and holes left in the socks. There would be up to ten rows of orphaned kids four or five abreast with a scrunched up blanket and brown liquid polish. The river Foyle was to our left, so they had these words, 'river, back', 'river, back', as we pushed the blanket to and fro together and inched along the passageway. The monitors would keep time and would come down on you if you faltered on the head, shoulders, arms, backside.

The Bishop used to come once a year, at Christmas, which meant that from October we would be up until 11 o'clock at night rehearsing for his concert. Everything had to be perfect, songs, hymns, the Christmas crib. I dreaded it. Then he would come in all his splendour and we would all line up and kiss his ring, calling him 'My Lord'. The nuns pampered the Bishop right, left and centre.

I remember making a very conscious decision that they would never make me cry. They had taken everything from me, but this one thing I promised myself they wouldn't do to me. Orphans learn things like that, never to cry. It used to gall Sister J.

I had a birth brother by the name of K at Termonbacca but it was never pointed out to me that he was my brother. I knew him, but not that he was my brother. I only found out when I was about eight.

I originally went to school at the Nazareth House in Bishop Street, where we were put in the same classes as the girl orphans who stayed there.

We weren't allowed to speak with the girls. We sat at opposite sides of the class and walked on opposite sides of the corridors. There was an invisible line always there between us.

I abhorred lunchtimes at Nazareth House. At the end of the passageway there were stairs down to a room where we spent our dinner hour while the girls were getting their lunch upstairs. The monitors were there to make sure we didn't talk. We just sat there. We didn't eat between leaving Termonbacca in the morning and going back up after school in the afternoon—that would be nine hours from breakfast. The aroma of the kitchens would filter through the passageway and down to the room we sat in. The pangs of hunger were devastating.

When I think about it now the most horrific thing was that I had five birth sisters there. At some time I must obviously have been sitting in the same classroom as one or more of them, but I was never told. When you put that alongside all the talk now of charity, of keeping families together, it doesn't seem to bear thinking about.

I can't even remember being shown any affection. Nobody ever put their arm around you and said, 'You are a good kid.' Everything that was done was done to keep you subservient. It is all deeply embedded in my memory.

Around 1958, for some reason we were not told about, we were transferred from Nazareth House to Bridge Street School. It was ordinary teachers there, not religious. There was a Mr Hutton, the headmaster, and his wife Mrs Hutton, and a Miss Jackson, a relief teacher, and a Mr Don Doherty. He was particularly excellent, brilliant to the orphan kids. We weren't beaten there, or belittled as orphans. I have fantastic memories of Bridge Street. We used to walk down from Termonbacca and along Foyle Road, in a long line. I remember passing the GNR railway station and we'd shout, 'Up the IRA, down the GNR.' The IRA campaign had started in 1956 and as children we thought it was fantastic. It would be different now. The GNR workers always had great time for us and would bring us over biscuits and stuff. I now realise their kindness to us orphans was because they knew the horrors of Termonbacca.

There was a shirt factory on Foyle Road, and we used to wave over at the women and they would bring us over sweets and biscuits too. I have a great love for the civilian people of Derry on account of that. Those were the happiest times of my childhood, the best part of 40 of us going along Foyle Road to Bridge Street, and laughing and waving at people.

There were still bad times, too, going back to Termonbacca after school. There was a senior monitor called MM who I believe is now in a mental institution in mid-Ulster, who, apart from the physical attacks, made homosexual assaults on the kids. I remember one specific occasion he took us on a route back from Bridge Street in through bushes and brambles alongside Braehead. It was a shortcut. I loved it in the summer because you could play and pick the berries. But this time, MM, who would have been maybe 17, lined up all the kids and had us stripped naked. Looking back and perceiving it now, it is reminiscent of those pictures of Jews lined up naked in the concentration camps. That was all that happened to me personally.

Before I was 12 I started to run away from Termonbacca. I spent many a night sleeping at the shirt factory on Foyle Road, where there was a big boiler house. On numerous occasions I was brought back by the RUC. I pleaded with them more than once and told them what was going on, but they didn't want to know. It was back to Termonbacca by the scruff of the neck and handed back to the nuns.

I was flogged every time, beaten with the rubber rod or with fists by the nuns. I was beaten until I could hardly walk, but I still didn't cry. It was the only dignity I had left. When I could walk properly I would run away, again and again.

Then came April 1960, which lives in my memory. It was a beautiful spring morning in Derry. I was told, 'You're not going to school today.' I stood there with my brother K for about half an hour. Then we were put into a car driven by a woman who must have been a social worker of some sort. She never spoke. We weren't told where we were going. I don't remember a single thing about that journey. I remember looking back and seeing Sister J standing at the front door, with a look on her face as if to say, 'I fixed you.'

And then I remember at about eight o'clock at night arriving at the industrial school in Galway, run by the Christian Brothers.

I was there until April 1964 and I can safely say that the violence was at least equal to Termonbacca, and more sinister. I remember the Brother Superior telling myself and K to go out into the playground and I was stunned by what I saw. There were 200-plus kids, some sent by the courts but generally speaking orphans, and suddenly a Brother blew a whistle and every one of them just froze.

Each orphan had a number and when the Brother blew the whistle for the third time each boy shouted out his number. I was number ten. You were always called by your number.

The routine of life was that the Brothers taught you in the school until five o'clock when you got your tea. Then you went to the shoemaker's shop, the tailor's or the farm and worked until about eight.

Brother A ruled with an iron fist. One of his ways of punishing you was to close his fist and to come down on your head with his middle knuckle in exactly the same spot over and over again. He could split your head like that and the blood would trickle and he would keep going.

On Saturday nights he would come up into the dormitory. We

had a civilian watchman but he was off on Saturdays. The kids didn't wear pyjamas but an overgown. He would turn the kid over and lift up his overgown and come down on him with the leather. Saturday night was a favourite night with the Brothers.

There was a Brother B, who was a hunchback, a Dublin man who was mad into soccer, which was quite against the ethos of the Christian Brothers. The other unusual thing about his was that he never carried a leather. It was the fist and the boot with him. Some young fellow might laugh or look at him and his skin would go deathly white and froth came out of his mouth and he would go totally insane, battering and kicking, resulting in him having to take an hour off to calm down.

Brother C, from Limerick, was a great lover of the rosary. He used to call a boy up to the table and sit him down and his hand would go in between the boy's thighs. The smile on his face would go from sadness to ecstasy. It didn't register at the time what was happening. I was never called up, but for the good-looking kids this was constant.

Brother D was a Kerry man and known as 'Mad Jack'. He used to call the time when the meal was over. He'd clap his hands and everybody had to freeze. You could have a spoon in your mouth and if you moved an inch you were dead.

A favourite of his was to lift a kid up in the air by the ears and then hop him off the dining room floor, which was a cement floor with tiles. Then he would proceed with the leather. I would say now that Brother D was insane.

Brother D never sexually assaulted me but I saw him many, many times sexually assaulting other kids. I saw him openly putting his hand up a boy's trousers and fondling his penis, talking to him all the time. He would think nothing of then giving him an extra cake or a few slices of bread. We would all sit looking at this, knowing that it was wrong but with nothing we could do about it.

One thing which has never left my mind was the terrible beating Brother E gave to a retarded boy called John B. He wasn't able to articulate in any way—he just made sounds and gestures.

There is no possible way John B could have recovered fully from what to me was the most violent assault I have ever witnessed in my life.

He would have been about ten. I don't know what he'd done. Maybe he'd done nothing. It happened in the playground as we all stood around watching. A number of the orphans had bowel spasms, dirtied themselves, from the terror. Brother E totally and absolutely destroyed that child. He beat him with his fists, and kicked him on the ground in his body and his head. The blood was gushing from him and he was whimpering and screaming for pity.

Everything came to a halt. Everybody stood rigid watching in terror. Nobody made a sound. There was only the Brother panting and the screaming of the child. There was nothing anybody could do. I never saw John B after it.

Brother F was another for the Saturday nights. He used to have 'parades' where everybody would have to turn their underpants inside out, and if there was any sign at all of excreta the boy would have to lift off his overgown and he would be put naked over the Brother's knee and the Brother would bring his hand down in a slap, but then the hand wouldn't leave. He would sit there with the naked boy across him and his hand on him.

The worst thing was when a Brother would come up to the dormitory and call a boy out to the toilet. It always happened at 11 or 12 at night. The kids would come back a long time later, when we'd be dead asleep. It never happened to me. It happened to a particular group, the good-looking ones: they were known as 'the pets'.

They were never beaten. They got all the prestige jobs like serving visitors and working around the Brothers' dining quarters. If the Brothers wanted a message done, it was one of them who would get it. Some of them went on holidays with the Brothers for the summer, too, to different locations which the Brothers had around Ireland. I think they were grateful to the Brothers for the softer time they had.

It was strange, thinking back on it now. It was general knowledge among all the kids that this was going on, but it was never spoken about. If it happened today in a conventional school it would be talked about. It would become well-known. Gardai would investigate and charges would follow.

My brother K was there all the time, and I knew now he was my brother, but we still didn't have any relationship. There was nothing to bring us together. We were never treated as being brothers, or put together in anything. There was no such thing as birthdays, no family occasions. So I knew he was my brother, but we didn't know what that was supposed to mean.

Maybe it was that nobody knew what was happening, but about

four years ago there was a fellow called Foran, a wino living rough in Dublin, up for killing a prostitute, and a psychiatrist giving evidence as to his condition told the judge that this man had been reared in St Joseph's Industrial School in Galway and had been subjected to sexual abuse including anal sex.

It was said that she had asked him for anal sex and, according to the psychiatrist, having anal sex with her brought back all the anger and hatred of what had happened to him and the way he released this anger was strangling her.

I read that and was able to believe it. I thought it might have caused an uproar. It was in every national newspaper, every single one.

It all left its mark which is manifested in the way many of the kids behaved afterwards. My brother K joined the government service too, but we never managed to become close like real brothers. There was always this distance. He developed extreme ideas and left. I haven't seen him since the early '70s and have no idea what has become of him.

My eldest sister L has been in a mental institution since 1963 when she was 18 years old. She had gone to England to study nursing but had come back and then had a nervous breakdown. Between her background in Nazareth House and the brutality inflicted on her by her birth father, she never recovered.

I tracked her down five years ago and went to see her. I visited her religiously for 14 months. Sometimes she was in good form. Other times her arms were cut up and bandaged and she was pumped full of valium. Sometimes in her better moments, when she had her composure, she would remember, for example, doing the dishes in Nazareth House and if it wasn't done right the nun would duck her head right down into the sink full of water, repeatedly. I remember her putting her hand into mine and saying, 'You were at the same school and we didn't even know one another.'

It was a great strain on me, going to see her, and eventually the specialist told me that it would be better if I could make the break. She was completely institutionalised and would never come out and had a full disability pension. I got her a new radio and a watch which she wanted and I walked away.

That was the hardest decision I ever made. That was the moment I fully accepted that I owed it to my birth brothers and birth sisters to expose the horrors of the holocaust inflicted on the orphans of Ireland.

Then there's my sister S. It will be 30 years next April since I have seen her. She was also reared in the Nazareth House. I met her for the first time when I went back to my birth village after I left the industrial school at 16. The first day I was back my birth father threw me out because I hadn't brought him money. But I went back again. I had it in my mind to try to make a go of it here. I spent four months in that house, which was a terrible experience.

S was 15, a good-looking girl. I remember coming in one day from getting my birth father's Woodbines in town and hearing screams. I can still see the scene. My birth sister was sitting all crouched up. Her hair had been chopped and my birth father was lashing her across the back with a real countryman's leather belt. My birth mother was sitting to his right, urging him on. The gist of what he was saying was, 'You'll never go with another fucking boy again.' There was a boy she had been fond of. She ran away that very day. It will be 30 years ago next April. I have never seen her since.

That's some of the brothers and sisters that I know something of.

In the four months I stayed I learnt a lot about my birth village. I remember the anniversary of the ordination of the parish priest, Fr M, and the number of opulent cars, the latest models passing the door of our house, such a humble run-down place, and wondering how this could be.

The parish priest, the doctor, the bank manager and the garda sergeant ran the village. I remember calling one day into the barber's shop for a message. The priest came in and everybody stood up, including the chap in the chair, who was half-shaved, who got out of the chair apologising to the priest and the priest sat down for a haircut. That the way it was at that time.

I became very deeply conscious of events in the world. I used to beg for three pence from my birth father to buy the *Evening Herald*. I remember the morning I went back after my birth father had thrown me out. The sun was belching out all over the countryside. This was in the '60s, of which I have vivid memories. Ireland was on the move, people all over Ireland had TV, they saw a new world and we wanted to be part of it.

People were standing up and saying we are going to fight back— we are not going to be walked on. I saw my situation in that context and I began to fight back to be something in life, to have my own self esteem and determined no other person would ever walk on me again.

I used to scour the papers when I got them, and I saw a job advertised for £4 a week at the Harcourt Hotel in Harcourt Street, Dublin. I was 16 years and four months at the time. I wrote off and sure enough the letter came back and I was away.

My health and outlook now are top class, thank God. But if I had children of my own there are two groups of so called religious people I wouldn't let them within a mile of and that's the Christian Brothers and nuns.

One person I would want to meet is Sister J. I would like to ask her face to face, without any threat to her: why did you inflict such venom on orphan kids? Why did you as a nun, as a Catholic, as a person who by your own profession and rules and the ethos of your order was supposed to give care and love to little ones, why did you batter kids and watch monitors batter kids? What was there for you to gain from the systematic physical and psychological terror you inflicted on helpless children? There must be a reason. What was it?

If I ever got the chance I would ask the Church, through the Nuncio or the Cardinal or whatever, could they not in all charity say that they are sorry? Could they not admit the grievous wrong they did, especially to orphans who had no parents to stand up for them?

I don't have any bitterness towards the nuns and the Brothers. I forgive them for what they did. And I know the Good Lord will forgive them. But I don't think history should forgive them, because if history forgave them they could do it again.

I await anxiously an apology from the Catholic Church. Can they in the interests of humanity bring themselves to say sorry?